Henry John Feasey

**Monasticism: what is it?**

A forgotten Chapter in the History of Labour

Henry John Feasey

**Monasticism: what is it?**
*A forgotten Chapter in the History of Labour*

ISBN/EAN: 9783744653619

Printed in Europe, USA, Canada, Australia, Japan

Cover: Foto ©Lupo / pixelio.de

More available books at **www.hansebooks.com**

# MONASTICISM:

## WHAT IS IT?

*A FORGOTTEN CHAPTER IN THE HISTORY OF LABOUR*

*By*

HENRY JOHN FEASEY

*Author of*
"WESTMINSTER ABBEY," "ANCIENT ENGLISH HOLY WEEK CEREMONIAL," ETC.

LONDON
SANDS & COMPANY
12 BURLEIGH STREET, STRAND, W.C.

MDCCCXCVIII

# MONASTICON

**Dedication**

*PAX*

TO THE PRIOR
*SUB-PRIOR*, AND MONKS
OF THE BENEDICTINE MONASTERY
OF

## ST GREGORY THE GREAT

DOWNSIDE, NEAR BATH

THIS VOLUME

IS RESPECTFULLY DEDICATED

BY

THE AUTHOR

# CONTENTS

## BOOK I

### PAGAN, JEWISH, AND CHRISTIAN MONASTICISM

Pagan, Jewish, and Christian Monasticism, 9—Fakirs, 10—Lamas, 10—Nazarites, 17—Essenes, 18-21—Paul of Thebes, 27—Anthony, 27-32—Macarius of Alexandria, 29—Stylites, 29-30—The Different Kinds of Monks, 31-32—Egyptian Monks, 32—Rules of Abraham, 33-34—of Pachomius, 35—of Monastery of Tabennæ, 35—of St Basil, 37—Eastern Monasticism, 27-38—Monastic Life, *temp.*—St Jerome, 38—Western Monasticism, 38—British Monasticism, 41-51—Rule of Celtic Monks, 43-47—Celtic Tonsure, 48—Rule of St Columba, 48—Book of Kells, 49—Gospels of St Cuthbert, 49—of St Chad, 49—Anglo-Saxon Monasteries, 49-51—Foundations for Women, 51—Paula, 52—Melania, 52—The Canonesses of the Holy Sepulchre, 52—British Nuns, 52-53—Double Convents, 53.

## BOOK II

### ST BENEDICT, FOUNDER OF WESTERN MONASTICISM

St Benedict, 54—Monastic Reforms, 55—Friars, 56-57—Rule of St Benedict, 58—Monks as Public Benefactors, 58-118—Cistercians, 65—Donations to Monasteries, 66-68—Tithe, 69—Glebe, 70—Mints, 81—Coining, 81—Wine Growers, 79, 118—The Monastery *v.* the Town, 84-87—The Monk *v.* the Bishop, 87—Monastic Schools, 89, 153, 173—Arts, Trade, and Commerce, 89-97—Hospitality, 103-7—Eminent Monastics, 107-18—Friar Bacon, 108—St Dunstan, 111—Peter Lightfoot, Mechanic, 111—Bede, 114—"Golden Legend," 115—"Speculum Majus," 115—"De Proprietatibus Rerum," 116—Dame Juliana Berners, 116—Monastic Libraries, 117-18.

## CONTENTS

### BOOK III

#### CONVENTUAL CONSTITUTION

Abbot, 119—Abbot's Officers (*Obedientiaries*), 123—Prior, 125—Prior's Lodge, 127—Novices, 130—Profession, 131—Novitiate, 132—Admission of Children, 137—Associated Brethren, 140—Burial in Monk's Habit, 140—Habit, 141—Foppery of Monks, 143 (*note* [1])—Abbot's Dress, 147—Discipline of the Cloister, 149—Quire Duty, 151—Schools, 153—Recreations, 156—Travelling, 158—Signs used in Silence Times, 160-61—Explorator, 160—Corporal Discipline, 161—Excommunication, 162—Prison, 165—Gate-House, 166—Porter, 167—Cloister, 168—Garth, 171—*Mixtum*, 172—Schools, 173—*Parliaments*, 175—Claustral Prior, 175—Externs, 176—Rastyr-House, 176—Precentor, 178—Sacrist, 179—Treasurer, 179—Seneschal, 180—Library (*Scriptorium*), 180—Chronicles, 184—Safe Depository, 186—Lending Libraries, 187—Carrels, 188—Kitchens, 192—Kitchener, 194—Table Supply, 194—Cellarer, 197—Refectory, 200—Weekly Reader, 204—Refectioner, 212—Misericord, 214—Longevity of Monks, 216—Almoner, 216—Almonry, 217—Hospitality, 219—Guest-House, 222—Hostiller, 225—Salutatorium, 226—Calefactory, 227—Chapter-House, 228—Lantern, 232—Lavatory, 234—Dormitory, 235—Cells, 237—Watchers, 239-40—*Necessarium*, 242—Chamberlain, 242—Infirmary, 243—Herbary, 243—Flebotomy (Bloodletting), 244—Infirmarian, 246—Physicians, 247—Death and Interment, 247-50—Terrier of House, 251—Seneschal, 251—Minor Officers, 252—Chequers, 253—Lesser Appurtenances, 254—Foreigns, 256—Conclusion, 256.

Note on the Dissolution of the Monasteries, 256—List of Religious Orders, 265-271—List of some Monastic Brasses, 272

LIST OF RELIGIOUS ORDERS, WITH NAME OF FOUNDER,
    DATE OF FOUNDATION, AND COLOUR OF HABIT . 265-271
LIST OF SOME MONASTIC BRASSES . . . . . . 272
INDEX . . . . . . . . . . . 273

# MONASTICISM—WHAT IS IT?

## BOOK I

#### PAGAN, JEWISH, AND CHRISTIAN MONASTICISM

BROADLY speaking, there is not another subject of which the average intelligent Englishman is so grossly ignorant than that of Monasticism. Of its method and scope; the various and component parts of its organisation; the classification and variety of its orders, each founded with a different end and object; he knows practically *nothing*. Ask him what Monasticism is, and he replies: It is Popery, or, at the best, Jesuitism in disguise!

This ignorance is very wide-spread. Even the Press, both secular and religious, is not entirely free from it; the latter frequently bewailing it as a most pernicious system of the most virulent Roman type; the germ, in fact, of that horror of horrors—Romanism!

It is proposed to deal exclusively with Christian Monachism, necessarily within a very limited area, for to give anything like an adequate idea of so vast and important a subject, would require a series instead of one single volume.

Evidence of Monasticism as a system is found in all the religions of the world almost without exception, be they Jewish, Pagan, or Christian. The Hindus have their *jogis*, or *fakirs*; the Buddhists their *lamas*, *phongyi*, or *shamans*; the Chinese their ascetics, with enormous finger nails, sixteen to eighteen inches long, and nuns with shaved heads, in grey cotton, priestly-shaped robes ministering before the idols.[1] Three hundred years before Christ came there were recluses, ἐγκεκλεισμένοι, in the temples of Serapis; and clay tablets, dug up on the site of Babylon, tell that among the ministers in Babylonian temples there was a body of monks who were forbidden to marry, and who lived in separate communities by themselves. Frequent allusions are made to them in the texts, and one of the tablets describes the consecration of three young men by their mother to this monastic life. In the classic days lived the Pythagorean recluse and the Neo-Platonic dreamer, the Vestal Virgins, and their Peruvian sisters, the Virgins of the Sun. In Judaism also were the schools of the Prophets, the Nazarites, and the order of the Essenes—societies which with many another were almost identical with that great system of European Monachism which had its rise in Benedict of Nursia.

Monasticism, therefore, belongs not exclusively to Christianity. Buddhism, the largest and most influential religion of the world, possesses monasteries to a vast extent. In Banghok, the Siamese capital, alone,

---

[1] The monastic is extolled as the only perfect life. Buddha's perfect path was: Right belief, believing in the Buddha and his doctrine; right resolve, the abandonment of wife and family as the best means of extinguishing the fires of the passions; right work, that of a monk; right living, living by alms; right exercise, the suppression of the individual self. Compare this with the "perfect life" of the Christian monk.

there are at the present time estimated to be upwards of 10,000 monks. Long before the dawning of the Christian era, hundreds and thousands of the followers of Buddha Gotama had lived and died under precisely similar conditions to what we now know as the cloistral life. Five hundred million of the followers of Buddha and Confucius accept the monastic life as the highest form of existence—possible, it is true, only to the few who aspire to the perfection of wisdom, of self-sacrifice, and philosophy. To Buddha and Confucius must be added Plato and Socrates,[1] and other giants among men, all testifying to Monasticism as being of essential value to the welfare of the community at large. To these we may add Elijah and John the Baptist as advocates among the Jews, and finally, the *positive* and *unequivocal* sanction of the Founder of Christianity Himself, in His Gospel for those aspiring to be "perfect," and "able to receive it." Nay, the Christ Himself has been claimed as the first Christian monk.[2] Then we have the gigantic minds of a Basil, a Jerome, an Augustine, an Ambrose, a Chrysostom, an Athanasius, a Benedict, a Bernard, a Bruno, a Francis d'Assise, an Ignatius Loyola, upholding and devoting their lives to the cause. Altogether, there is very good ground to go upon in the consideration of this great subject, for beyond all shadow of doubt, the founders of the various religious orders were all great men, all remarkable men, all good men, men of no ordinary calibre, but quite

---

[1] DIOGENES, being asked who were the noblest men in the world, replied, those who despised riches, glory, pleasures, and lastly, life, and who overcome the contrary of all these things, namely poverty, infamy, pain, and death, bearing that with an undaunted mind. Temperance of mind and body was also SOCRATES' idea of true nobility.

[2] St Chrysostom calls Monachism "The Divine Philosophy, introduced by Christ."

wonderful in their depth of thought and keen insight into human nature and affairs; men of amazing genius, of enlarged sympathies, of an indomitable strength of will, together with the highest of aspirations; poets and philosophers, every one of them, who not only created but realised and lived up to their grand ideals; and yet, all differing from one another in character and temperament, just as the communities they formed differed from each other in name, scope, and purpose.

"We are outliving," adds Mrs JAMESON, the talented author of "Legends of the Monastic Orders," "the gross prejudices which once represented the life of the cloister as being from first to last a life of laziness and imposture; we know that but for the monks, the light of liberty, and literature, and science had been for ever extinguished; and that for six centuries there existed for the thoughtful, the gentle, the enquiring, the devout spirit, no peace, no security, no home but the cloister. There Learning trimmed her lamp; there Contemplation 'plumed her wings'; there the traditions of Art, preserved from age to age by lonely, studious men, kept alive, in form and colour, the idea of a beauty beyond that of earth, of a might beyond that of the spear and the shield, of a Divine sympathy with suffering humanity. To this we may add another and a stronger claim on our respect and moral sympathies. The protection and the better education given to women in these early communities; the venerable and distinguished rank assigned to them, when, as governesses of their order, they became in a manner dignitaries of the Church; the introduction of their beautiful and saintly effigies, clothed with all the insignia of sanctity and authority, into the decoration of places of worship and looks of devotion—did more, perhaps, for the general cause of womanhood than all the boasted institutions of chivalry."

Women, who, like our own St Hilda of Whitby, the advisers of bishops and princes, sitting in their councils, and voting with the noblest and greatest of the land.

"Whatever reproach," writes Lord MACAULAY, "may at a latter period have been justly thrown on the indolence and luxury of religious orders, it was surely good that, in an age of ignorance and violence, there should be quiet cloisters and gardens in which the arts of peace could be safely cultivated; in which gentle and contemplative natures could find an asylum; in which one brother could employ himself in transcribing the "Æneid" of Virgil, and another in meditating the "Analytics" of Aristotle; in which he who had a genius for art might illuminate a martyrology, or carve a crucifix; and in which he who had a turn for natural philosophy might make experiments on the properties of plants and minerals. Had not such retreats been scattered here and there among the huts of a miserable peasantry, and the castles of a ferocious aristocracy, European society would have consisted merely of beasts of burden and beasts of prey. The Church has many times been compared by divines to the ark of which we read in the book of Genesis; but never was the resemblance more perfect than during that evil time when she alone rode amidst darkness and tempest on the deluge beneath which all the great works of ancient power and wisdom lay entombed, bearing within her that feeble germ from which a second and a more glorious civilisation was to spring."

Thus, though comparatively we know so little of its real nature, this so far removed, old-world Monasticism still exercises a singular fascination upon the minds of the generality of us moderns, Catholic, Protestant, and Atheist alike, for somehow one and all seem awed by the mysterious, subtle charm which attaches itself to the very words, monk or nun, hermit, cloister, or cell. Let us "take a walk down Fleet Street" and enquire of that most amiable and delightful of old Englishmen, stanchest of Protestants, Dr JOHNSON, what he thinks of Monasticism. And he tells us that "he never thought of a monastery, but in imagination he kissed its stones, or of a hermit, but in imagination he kissed his feet." While, on the other hand, we find

VOLTAIRE, that great French savant, declaring, that could the great void of his yearning, Christless heart have been filled with the love flowing from the atonement of the God-man, he would have had no other alternative than that of being a monk; and it remains a well-known fact that the learned Benedictine, Calmet, remained to the last one of his most cherished friends.

We walk through the ruins of Tintern, of Fountains, of Grace Dieu, and the hundred other remnants of those mysterious, long-departed, good old days of "Merrie England," of which the monastic economy formed no inconsiderable a part, and are strangely moved by the silent grandeur of the stately magnificence of these structures, even in their decay. They seem to speak to us in a language which penetrates to the very soul, awing us too, as it were, into a silence of admiration, so that we can only wonder, and listen, and sympathise with them in their desolation. How strangely we learn to love these desecrated sanctuary homes of industry and peace—peaceful and beautiful in life, and in decay no less beautiful and reposed—whose very stones seem to live again, and to gush with life and long-past memories at our approach, each with its own sad story of faded glory or sacrilegious spoliation.

The old fable which so erroneously supposed the misnamed "Dark Age" as a period when the world was cloaked in ignorance and sloth has long since been happily exploded, and the men of to-day are beginning to see things as they really existed.

"We refuse," says a recent writer on this subject, "to believe that human heroism belongs exclusively to any time." Yes, we do refuse to believe any such thing, for are not men the same all the world over?

Are not the hearts of our nineteenth-century men beating with the same high enthusiasm, the same laudable endeavour? Are they not consumed with the same passions, the same ardent yearnings, the same aspirations for all that is good, and noble, and true? the same hopes and fears, and, alas! with the same temptations, and the same failings, too, as the hearts of their brethren of the so maligned Middle Ages pulsed to then? Yesterday and to-day—ay, as long as the world endures—there will be the same striving for the mastery in things both civil and ecclesiastical, the same *decided* call for sacrifice, the same fierce battle for the right, the same abhorrence of all things evil, the same bitter disappointment and hopeless failure. But one thing they had in those mediæval days which we, in these harum-scarum, brummagem days of ours alas! lack so sorely—*sincerity*; a great, firm, stern, and terrible sincerity in all they took in hand. Once having put their hand to the plough, they seldom, if ever, looked back, be the way ever so weary; they toiled patiently on till the poor, tired body refused to bear its burden any longer. No one class was affected. Kings, princes, and nobles, being equally caught with their people in the strange spell, came down from their thrones to beg the poor habit of the monk, and to delight in the crust that supplied his daily food. No work was esteemed too menial; monarchs, the terror of nations, waiting meekly in an ante-room while a Bernard of Clairvaux washed the crockery in the monastery kitchen, or an Elizabeth of Hungary the sores of scrofulous beggars.

Not a few of the inhabitants of early and mediæval monasteries had been men and women of considerable rank and standing in the world. Quite a number of the Irish petty kings threw off the trappings of royalty to assume the rough garb of the monk.[1] Bangor, the White Quirê, formerly the Vale of Angels, was an "asylum for kings and princes," and later, many scions of royal houses presided over, or were numbered in the community of many an Anglo-Saxon religious house. Nay, of such a power was Monasticism in the land, that it drew within its fascinating influence even great kings, as the Emperor John Cautacuzene, Domitian, and Charles V. of Spain, and even in these latter lukewarm days it has not diminished in its power, as the retirement from the world of Prince Hazlitt and several others has proved.

"Of these," says Peter de Roya, writing of the monks of Clairvaux, "who were now poor, some had been of Episcopal rank, and others of baronial, knightly, and other dignities, some others also illustrious by their great knowledge, and others, again, were young men of noble birth;[2] but now, by the grace of God, they are dead to every acceptation of persons, so that, inasmuch as each was thought of loftier station in the world, so much he considers himself less than the least in this congregation, and though to the outward eye they appear fools and speechless, the reproach of men and the rejected of the people, yet their heart has a strong and well-founded belief that their life is hid with Christ in the heavens. . . . Thus, eagerly bearing the spiritual yoke, and feeding upon the Word of Life for which they always hunger, they eat and drink reverently the other gifts of God which are set for each of them; nor do they need costly delicacies, but the fruit of the labours of their hands, pulse and other vegetables. Their drink is beer, but if they have not this, they gladly take pure water—for they rarely use wine, and that mixed with

---

[1] *Flaithbheartagh* (724 A.D.); *Niall-Freasach* (782); *Daniel* (984); *Muriertagh*, or Murtough (1110); *Flaherty* of Tyrconnell (1197); *Cathol O'Connor* of Connaught (died 1224); and *Daniel O'Brien* of Dublin (1135).

[2] St Bernard himself had brought with him into the novitiate many of the knightly youth and flower of chivalry of his day.

much water. Thus they eat and drink as rendering to the body its due, not to taste or for gluttony, but only for the supply of natural weakness, and to God, as it is written."

Peter de Roya gave the best possible proof of the sincerity of these praises of the congregation of Clairvaux, by himself becoming a novice there.

The term "monk" comes to us from the Greek word *monus* (μοναχός), which means a solitary, *i.e.* one who had abandoned the world, and separated himself from the human race for a specific object, that of the Christian monk being to spend his life in devotion to the Redeemer, either personally by unceasing worship, or in ministering to Him in the service of His poor. The former is known as the *Contemplative*, the latter as the *Active* life. To the former, the term "monk" is *alone* applicable; to the latter, the proper designation is *friar*, though it is customary to mix them indiscriminately. With but rare exception such a life was adopted under the threefold vow of Poverty, Chastity, and Obedience, and all this in imitation of the Christ, the Perfect Man, interpreted by His own earthly life and precepts.

The question of vows is, at the present time, a most disputable one, yet Old Testament Scriptures show God Himself not only sanctioned "vows" in the system of Monachism among the Jews, known as that of the "Nazarites," but also gave special rules for the guidance of those who followed it.[1]

This order of "Nazarites," or "Nazarenes,"[2] is the only

---

[1] *See* Lev. xxvii. 1, 2; Num. vi. 1-3, xxx. 2; Eccles. v. 4, 5; Jer. xxxv. *Compare* Acts xviii. 18, xxi. 23, 24; and the indispensable vows made in Baptism, Confirmation, and Holy Matrimony.

[2] "Nazarene" and "Nazarite" are distinct words, the former being derived from ناصرة (Nazareth), the town; the latter from نازر (nuzur, nazar), a vow or offering, something separated.

society of the kind mentioned in Old Testament History (Num. vi.). The other sects seem to have been merely religious societies of varying views or doctrines, standing in somewhat the same relation to Judaism as the various sects of to-day stand in dissenting from the Catholic Church, and not at all of a monastic nature. JOSEPHUS, Israel's great historian, thus describes the life of one of these Nazarites, with whom he declares he spent three years, and whose mode of life seems to savour more of the eremite, than that of the Essenes.

"His home the desert; his only clothing the leaves and bark of trees; his only food what grew of its own accord; his only drink the brook; and his daily and nightly practice to bathe in cold water."

To this society, Samuel, Samson, Saints John Baptist and James the Just belonged, the former having gone into the desert to embrace the life at a very early age.[1] Elijah is another great Biblical character who stands out as a remarkable example in the intense fervour of his eremetical devotion. The Carmelites claim him as their patriarch and founder.

"We have," says St Jerome, founder of the Bethlehemite order of monks, "our examples in Elias, the Prince of Monks; our Chief in Eliseus; our leaders the prophets, who dwelt in fields and solitudes, and built their tents along the streams of the Jordan."

It is from Josephus ("Antiquities," xviii. 2) also that we gain an account of the society, or order, of Jewish

---

[1] There were two classes in the constitution of this order: those dedicated by their parents in infancy, like St John Baptist, and those who dedicated themselves for life, or for a specified period, as did Samson.

monks known as the *Essenes* (Greek, ὅσιοι, pure and holy). Their mode of life was almost exactly similar to that prescribed by the Rule of Saint Benedict, the great patriarch of Western Monachism. They dwelt in the caves of the oases and the desert, leading there a purely religious and contemplative life. Like the Christian monks, they renounced all the pleasures of life, and abstained from marriage, making themselves "eunuchs for the Kingdom of Heaven's sake,"[1] possessing all things in common (all being supported from a general purse), and rendering explicit obedience to their head, or superior. They studied the Scriptures, and engaged in manual labour. Their one great aim was personal purification, and to effect this end they did much bathing. The "Synagogue" was to them "the world," consequently of the earth—earthy. They even abstained from pilgrimage to Jerusalem. From all who were not pure like themselves they stood utterly aloof. When any died among them, all who had come into contact with the deceased underwent a long course of purification. Save when they themselves drew aside the veil which hid them in its strange, mysterious folds, the outside world knew them not. They went out from each other only to heal and help, to visit and nurse the sick. They were the extreme religionists, the "Perfectionists" of their day, perfect Jews fulfilling the whole law.[2] They were sober, virtuous, and unselfish, their conduct most exemplary. They were Communists (even as all true monks are Socialists from their very mode of life). If

---

[1] St Matt. xix .12.
[2] They are said to have originally spread from Egypt, and to have numbered about 4000 devotees. They are presumed to have represented Judaism in its purity, and to have exercised some influence on Christianity itself.

one fell ill, the others cared for him at the common expense. They clothed in white and wore the tonsure. Beyond all doubt, for they had life vows upon them, the Christ, though not himself an Essene, knew of them, and met them, for they flourished in His day, but never to upbraid or condemn as He so frequently did the Pharisees, Sadducees, Scribes, and others.

PHILO of ALEXANDRIA, writing about twenty years after the death of Christ, says of the Essenes :—

"They are called 'Essenes,' which name, though not in my opinion formed by strict analogy, corresponds in Greek to the term 'holy.' For they have obtained the highest holiness in the worship of God, and that not by sacrificing animals, but by cultivating purity of heart.

"They live principally in villages, and avoid the town, being sensible that as disease is generated by corruption, so an indelible impression is produced in the soul by the contagion of society.

"Some of these men cultivate the ground, others pursue the arts of peace, and such employments as are beneficial to themselves, without injury to their neighbours. They seek neither to hoard silver nor gold, nor to inherit ample estates in order to gratify prodigality and avarice, but are content with the mere necessaries of life. They are the only people who, though destitute of money and possessions (and that more from choice than the untowardness of fortune), felicitate themselves as rich, deeming riches to consist not in amplitude of possessions, but, as is really the case, in frugality and contentment.

"Among them no one can be found who manufactures swords, cutlasses, shields, or any other weapon useful in war, nor even such instruments as are easily perverted to evil purposes in times of peace.

"They decline trade, commerce, and navigation altogether as incentives to covetousness and luxury. Nor have they any slaves among them; all are free, and all in their turn administer to others. They condemn the owners of slaves as tyrants, who violate the principles of justice and equality, and impiously transgress the dictates of nature, which, like a common parent, has begotten and educated all men alike, and made them brethren, not in name only, but in sincerity and truth.

"As to learning, they cultivate natural philosophy only so far as respects the existence of God, and the creation of the Universe. Other parts of natural knowledge they give up to vain and subtle metaphysicians, as really surpassing the powers of man. But moral philosophy they eagerly study conformably to the established laws of their country, the excellence of which the human mind can hardly comprehend without the inspiration of God.

"In discussing these objects, the ends which they have in view are the love of God, the love of virtue, and the love of man. Of their love to God they give innumerable proofs of leading a life of continued purity, unstained by oaths and falsehoods; by regarding God as the Giver of every good, and the cause of no evil.

"They evince their attachment to virtue by their freedom from avarice, from ambition, from sensual pleasure; by their temperance and patience; by their frugality, simplicity, and contentment; by their humility, their regard to the laws, and other similar virtues.

"Their love to man is evinced by their benignity, their equity, and their liberality. There exists among them no house, however private, which is not open to the reception of all the rest. And not only the members of the society assemble under the same roof, but even strangers of the same persuasion have free admission to join them.

"There is one treasure whence they derive all their subsistence, and not only their provisions, but their clothes are common property; even the daily labourer keeps not for his own use the produce of his soil, but imparts it to the common stock, and thus furnishes with a right to use for himself the profits earned by others.

"The sick are not despised or neglected because they are no longer capable of useful labour, but they live in ease and affluence, receiving from the treasure whatever their disorder or their exigencies require.

"The aged, too, among them are loved, revered, and attended as parents by affectionate children; and a thousand hands and hearts prop their tottering years with comforts of every kind. Such are the champions of virtue (which philosophy, without the pride of Grecian oratory, proposes as the end of their institutions), and the performance of those laudable actions which destroy slavery, and render freedom invincible."

In the mode of life of the Prophetess Anna, abiding in the temple day and night, absorbed in worship, prayer, and fasting, and in that of St John the Baptist, an eremite from his youth up, the connecting link is found between the Monachism of the Old and New Dispensations.

In the Christian Dispensation no less a claim is made than that of the Founder of Christianity Himself as the first Christian monk, not only as sanctioning the system, but by following out in His own Person such a monastic life. Was not His earthly life the most perfect exemplification of voluntary poverty, of voluntary virginity, and of voluntary obedience, in each of the two phases of monastic life, both contemplative and active?—the former for the long period of *thirty* years, which from Biblical silence we cannot but infer that He passed in a secluded life of devotional preparation for His ministry, and the three years spent in the latter. "JESUS did not advance beyond this first and *entirely* monachal period," says RENAN, in his "Life of Jesus," in which it was believed that the impossible could be attempted with impunity. He made no concession to necessity. He boldly preached war against nature, and total severance from ties of blood. "Verily I say unto you, there is no man that hath left house, or parents, or brethren, or wife, or children, for the kingdom of GOD's sake, who shall not receive manifold more in this present time, and in the world to come life everlasting" (St Luke xviii. 29, 30).

Then again, by His teaching and "counsels of Perfection," He not only invites but encourages *some* to "*forsake* father and mother" for His sake, and the Gospel's, and declared that "he that loveth father and mother more than Me, is not worthy of Me." His reply to the rich young man is crushing in the extreme (St Matt. xix. 16-30). Having kept "all these things," *i.e. God's* commandments, he asks: "What lack I yet?" Whereupon our Blessed Lord, "beholding him, loved him," calls him to the higher life of perfection, "If thou wilt be perfect, go and sell that thou hast . . . and come and follow Me."

In this nineteenth chapter of St Matthew, as also in St Mark x. 17-31, and St Luke xviii. 18-30, JESUS preaches this doctrine of perfection to His Apostles. "Lo!" says St Peter, "we have left all and have followed Thee." To which our Lord replies: "Verily . . . there is no man that hath left house, or brethren, or sisters, or father, or mother, or wife" (as St Peter himself had done), "or children, or lands, for My sake and the Gospel's, but he shall receive an hundredfold now in this time, houses, and brethren, and sisters, and mothers, and children, and lands, with persecutions, and in the world to come eternal life." With *persecutions* is very significant, for He foresaw all the trials and sorrows, the rending of hearts, which this forsaking of father and mother and *all* had in store for those who would follow the more perfect way. Thus we come back to the definition of a Christian monk, as being a man who has forsaken the world, or left *all*—home, kindred, possessions—nay, even to the sacrifice of his own individuality by his vow of obedience—and who, by solemn, irrevocable vows, after a suitable novitiate, has consecrated himself and all he has, or is, or shall be, to the service of God by an imitation, as far as possible, of his Saviour's life on earth, emphatically believing that that state *must* be the most *perfect*, which the Son of Mary, the PERFECT MAN, chose. Thus he finds that the Monk's great Example, the Perfect Man, dwelt in a state of virginity, or celibacy; *therefore*, virginity is proven to be the most exalted, or the institutor of the Holy Sacrament of Matrimony would not have preferred to live a celibate or virgin life Himself, and the reason is that though marriage be holy, yet there is still a holier state, and that is *virginity*. He applies the same reasoning to his embracing an existence of *voluntary poverty* and *voluntary obedience* to his superior, who is *God's* representative to him. This latter is the very essence of self-denial and self-conquest, more especially at such times as the present, when men are seeking self, and *self* alone. "Self" is, indeed, the idol which the prince of this world has set up for nineteenth-century men to worship.

Next, in the Apostles themselves we find the first community of Christian monks, in that they adopted the mode of life of their Master, and acted upon His sayings. They *left all*. Saints Matthew, Andrew, James, and Peter, we are told, instantly abandoned *everything* to follow Him. St Barnabas, we learn, gave up large possessions to follow their example, distributing them to the poor by the command of Christ, even as, in after days, the early Franciscans did, who professed to copy the lives of the Christ and His Apostles. St Peter left his wife to live a life of celibacy, and the others, if similarly situated, must have doubtless done the same. St Paul, in writing to the Corinthians (chap. vii.), commends the superior sanctity of the unmarried state.

From the continuous references in the sacred narrative of the Apostles and Disciples abiding, or being found together, a reasonable inference may be drawn that they—or at least some of them—lived in a conventual manner.[1]

. . . . . . . .

Christian Monachism, like the Gospel itself, came originally from the East. During the first three centuries of the Christian era all Christians retained a more or less communistic or monastic character, their lives being lived and hidden amid Pagan society. From a very early period obscure and uncertain traditions of solitary persons living the life of ascetics [2] and hermits, and even in a kind of religious community, have survived, but the true birthplace of the eremetic life, lived either singly or in groups, may be said to be Egypt.

Various combined circumstances connected with the world's history, and the happenings of the times, brought about a vast increase in the numbers of men and women (and whatever advance in the monastic life was made by men was equally shared and followed by women) who flocked to lead a life of devotion in the deserts.

Towards the end of the third century the concluding volume of the history of the great Roman Empire was being rapidly brought to a close. Though still holding together by the concentrated forces hastily withdrawn from its outer limits, it was fast rushing to its dissolution—the dissolution of a Goliath amongst empires, whose death-throes were to be simply awful. At the very core the rot had begun, and the corruption had

---

[1] *See* St Matt. viii. 21, 37 ; ix. 10, 37 ; x. 1 ; xii. 1-7 ; xiii. 11, 16 ; xv. 1-3 ; xvii. 24-26 ; xxvi. 18, 20 ; St John xi. 2 ; xii. 8, 54 ; xvi. 27, xvii. ; xx. 19, 30 ; xxi. 1, 2, and the Acts of the Apostles generally.

[2] Ascetic, a *Scete*, a dweller in the desert of that name ; the house of Ascetics.

spread with a terrible, far-reaching activity, throughout the extreme dependencies of the empire. Utter disorganisation reigned everywhere, and famines, tyrannies, and internal feud and bloodshed, desolating the provinces, left no security for either property or life.

In the days of the beginning of the end came the religious persecutions under the last heathen emperors, when, amidst a darkness which preceded an eruption as of a Vesuvius, burst that desolating flood of confusion, and strife, and bloodshed, which laid the giant empire and its marvellous civilisation in the dust.

For a moment only was there a lull in the storm, when, in the early days of the fourth century, the Emperor Constantine, throwing aside the traditions of the Pagans, openly embraced the religion of the Christ. Truly that was a happy moment, when once again the sun shone out from amidst the awful darkness, upon what may be called the bridal of the Church and the world! The bloody sword of persecution was sheathed and crossed with the olive of peace. The Church, now no longer forced to seek a refuge in deserts and mountains, in dens and caves of the earth, came out boldly and took possession of the great basilicas for the worship of the once despised Nazarene, and her bishops and priests, casting off their "sheep-skins and goat-skins," assumed gorgeous robes, and proceeded in stately equipages to the discharge of their sacred functions therein. Christianity became, by the acclamation of the multitude, the popular religion, and extravagance, luxury, worldliness, and pride rolled into the Church as a flood, swamping the love of Christ in the very heart of Christendom.

The awful state of the crumbling empire of the world was enough, but the horrible corruption of the

Church, the bride of Christ herself, by that very world she had so recently almost agonised to save, pointed only too surely to the speedy coming of that day which would bring the end of all things.

Men and women within whom the slightest degree of sincerity remained became alarmed, and fled away as from another Sodom and Gomorrah, to people the deserts and wastes of Nitria and the Nile Delta, which soon swarmed with the huts of the ever-increasing number of arrivals, forming, as it were, not only abodes of a higher and more spiritual life, but also cities of refuge for all interests worth preserving, whether spiritual or temporal, sharing a common creed, a common hope, common interests, pleasures and sorrows, and to ponder undisturbed on duty, judgment, death, and eternity.

Foremost amongst these "Fathers of the Desert" of this exodus of the third and fourth centuries was PAUL OF THEBES, a Christian youth of noble family. Terrified by the allurements tried and tortures threatened to induce him to deny the Faith, he had fled to the desert, pitching his abode on the east of the Nile. For ninety and eight years he lived in this retreat, subsisting on the fruit of the date-tree, and the water of a spring, covering his nakedness, when his clothes failed him, with a garment of palm leaves woven together.

Of equal celebrity were Anthony, Pachomius, Amon, Basil, the two Macarii, and Jerome, all prominent figures in this cenobitic host. Paul is regarded in point of time as the first hermit, Anthony as the most noted, and "father" of all monks and hermits. He was the first to gather together the scattered recluses into communities (*lauras*), collections of huts spread over the waste of the Thebaid. Pachomius, Anthony's first disciple, was equally zealous in the work, being the founder of eight monasteries, or congregations of monks, each with its abbot, rendering obedience to one superior. Hilarion, a native of Gaza, in Palestine, studying philosophy at Alexandria, was also a convert of St Anthony, and, eventually, the founder of the first monastery in Syria. Basil, his disciple, carried the work into Asia Minor, and Jerome, who had visited Anthony in his desert, carried the fashion into Italy and Gaul. Thus, originating in the hermit life in Egypt, a system of Monachism had, in a short time, spread over the whole of Eastern and Western Christendom.

The writings of St Ignatius, Bishop of Antioch, and disciple of St John the Divine, martyred in the first century, show the existence of communities of women even in those days. He writes (A.D. 107) to the convent of virgins—*susteema ton parthenon.* St Paul also wrote to *tas parthenas tas legomenas keeras,* or "the virgins whom ye call widows," *i.e.* being espoused to Christ, were called "widows" in His absence. The Ecumenical Council of Chalcedon, held A.D. 154, a council acknowledged by the whole Catholic Church, not only sanctioned the institute of Monachism, but laid down rules for the guidance of those who gave themselves up to that life, and of the method in which they should be treated by the bishops. The canons passed at the Ecumenical Councils of the first ages prove how closely Monachism had become interwoven with Christianity.

The first hermits established their cells on the shores of the Red Sea. Next in point of antiquity come the monasteries of Nitria, of which accounts are preserved as far back as the middle of the second century, when, about the year A.D. 150, it is recorded that Fronto, with seventy of his brethren, retired to the valley of the

Natron Lakes.[1] The chief and pattern of all the recluses of Nitria was the great MACARIUS OF ALEXANDRIA, who, after sixty years' austerities, first in the Thebaid (A.D. 335), and afterwards in various deserts, died in 394. The reputation of his sanctity drew large numbers to a similar life. Rufinus, visiting them in the year 372, mentions fifty of their convents or congregations, and Palladius, in 387, reckons on the spot the devotees at five thousand, a number seemingly kept up without much diminution for several centuries.

As may be expected, the first recluses observed no definite rule, each and every one following the course of his own individual will and inclination. Being bound by no vows they wandered about in companies, sometimes into the towns, mingling with the people. All human learning they held in scorn, and founded their notions of orthodoxy on what was, or was not, true piety. It has been said, State laws presented to them no barriers; the authority of civil magistrates they ignored; while, to their religious fanaticism was added a cynical indifference to social duties and the proprieties of life.

Consequently there was no end to the vagaries of some of them, actively engaged, as many of them were, in the one endeavour to outstrip each other in their absurdities. Some shut themselves up in dens, wherein they could neither stand nor sit upright, nor lie with any comfort. Others abode in rocks, in hollow trees, or upon the tops of high columns (such as the Stylites), exposed to all the variations of climate, refusing meat, drink, and sleep, save the morsel absolutely necessary to ward off actual death. Others again lay motionless

---

[1] Some kind of recluses called "Therapeutæ" had inhabited Egypt long before the coming of Christ.

day and night upon narrow planks, half naked, and loathsome from dirt and disease, for they esteemed the body only as a target for torture and penitential practices. To them this present world was nothing, their whole thoughts being centred on the life of the world to come. Altogether, it is to be feared many of their absurdities can only be compared to those of the religious fanatics of the modern East.

Condemned as such a method of procedure must ever be, yet there is some justification in what they did, seeing it was a means to an end—the bringing back to itself a world *utterly* gone astray. Consider the state of the period; the acme of art and civilisation; the population of the cities, sunk in the lowest depths of sensualism, lived only for pleasure. Having exhausted all the refinements of luxury and sensuality, they were greedy and eager for any novelty which might arise.

That opportunity presented itself in the painful austerities of many of the ascetics, and, as a natural result, the attention of these exquisites was arrested, and they stood and wondered, flocking to visit these wonderful specimens of humanity, who, without pity or mercy for themselves, were ever ready to participate in the suffering of others, consoling the sorrowful, and interceding at request for the recovery of the sick and afflicted.

The result was at once apparent. Their goodness won many, and the mighty force of their example was more eloquent than the burning words which they addressed to the assembled crowds on the vanity of pleasure, and the capabilities of their immortal souls for a higher destiny in a better world, where eternal happiness was to be gained by the exercise here of Christian virtues.

Thus, both by word of mouth, and the attractive power of their example, they, in reality, preached the Gospel. Drawn at first by curiosity to gaze at these men and be amused, they became converted, and, from admiration, imitation became the order of the day. As a natural consequence, in a few years, the deserts were swarming with their disciples, a great cenobitic multitude, giving themselves up to abstract meditation and prayer, and, as far as was needful, manual labour.

St Benedict, the great founder of Western Monachism, in the opening chapter of his famous Rule, treats of the several kinds of monks and their way of life in his day.

"It is well known," he says, "that there are four kinds of monks. The first are Cenobites—that is, monastic or conventual, living under a rule or abbot. The second are anchorets, or hermits, who, not in the first fervour of devotion, but after long probation in the monastic life, have learnt to fight against the devil, and after being aided by the comfort and encouragement of others, are now able, by God's assistance, to strive hand to hand against the flesh and evil thoughts, and so go forth from the army of the brotherhood to the single combat of the wilderness. The third and worst kind of monks are the Sarabites, who have never been tried under any rule, nor by the experience of a skilful master, as gold is tried in the furnace, but, being soft as lead, and by their works still cleaving to the world, are known by their tonsure to be disloyal to God.

"These in twos and threes, or perhaps singly, and without a shepherd, are shut up, not in our Lord's sheep-fold, but in their own; the pleasures of their desires is to them a law, and whatever they like or make choice of, they will have to be holy, but what they like not, that they consider unlawful.

"The fourth kind of monks are called 'Gyrovagi,' or wanderers, who travel about all their lives through divers provinces, and stay for two or three days as guests, first in one monastery, then in another; they are always roving, and never settled, giving themselves up altogether to their own pleasures, and to the enticements of gluttony, and are generally in all things worse than the Sarabites. Their miserable way of life is fitter to be buried in oblivion than to be the subject of our discourse." [1]

ST ANTHONY was the first among the Fathers of the Desert to abandon for a time his solitude of thirty-five years, which he did at the urgent request of St Athanasius, when the Church was endangered by the Arians. For this purpose he established himself at Alexandria, where the brilliance of his arguments won for him even the admiration of the philosophers, and the respect of his adversaries. His work accomplished, he returned again to his desert home in Mount Colzin, taking with him his illustrious disciples, Maccarius and Amathas, and many another, whom his saintly life and example had drawn to follow him into his solitude. [2]

These monks all lived entirely by their own labour, principally on bread, fruit, and vegetables, and whatever they gained beyond what was actually required for their own immediate necessities was given to the poor. At first all lived separate in little huts scattered about the locality of the cell of the superior, who among the Egyptian monks was called "David." On Sundays they all met together for prayer, which, with abstinence and self-denial was their chief occupation. Fasting played a very prominent part in the monastic regimen. It was to be diligently cultivated, for it "is the origin of all virtues, the fountain of all excel-

---

[1] "Rule of St Benedict," from the Old English Edition 1638, chap. i. pp. 17-19.
[2] Monasteries of St Anthony's own foundation are said to have contained upwards of 15,000 cenobites. In the early part of the fifth century 5000 monks and 366 monasteries were in the Desert of Scete (Natron) alone.

lence, and a guide to true life." Some fasted the whole, others part of the year, except Sundays and Eastertide, which lasted to the Feast of Pentecost. Saint Macarius of Alexandria fasted all day during Lent, and sometimes for two or three days together. On Sundays he was wont to *indulge* in a raw cabbage leaf. The observance of a strict silence was another chief point, none attempting to hold intercourse with a stranger without leave.

By the "Rules" of Abraham, abbot of the great monastery on Mount Izla, near Nisibis, in the sixth century, the monk was enjoined before all things to lead a life of contemplation and retirement in his own cell; for "when a fish is taken out of the water it dieth, even so the solitary who is brought outside his cell." Idleness was to be rigidly eschewed, "for it begetteth a multitude of evils," and to this end a monk's time was to be filled by constant reading and prayer, when not engaged in the recitation of services or the Psalms. He that would do excellently must pray seven times a day, as did the Psalmist. Thus they rose at midnight, and remained praying till sunrise, often till mid-day.

Silence, as has been said, was to be zealously guarded. When the voice of the Lord bade Arsenius to lead an ascetic life, it said: "Flee, Arsenius, be silent, and live a life of solitude and contemplation"; while to another brother it was said: "Be silent, and count thyself nothing."

During the forty days' fast, no brother might leave his cell, nor at other times visit another monastery, town, village, or even eat with believers without the express permission of the abbot.

After satisfactorily passing through a three years'

novitiate, a brother might leave the central house and establish a home for himself in a separate cell, built by the monastery, or by himself.

On Sundays and festivals, all belonging to the monastery were bound to appear in church, unless prevented by illness, or possessing the abbot's permission to be absent.[1]

Having gathered together for service, the time before its commencement was to be spent in listening to edifying discourse, or meditation, and none were to "turn aside to speak upon matters which are alien [to the day], or to narratives and rumours of battles and wars, or to conversation upon worldly matters, or to vain stories which do harm to the soul."

A number of these separate cells, each tenanted by a single recluse, hermit, or anchorite, was called a *laura*, or monastic village—from the Greek Λαβρα, or Λαυρα, an avenue, labyrinth, or cluster of hermitages—in contra-distinction to a convent or monastery, at that period called a *cenobium*, where the brethren lived together under the rule of one as superior, in one building.

These monasteries frequently sprang into existence by the settlement of a hermit, or a hermit and a few companions, who, as time went on, gradually drew others into a common life with them, the arrivals taking up their abode in rocks and caves, or any shelter that happened to be handy, exposed to all the violence of the weather. This species of Monasticism appears always to have been a peculiar

---

[1] They were summoned from their cells to church by the sound of a board struck with a hammer; the order to strike the summons could only be given by the head of the monastery. *See Frontispiece*, Curzon's "Monasteries in the Levant," and p. 332.

characteristic of the Eastern Christians, and remains so down to the present day, when Greek, Copt, and Abyssinian skin-clad hermits still inhabit eyries, clefts in the rocks, and similar desert places of Asia and Africa.[1]

ST PACHOMIUS was the great advocate and indefatigable labourer in the monastic cause in the East. As the founder of the great monastery of Tabennæ, in the Thebais, he drew up the first complete set of regulations for the use of·cenobites that has come down to us.[2]

The constitution of this monastery may be taken as an example of what conventual foundations were at this period.

The monastery of Tabennæ was built up of a vast network of cells or small houses erected one after another. The establishment was presided over by a supreme head, to whom the religious administration was delegated. In his work he had assistants whose duty it was to look after material and secular affairs, or to take his place in his absence. Each of the houses which went to the composition of the monastery contained a prescribed number of cells, or chambers, each tenanted by three monks. Each house was under the supervision and management of a prior, three or four of such houses going to make up a *tribe*, or monastery.

---

[1] *E.g.* the monasteries of Megaspelion, Gulf of Corinth, Meteora in Thessaly, and Mount Athos, the Holy of Holies of the Greek Church, on the summits of inaccessible rocks, and the awful precipices of the mountain of Quarantina, the scene of our Lord's forty days' temptation, in the Jordan Valley, which is pierced all over with the caves excavated by the ancient anchorites, the Lavra of Kief (Russian) has 1500 religious.

[2] Many celebrated ascetics arose about this period, doctors and fathers of the Church, as Saints Gregory Nazianzen, John Chrysostom, Jerome, and Cyril.

Some of the great monasteries had thirty or forty houses, with an average tenancy of forty monks to each, and from seven to eight hundred persons altogether. That of the Tabennæ at the death of St Pachomius is said to have numbered seven thousand monks, and further, that Pachomius was superior at twenty-two years of age.

According to Palladius, catechumens preparing for baptism, children, youths, and men of all ages were received there. The study of the New Testament and the daily recitation of the whole Psalter was strictly obligatory on all. For those requiring it, wholesome instruction was dispensed thrice a day. Three times a week the prior assembled the whole of his house to converse with them, such conversation being known as catechising, or arguments. Afterwards they discussed the questions dealt with amongst themselves.

Besides the catechising and lessons which the chief or general of the order himself took charge of every week, the mysteries of the Faith were explained to the monks by the prior once on Saturdays and twice on Sundays.

This teaching of the monks was not confined to themselves, but extended to the instruction of the faithful and others of the surrounding districts.

It will be observed that St Pachomius, and other great monastic leaders, did not confine themselves to mere development of the moral principles taken from Holy Scripture, but entered upon an exegesis of them, extending to their audience the right of replying, of putting questions of their own, and discussing their statements, and afterwards had the further liberty accorded them of answering all objections so made in writing.

One of their chief studies after Holy Scripture was the writings of the great men of their day, known to us as the "ancient fathers," by which means they were trained and made eloquently capable to defend the truths of the Christian religion against its detractors, which they were frequently authorised by their superior to do individually, or by a series often of public lectures.

The monastic discipline, originating under St Basilius, or Basil, regarded as the founder of Eastern Monachism (as St Benedict was of the West), and author of the great Rule named after him, was somewhat similar to that of St Pachomius. Under it children were likewise taken as pupils, and, when of sufficient age and proficiency, were sent back to the world to choose a profession, and to start life on their own account.

In the monastery proper was the abode of the young men in training for the ascetic life by the three years' necessary probation. Here, besides learning the Rule, which henceforth was to guide their life, they ploughed the fields, sowed the grain, and reaped the harvest, gathered the grapes and the olives and pressed out the wine and oil—in short, the larger part of the manual labour was performed by them.

From Egypt the monastic institute spread into Palestine, Syria, Mesopotamia, Asia Minor, and even beyond the limits of the Roman Empire. By the fourth and fifth centuries the examples and rules of the anchorites and cenobites of the Orient had overrun Greek, Italy, and Gaul. Already, in the middle of the fourth century, a single Mesopotamian monastery alone had sent forth seventy missionaries, *i.e.* founders and preachers of the monastic idea, and by the opening of the century following, monasteries were founded all over Armenia, Mesopotamia, Persia, and along certain parts of its gulf.

In 401-5 A.D., the ascetics of Constantinople are spoken of in high praise as keeping up a perpetual psalmody, and a multitude of hermits, under the guidance of St Euthymius, practised the most rigorous abstinence in Palestine, not far from Jerusalem. In the following century (501-23), St Fulgentius, exiled in Africa by the Arians, promoted there the observance of primitive discipline by preaching a strict observance to monastic rule.

There were monks in the West from the days of St Jerome, who records that "we daily receive troops of monks from India, Persia, and Ethiopia."

In the years 352-360 A.D., St Martin founded the most ancient monastery at Poitiers, in Gaul, and the famous Abbey of Charmontiers.

St Athanasius, one of the most illustrious of the followers of St Jerome, continued the work of his great master not only by preaching and writing, but by following his example, and becoming a most untiring promoter of the monastic institution in the West of Europe. St Augustine also, in his diocese of Hippo, founded convents for both men and women, placing them under the Rules of Saints Anthony and Pachomius as to common life and poverty. "There were at this time," says their illustrious founder, "monks all over the world."

Still further West, from the midst of the Romagnal Alps, in the towns of Arles and St Maurice d'Agaune, three model monasteries sprang into existence, over which ruled the noted abbots, Saints Hilary, Cæsarius, and Severinus, and which could number such men as

Theodoric, King of the Goths, Theodoric, the Great, and Sigismund, King of Burgundy, among their benefactors.

With so many differences of mind and temperament, it was but natural that the first purity of the monastic idea should become sullied, and the monastic rule itself undergo a great change as relaxations from ancient severity crept in. The combination of the monastic with the clerical order was greatly conducive to this, the services of the latter being often in request in consequence of the deficient number of the clergy; a state of things bringing about, among other things, an interruption of the monastic rule.

In the course of time, it further brought about a precedency of the cleric over the simple monk.[1] Thus, in the East, the abbots became archimandrites, being raised to the priesthood, and thence to the episcopate, the exercise of which functions, and the duty of attendance in church councils, interfered greatly with their observance of the cenobitic life.

St Eusebius, Bishop of Vercelli, was the first prelate of Western Christendom to associate the clerical with the monastic life, his own clergy living in community, and passing their time in prayer, fasting, reading, and manual labour.

Yet this apparent infraction of primitive discipline, though derogatory to the moral position of the monk, raised him, on the other hand, to a standing of social importance in the world, a temporary distraction from the original intention which did not prevent the

---

[1] All monks were originally lay brothers; but in the sixth century the majority were in some kind of orders. When the monks began to take the cure of souls outside their monasteries, the servile occupations naturally fell to the share of the generally unlettered serving brothers. In the West, however, laymen held the office of abbot as late as the eleventh century.

production of men of great piety and learning, who, both by teaching and example, maintained the true position and features of monkish life. Men like Saints Honoratus, Maximus, Hilary, Dalmatius, the two brothers Romanus and Lupicius—just to name a few —and such famous abbeys as Lérino and Mount Jura.

A general idea prevails that there were no monks in Western Europe prior to the advent of St Benedict. At Subiaco, St Benedict himself found monks, one of whom (Romanus) gave him, as a boy eremite, his first monastic habit, and Benedict himself ruled for a time the monks of Vico-Varo. The monks of St Equitius in Italy and St Severinus in Gaul have already been mentioned, while still further West were the monastic colonies of the Britons, founded in Armonica by Saints Sampson, Gildas, Briene, and Malo; the Columban monks of Benchor, Iona, and Lindisfarne, and the nuns who lived under the Rule of St Cæsarius of Arles, and those of St Bridget of Kildare, all belonging to the same period (sixth century), and, as a rule, practising greater austerities than those commanded by St Benedict.

In considering the monastic history of our own country, the mass of unauthentic pious legend may be dismissed at once. Let it be sufficient that by the third century Christianity had established so firm a footing here as to be in a position to send three representative bishops to a council at Arles (314 A.D.), and that some years later St Athanasius could reckon the British Church as true to the Catholic faith as against the attacks of Arianism.[1]

---

[1] King Lucius (A.D. 180) has been credited with establishing an early abbey, a kind of laura, of twelve religious, residing as anchorites (at Glastonbury ?).

The introduction of Monachism into Britain must have been almost coeval with the preaching of the Faith. At the close of the fifth century St Bridget had founded a convent for women at Kildare, and houses of both monks and nuns sprang up over Ireland under her rule. Indeed Monasticism, as applied to men, had reached at this period a high state of development, and by the middle of the sixth century was strong enough to send numerous missionaries, including many women, into Cornwall, and later into what is now Brittany.

The Monasticism of Ireland—for it is there that we must look for the springing of the seed, evidently brought from the East—was founded on the Egyptian Rule, according to the Institutes of Pachomius. All the various kinds of monks described by St Benedict —Cenobites, Anchorites, or Hermits, and Sarabites (itinerant monks who travelled about all over the country and beyond the sea), were to be found.

Again, the homes of the Irish monks—rude villages of wattled huts—were remarkably similar to the lauras of the desert, where the recluses lived, taught, and studied practically in the open air, as did their *confrères* of the Emerald Isle.[1]

The likeness is seen again in the anchorite system, apart from the community life, which formed so essential a part of the Monachism of the Celts. The land abounded with them—these anchorites—a fact supported by the frequent appearance of the word "desert" or "disert" as a place-name in town and parish, and no circumstance appears oftener in the lives of the early Irish saints than the departure of

---

[1] This was the case with St Martin of Tours, who resided in a cell of interwoven twigs, many of his disciples occupying caverns. The Rule of St Martin has been pronounced to be Egyptian.

devotees, aspiring to a still greater perfection, from their monasteries to an abode of their own seeking among the desert places of the land.

The constitution of the early Celtic Church in Britain was thoroughly monastic, and hence the secret of its marvellously rapid success, that was the crowning glory of Celtic Monachism—its *intense* missionary zeal, which has left an indelible mark upon the European Continent, from Iceland in the north, to Taranto in the south of Italy, where St Cathaldus, an Irish bishop, returning from a Roman pilgrimage, turned aside to convert the Taranto heathen, and founded the See.[1]

The vast number of monks which filled the Celtic monasteries appear to us moderns as almost incredible. St Brandan, a Scotch abbot (577 A.D.), is said to have been the spiritual father of as many as three thousand monks. The great monastery of Bangor Iscœd, near Wrexham, founded in 530 A.D. by St Congal, had a population of twelve hundred monks, employed in manual labour on the farms, study, and in various other offices.

In the days of St Asaph, the city, afterwards named in his honour, is described as "a hive of very saintly bees." Its founder had been Kentigern (Mungo, "the Amiable"), Bishop of Glasgow, who, after his flight southward from his own savage Strath Clyde Britons, had returned north from Menevia, with the blessing of Saint David, to found in the Vale of Clwyd a religious community, which soon numbered nearly a thousand members, "all living together in monastic discipline, and serving God with great abstinence." A third of their number tilled the soil; a third looked

---

[1] His pectoral cross of gold, with an ancient Irish inscription, is still shown at Taranto.

after the needs of the establishment, and the remainder were occupied with the perpetual service of the sanctuary. When Kentigern, on his return to his repentant flock, handed his work over to St Asaph's oversight, it was a large monastery over which he was called to rule as the second bishop of the See.

In Ireland, the number of religious equalled those of other parts of Britain, and, in some instances, even surpassed them. Leighlin, in the seventh century, had its fifteen hundred monks, as did Mungret (Limerick), five hundred of whom were preachers, five hundred psalmists, and five hundred occupied in spiritual exercises. Killamary (Kilkenny County) had a thousand under St Gobban, and Cork (in the eighth century) seven hundred, and in addition seventeen bishops, all living the contemplative life. To Mayo came St Gerald and his three brothers with a great company of three thousand disciples.

In short, these communities were little else than great spiritual clans, of which the abbots became heads, having under their direction many bishops, who, while living in community, exercised their episcopal functions at their bidding.

The monks of the age of St Jerome professed obedience to a head, or superior. The whole body was divided into companies of tens and hundreds, each officer of a hundred having nine deans under him. Each monk had a separate cell (sometimes three shared a cell), but possessed no private property, having all things in common. A daily proportion of work was assigned to each, which, when finished, they gave to the dean, who deposited it in the store-house. At a time corresponding to the modern 3 P.M., all assembled at the church, and after the singing of Psalms, and reading of Scripture, and prayer, they seated themselves to hear the lecture begun by the abbot. In their worship the custom was to stand, hence the introduction of the tau, or crutch staff, as a support during the long hours spent in devotion.

Lecture finished, every Decury put themselves at table with their Deans, and took their meal of bread, pulse, herbs, and water—for wine, then the general drink of the people, was strictly precluded from the monastic economy, save to the sick. What remained of the meal was the portion of the poor.

After grace, all withdrew to their cells, where they conversed till evening. No art, except that of writing, appears to have been exercised, and in this the juniors only among the monks were occupied. The cells were rarely left, unless it was to assemble at the place of prayer. As to clothing, many were clothed with bristles of camels and other skins, a soft raiment being esteemed as criminal. When skins were not worn, garments woven of hair, generally that of the camel, and hats of the same material were adopted.

One of the great monastic colonies of Wales was that of the Rose Valley, founded by St David (*Dewi*), who was born about the middle of the fifth century, and died *circa* 601. His reputation for sanctity, no less than of learning, brought about him a considerable number of scholars. The discipline of the rule established for observance by his followers was unusually strict and severe, being very similar to that followed by the Egyptian monks.

A person applying for admission to the monastery was to stay at the gate for ten days, exposed to rebuke and insult, in order to prevent pride. Enduring this humiliation in patience, at the expiration of that period, he was admitted and consigned to the care of the senior in charge of the gate. To this officer he became as a servant, condemned for a long time to hard, manual labour, and no less intellectual affliction, which probation, bravely endured, at length insured him admission into the community.

The "intellectual suffering" was the committal of the Lord's Prayer and many Psalms and other things to heart, for in those days a monk's head was the only Prayer Book to which he had a ready access. The recitation of the Psalter was one of the chief devotions of monastics. In the days we are writing of, it was almost everywhere recited entire every day, and in several places an unceasing psalmody was kept up by constant relays of monks devoted to the purpose.[1] Even in latter monastic days, when the Rule of St Benedict had entirely superseded all others in the West, the individual coming to conversion, *i.e.* to the monastic life, was supposed to know the whole Psalter by heart.

In this period of trial, the fitness of the applicant was severely tested in regard to his renunciation of the world and other monastic pre-requisites. If found fit and worthy, he was further instructed in the remaining ordinances, clothed in the habit, and handed over to the porter, who, at the hour of prayer, put him in his appointed place.

The head (St David and those after him) was called "father," and not "abbot" as of old,[2] to whom all rendered an implicit obedience. St David established the following consuetudinal.

Every monk was to pass his time in common, labour-

---

[1] As at Bangor.
[2] Among the Egyptians he was called "David," whence perhaps the name of the Welsh saint.

ing with his own hands for the common welfare, according to the apostolical direction, that he who would not labour should not eat. The labour was that of husbandry. During their employment there was to be no other conversation than what the occasion necessarily required; but every one "performed his task, either praying, or rightly thinking."

Concluding their appointed work they returned to their monastery, and passed the remainder of the day till evening (3 P.M.) in reading, writing, or praying. At the sound of a bell, without a moment's delay, they proceeded to the church in silence, where, after the psalmody, they remained in genuflection (bending or bowing of the body, the ancient attitude for prayer [1]) until the appearance of the stars proclaimed the close of the day, when all retired to the refectory to eat sparingly, and not to satiety. When all had withdrawn, the abbot alone remained praying in private for the good of the Church.

Their food was bread, with roots or herbs, seasoned with salt, quenching their thirst with a mixture of water and milk. This, according to EUSEBIUS, was the fare of the Oriental monks, who subsisted on bread, water, salt, and herbs; the latter being included by St Chrysostom among the luxuries.

Supper being ended and grace said, they returned to the church, and continued for about three hours in watchings (vigils), prayers, and genuflections, during which it was not permitted to any to slumber, cough, sneeze, spit, etc. After this they went to partake of the nocturnal recreation of sleep, but only to rise at cockcrow for prayer till daylight. "At sunrise—nay, many

---

[1] Some Orders still only kneel at their devotions in Lent.

hours before daylight," says St Chrysostom, writing of the monks of his day, "they rise from their beds, and, forming a choir, diligently praise God with hymns."

The father, or abbot, passed the day in attendance upon the sick, at the schools, among visitors, the poor, widows, and orphans, and in other offices of regulation and inspection, in prayer and ascetical severities, among them the consecration of the Eucharist, and a succeeding immersion in cold water (a favourite austerity), " to subdue all carnal provocations."

All gifts or possessions offered by unjust men were refused, and a hatred of wealth cherished; nothing could be called their "own" without immediate subjection to severe penance. All inward sensations and thoughts were discovered to the superior, and from him was demanded permission in all things. Their clothing was the skins of beasts,[1] *i.e.* common leather jerkins,[2] usual also with the Egyptians, and white cowls.[3] The Egyptian monks wore the short cloak of the Greek philosophers (*tribonium*). In the fifth century the monks of Gaul had, besides cloaks, girdles, and walking-sticks, a hair-shirt, according to St Chrysostom, which was also a part of the Oriental monk's habit, worn perhaps in all instances, as in mediæval days, as a penance. These shirts, reaching from the elbows to the knees, were made of goats' hair, worked into fine threads, and woven by the wearers for this especial purpose. That worn by St Thomas à Becket was washed by his chaplain, and it is recorded to have been rare if there was no vermin in it. Feet and legs were bare.[4]

---

[1] *See* "Acta Sanctorum Martyrum."
[2] RICEMARCH.   [3] REYNER.
[4] Pachomius orders the feet of visitors to be washed, even if clerks or monks. This was also an Anglo-Saxon custom.

The mode of shaving the head among the Celtic monks differed altogether from what is known as the Petrine or Pauline tonsure. The former shaved the head from the top to the level of the ears, leaving the hair entirely covering the back of the head; the latter the entire surface of the skull in a broad circular fashion.

Their houses were of wattle-work, thatched; stone buildings being deemed miraculous by the Britons.

St Columba is credited with the compilation of the first set of Monastic Rules, which were very generally adopted in France, even as the Rules drawn up by St Isidore, Bishop of Seville, and those of St Augustine of Hippo were followed in the British Isles. In general principles these Codes bore much resemblance to one another, though they varied in many particulars, one of their chief merits being their applicability to religious persons living in different countries. Those who practised the Rules of St Columba lived much the same life as that followed afterwards in the great Benedictine houses; prayer culture of the mind, and labour with the hands, were the invariable employments of the cloistral life. And again the Benedictine Code was in substance the same as the Egyptian, but mitigated and rendered more efficacious.

So deeply had these Rules of Saint Columba and his imitators, Saints Isidore and Augustine, laid hold of their observers, that they maintained their hold and authority even into the eight century, though everything was done by the new system imported from Rome, and zealously propagated throughout the land by the Anglo-Saxon monk, St Wilfred (634-709), to crush them out. The great monastery of Iona was the very last to submit to the powers from Rome after a valiant withstanding of some hundreds of years.

In a comparison of these monastic systems—I mean the system of the old Egyptian anchorites and that of the Celts—one very striking difference is observed between them. This is in regard to art and learning. The ancient Easterns utterly tabooed art in all its aspects, probably on account of its close connection with Paganism, but with the Westerns the case was the exact opposite. They not only loved it, but practised it, nay, brought it to such a pitch of perfection that their skill in this department is the wonder of to-day.

What words can describe the incomparable beauty of the Book of Kells, treasured in Trinity College, Dublin, the Gospels of Saint Cuthbert and Chad, and many a like precious treasure, stored up in the public museums and the cabinets of the wealthy? What of the gold and enamel work, such as that, for instance, in the museum of the Royal Dublin Society?

Their schools were famous even on the Continent. In the seventh century, Dagobert II., King of France, was educated at Slane Abbey, in Meath; and Alcuin corresponded from the Court of Charlemagne with Colcu, the chief teacher of the school of Clonmacnois, the letters showing Alcuin's high estimation of the learning of Colcu, and the excellence of his school.[1]

The monasteries of the Anglo-Saxon era were at first mere assemblages of devout people, secular clerks drawn around the habitation of one leading the eremetical life, but bound by no certain rules, daily

---

[1] For further particulars of Irish teaching at this period see (Dr) Stokes, "Greek and Hebrew Learning in Irish Monasteries."

performing the sacred offices, yet enjoying all the privileges of our clerks in holy orders, and were even married, who exercised a kind of abbatial supervision over them.

Frequently, at first, this individual, and afterwards his companions with him, acted as a preceptor of youth.[1] The habitations were clustered around the dwelling of the chief or head, to the number of twelve, each with its chapel, tenanted by a like number of religious, the whole enclosed by a high wall. The strictest of enclosure prevailed, none going to the gate, or the house beside it, where they held converse with friends and acquaintances, without the express license of the abbot. On Sundays all assembled together for the Eucharist, after which they ate together.

The venerable Bede observes that it was the fashion in his day for noblemen to purchase crown lands upon the pretence of founding a monastery, and making themselves abbots, collected a convent out of expelled monks, and their own servants, and led a life perfectly secular, even to "bringing wives into the monastery," and being husbands and abbots at the same time. The courtier-servants of the king also adopted the same fashion, and became abbots and ministers of state at one and the same time.

The Danes, lest the number of their effective troops should be diminished, and the convents refuse to take up arms against their masters, not only discouraged conversion, but rigorously persecuted the monks to that end. So much so, that in King Alfred's time

---

[1] The religious congregations of Abingdon, Bath (in its refoundation), and Malmesbury had such an origin, and that of St Gall, Switzerland. Lucerne began with a settlement of monks in an orchard, the first house being the monastery erected by the lake, thence it grew into a village, then a town, then a city.

none but boys were willing to become monks, and thus Monasticism in England was well-nigh extinct. It is said that in the tenth century there were no monks in England except at Glastonbury and Abingdon. This statement it is presumed only applied to monks proper, and not to canons who occupied the monasteries, and whose secular mode of life eventually brought about their overthrow.

On the other hand, the Britons, in their hatred of the Angles, would not impart what knowledge they possessed of the Christian Faith to them; and hence, among other reasons, we hear of no such enormous establishments as are recorded to have existed in Wales and Ireland.

King Alfred, we are told, founded a monastery with different orders intermixed; and Osbern, a Norman monk, says that before Archbishop Dunstan's reformation, in the reign of King Edgar, "there was no common rule of living, and that the name of abbot was scarce heard of."

Religious houses or convents for women, as has been said, came into being with the establishments for men. The first female religious in the early Church were of three classes—the virgins devoted to the Church, the young widows, and the deaconesses. They led a similar life to that of the monks—a life of seclusion and contemplation.

In Egypt and Palestine the sisters both of St Anthony and St Pachomius presided as head over two congregations of virgins, having been placed in that position by their venerable brothers. In Pontus, and Cappadocia also, St Basilius founded several houses for women, his sister, Machrina, assisting in developing the work, and their number so greatly increased that, at the opening of the fifth century, one single convent (or cenobium) contained two hundred and fifty virgins.

Their increase was no less rapid in Europe. In the days of St Anthony himself, two religious houses were established in Rome. Eusebius, Bishop of Vercelli, founded a similar institution adjacent to his own Church; and another was the remarkable convent at Milan, which owed its establishment to St Ambrose, bishop of that city, in which his sister, Marcellina, and her faithful companion, Candida, took refuge. Ere the close of the fourth century St Paula, who lived under the direction of St Jerome, at Bethlehem, had caused three convents and a monastery to be erected in Africa, placing the management in the hands of the celebrated "father." At Jerusalem, Melania, a lady descended from one of the most noble families of Rome, founded another house for women, and her grand-daughter of the same name, at Tagaste, near Carthage, a monastery of one hundred and thirty nuns, maintaining herself by the transcription of manuscripts. From Tagaste, Melania the younger went to Egypt, and thence to Jerusalem, where, though not yet thirty years of age, she lived as a recluse on the Mount of Olives, subsequently founding there the order of the Canonesses of the Holy Sepulchre, which, after a variety of vicissitudes, has survived to the present day.

With regard to religious houses for women in the primitive British Church, very little information is forthcoming. Dean Milman, in his "History of Latin Christianity," speaking of the period of the Saxon invasion, says they "must have existed in considerable numbers." The suppression of a convent at Malmesbury, under the direction of Dinoth, abbot of Banchor by St Augustine, for the misconduct of its inmates, lends support to this statement.

The earliest establishment for women, erected after the coming of the Benedictine monk, Augustine, was that founded at Folkestone in 640 A.D., by Eadbald, King of Kent, for his daughter, Eanswitha. Close upon the same period dates the convent erected at Hartlepool (645 A.D.) by Hien, who became its first abbess, to be subsequently succeeded by that most prominent figure of Anglo-Saxon church history, St Hilda, the founder (657-8) of the celebrated house of Whitby. This, as was generally the case in the Celtic and Anglo-Saxon Church, was a double convent, that is, a house for both sexes under one roof, and not infrequently under the government of women.

Such was the general position of cenobitism, Monasticism, or by whatever designation it has been known, when St Benedict, the future patriarch of Western Monachism, and supreme legislator for, and institutor of the first regular monastic order, came forth from the seclusion of his cavern at Subiaco, in the year 528, to found that glory of after ages—the famous Abbey of Monte Cassino.

# BOOK II

## ST BENEDICT, FOUNDER OF WESTERN MONASTICISM

AT Nursia, one of the many white hillside cities of Umbria, Benedict, "blessed by nature and in name," was born in the spring of the year 480 A.D.

In early boyhood he was sent to Rome, the then centre of all civilisation, to study the sciences and to become familiar with the manners of the world, but horrified by the fearful vices prevailing on every side, he fled away lest the shameful city should be destroyed like another Sodom.

Journeying on and on into the far-reaching desert, the youthful enthusiast of sixteen years took up his abode in a cave, and gave himself up to prayer for the city and its sinners he had left, and to the contemplation of the devout life. In short, he did what many another had done before him, fled the world and took refuge from its snares and temptations in the solitary wilds of the desert.

Naturally, the fragrance of the sanctity of such a life could not long remain hidden. The first years of trial over, he gathered strength upon strength ere he came forth from the wilderness to strengthen and to conquer.

First his fame reached and attracted the recluses living the eremetical life in his vicinity, and gathered them to him; then it went still further afield, drawing people out of the world to a life similar to his own, until it became absolutely necessary that something like order should prevail among the heterogeneous number of devout persons by whom he was surrounded.

To this end he begun by gathering them together into companies, and for their guidance he drew up his famous "Rule," which has ever since been the guide and groundwork of all monks and monastic constitutions. It differed from all others in that it gave stability to the system by the imposition of life-long vows. This system spread with marvellous rapidity, and primitive discipline and fervour flourished for a long period; only at the end of the third century of its existence did the purity of its first devotion begin to grow lax.

Then arose a series of reformers and revivalists of primitive rule, chief among them Odo of Tours and Berno of Cluny,[1] who started what is called the Cluniac reform, from the great Abbey of Cluny in Burgundy, early in the tenth century; the Carthusians and Cistercians, under Bruno and Bernard of Clairvaux, taking up the work of reform of the then laxed Cluniacs, and the revival of ancient discipline in the latter part of the following (eleventh) century.

All these were not by any means destroyers. They were purely and simply reformers of abuses which had crept into the order with the roll of years, and valiant revivalists of the primitive observance of the days long past. Their one all-absorbing idea was not to found

---

[1] Hugh, abbot of Cluny (1049-1109) held office for the long period of sixty years. Ten thousand monks are said to have been under his superintendence.

fresh orders of religious, who should live under a newer rule more adapted to the needs of their times, but to make the ancient Rule of St Benedict more efficient, and to guard against the entrance and recurrence of abolished abuses, and to prevent relaxed observance by additional regulations and a more strict observance of the law of the great patriarch.

The early part of the thirteenth century saw the foundation of a new army of religious in the orders of Friars Franciscan, Dominican, Carmelite, and Augustinian who, ere the close of the century, counted by hundreds. While still religious, living the conventual life, and bound to it by the three irrevocable ties of poverty, chastity and obedience, the mission of the friars was altogether a new one. The Franciscans and Dominicans, scorning the possessions of lands, revenues, and magnificent houses, were to be poor men, living with and amongst the poor, and as the poor, and for the poor. The one great object of their founding was to rescue the great " submerged tenth," by example and precept, from that woeful state of social misery, moral degradation, and spiritual destitution which the violence and arrogance of the rule of their masters, spiritual and temporal, had plunged them. They came, more particularly the Franciscans, or Grey Friars (so called from the colour of their habit), avowedly organised to do what the regular ministry of the Church of those days had neglected or failed to accomplish.

And yet, although by their very mode and object of life antagonistic to the regular clergy, or the old monastic orders, even the friars were not destroyers or overthrowers of that system which had been from of old. They, too, were very zealous for the pure and single-eyed observance of the precepts and example of the Christ which had inflamed the hearts and souls of their brethren in the early monastic days. They came with all the burning zeal of their first enthusiasm to infuse new life into the old monastic tree, which the wear and tear of ages had began to render decrepid and dry. That after the unusually fair promise of spring, the grand short summer of success, and the unparalleled ingathering of a great harvest, the sharp, stern winter of ultimate failure should overtake the friars, as it had their predecessors, was but a repetition of all history from the beginning of the world, and will be till the end. That they should be degraded by that very world they so zealously laboured to save, that they became at length not one whit the better than those old monks whom they rebuked so sternly, and against whose errors they had so fiercely preached, was only what had happened to many great institutions before, and will repeatedly happen again.

But for all this, the work of the monks and friars was a grand and noble one, and the history of the world would be lacking, indeed, were the record of it obliterated from its pages. It has been truly said that "the world has never been indebted to any body of men as the illustrious order of Benedictine monks." The pages of history literally blaze with the great names of the mighty ones of this celebrated order.[1] From its first foundation, in the early part of the sixth century, it has produced nearly half a hundred popes, cardinals four times as many, hundreds of patriarchs and archbishops, thousands of bishops and canonised saints, while emperors, kings, and their consorts, not

---

[1] St Wilfred of Ripon is accredited with the introduction of the Benedictine Rule into England.

a few, have abandoned their crowns and thrones for the cloisters of this order. In the council chambers of princes, at the helm of the state, in schools and colleges, on the papal throne, and in the far-away lonely mission-field, the sons of St Benedict have been found proclaiming, in no uncertain language, the Gospel of Peace.

Of the Benedictine Rule, Constitution, or Code of laws for the government of monks, it is said to be the result of profound physiological and philosophical studies; a work of moral science, wisdom, and piety, which divided the monk's time between prayer and manual labour, to be succeeded by the cultivation and exercise of the intellect whenever the glory of God, the interests of the monastery, and the education of the people might require it.

This latter part—that of intellectual study—was an after-thought of the subsequent legislators for the order, and no part of the original ordinance of the great patriarch, who, like his great mediæval counterpart, the seraph of Assisi, held the acquisition of worldly learning as quite of secondary importance. To know the Psalter well, and a fair acquaintance with the Scriptures, was about the sum of knowledge required of the postulant for admission to the order.

Of this admirable "Rule," the late Cardinal Newman writes :—

"Its spirit indeed is one, but not its outward circumstances. It is not an order proceeding from one mind at a particular date, and appearing all at once in its full perfection, and in its extreme development, and in one form and the same everywhere, and from first to last, as is the case with other great religious institutions; but it is an organisation, diverse, complex, and irregular, and variously ramified, rich rather than symmetrical, with many origins, and centres, and new beginnings, and the action of local influences, like some great natural growth, with tokens, on the face of it, of its being a Divine work, not the mere creation of human genius. Instead of progressing on plan and system, and from the will of a superior, it has shot forth and run out, as if spontaneously, and has shaped itself according to events from an irrepressible fulness of life within, and from the energetic self-action of its parts, like the symbolical creatures in the prophet's vision, 'which went, every one of them, straightforward, whither the impulse of the spirit was to go.'[1]

"He" (St Benedict), adds Cardinal Newman, "found the world, physical and social, in ruins, and his mission was to restore it in the way—not of science, but of nature; not as if setting about to do it, not professing to do it by any set time, or by any series of strokes, but so quietly, patiently, gradually, that often till the work was done, it was not known to be doing. It was a restoration rather than a visitation, correction, or conversion. The new world he helped to create was a growth rather than a structure. Silent men were observed about the country, or discovered in the forest digging, cleaning, and building; and other silent men, not seen, were sitting in the cold cloister tiring their eyes, and keeping their attention on the stretch, while they painfully deciphered, then copied and re-copied the manuscripts which they had saved. There was no one that *contended or cried out*, or drew attention to what was going on, but by degrees the woody swamp became a hermitage, a religious house, a farm, an abbey, a village, a seminary, a school of learning, and a city. Roads and villages connected it with other abbeys and cities which had similarly grown up, and what the haughty Alaric or fierce Attila had broken to pieces, these patient, meditative men have brought together, and made to live again. And then, when they had in the course of many years gained their peaceful victories, perhaps some new invaders came, and with fire and sword undid their slow and persevering toil in an hour.... Down in the dust lay the labour and civilisation of centuries—churches, colleges, cloisters, libraries—and nothing was left to them but to begin all over again; but this they did without grudging, so promptly, cheerfully, and tranquilly, as if it were by some law of nature that the

---

[1] "The Mission of St Benedict."

restoration came, and they were like the flowers, and shrubs, and great trees which they reared, and which, when ill-treated, do not take vengeance, or remember evil, but give forth fresh branches, leaves, and blossoms, perhaps in greater profusion, or with richer quality, for the very reason that the old were rudely broken off."[1]

"The greatness of the Benedictines did not, however, consist either in their agricultural skill, their prodigies of architecture, or their priceless libraries, but in the parentage of countless men and women illustrious for active piety, for wisdom in the government of mankind, for profound learning, and for that contemplative spirit which discovers within the soul itself things beyond the limits of the perceptible creation."

Thus Sir James Stephen [2] sums up the highest claims of the Benedictines upon the gratitude of succeeding times.

Soon after the amalgamation of the various monasteries or establishments of recluses, St Benedict found himself at the head of a vast army of monks, who, with almost amazing rapidity, spread throughout the whole Christian world the Rules of their illustrious chief. St Maurus, whose father had been minister to Theodoric the Great, and Cassiodorus founded respectively the great branch monasteries of St Maur-sur-Loire in France, and Vivieri in Calabria, whose library was one of the richest in the kingdom. To collect books, Cassiodorus put himself to great pains and expense, not confining himself to the Scriptures, with their commentaries, the Greek and Latin Fathers, and Jewish historians, but adding the principal works on geography, grammar, and rhetoric, and the best treatises on medicine, in order that the monks attached

---

[1] Cardinal Newman, "Historical Sketches: The Mission of St Benedict," Vol. III. pp. 410, 411.
[2] "Essays," 371.

to the infirmary might be fully capable of attending the sick.

In these collections of Cassidorus remarkable homage is paid to the calligraphy of the monks of that day.

"I confess, my brethren," he says, "that of all your physical labours, that of copying books has always been the avocation most to my taste; the more so, as by this exercise of the mind upon the Holy Scriptures, you convey to those who will read what you have written a kind of oral instruction you preach with the hand, converting the fingers into organs of speech, announcing silently to men a theme of salvation; it is, as it were, fighting the evil one with pen and ink. For every word written by the antiquary[1] the demon receives a severe wound. . . . In his seat, as he copies his books, the recluse travels through many lands without quitting his room, and the work of his hands has his influence in places where he has never been."

Calligraphy and illuminating were the favourite employments in many monasteries long before St Benedict had enjoined manual labour as one of the chief characteristics of his Rule. In the monastery of Kildare, governed by St Bridget, and in the monastery founded by St Columba, the teaching of Christian art, of Church lore, and profane literature was unequalled in its perfection, its fame reaching even to Gaul.

Thenceforward, throughout every succeeding age, learning and civilisation was carried on by the monks. Barbarians—Vandals, Goths, Huns—one after another swept down and overran the Roman Empire as a devastating torrent—a torrent which the strong bulwarks of Monasticism alone could stem—savage hordes nurtured and maintained on blood and slaughter which only the monk, like another Orpheus, could charm and tame. The fire and sword of the barbarian went out

---

[1] *Scribe.*

after them with a terrible ferocity it is true, wiping them out from their settlements in the land, but for all this they rose again and again, Phœnix-like, from their ashes, to carry on still further their noble work.

The monk alone, throughout all these dark ages, cast himself forward into the gap to stay the course of these wild boars out of the wood, and to bring them down to the nailed-pierced feet of the crucified Saviour. Every stage of the ninth century, it has been said, exhibited deep and lasting traces of the monk. To him all Europe owes a debt of gratitude which it never can repay.

Having nothing better to occupy their hands, petty warfare was the general employment of the great and noble of all countries in those semi-barbarous times, and for the rest, quiet gentle souls, if they preferred the way of peace they must necessarily engage in a different kind of warfare to that of the bloody massacres of highly vaunted knight-errants of early mediæval days. To such as these the safe, calm refuge of the cloister offered a spiritual battle-field whereon they could combat to their hearts' content the allied forces of the World, the Flesh, and the Devil.

Shufflers from the world's responsibilities, say you? Cowards slipping the yoke which tied their brethren to the burden and heat of the day? Be it so. Yet the cloistral life was anything but a "bed of roses." It could hardly be where toil and hardship, endurance and silence went to make up the monk's daily portion. Once within the monastery, the monk's neck was fitted to the hard yoke of the Rule which, with an almost harsh sternness, declared no one was to be idle. The chief enemy—the Goliath of the monk—was Idleness, the breeder of Sin, and the weapons wherewith he was to be combated were Manual Labour and Prayer. The monk's life-existence was to be woven up of a woof of Labour and a web of Prayer.

The postulant, weary of the strife and clang of the world, came seeking peace, and in a life of unceasing labour by a strange coincidence found it, for the life of the cloister had yet another and more beautiful side. The old monkish chroniclers, themselves, bronzed by the sun, with hands corned, wrinkled, and knotted by this self-same labour, have sketched the picture for us. In the charming prose-poetry of the day they describe for us, with the minutest detail, the pastoral life of the brethren — for in the cloister all were brothers, whether they had been nurtured in castle or field—the hay-making, the reaping, the pruning, in the sweat of the brow, in the heat of the day.

"Everything was rural," says a writer on the subject, "and the silence of countryside was broken only by the sound of the Psalms. Then you might see the monk guiding the plough and singing 'Alleluia.' The reaper sweating to the harvest repeats the Psalms, and the husbandman in the vineyard uses the pruning-hook while he sings the Canticles of David.[1] These are the songs, and, as the phrase is, the love-ditties of the monks. These are the pipings of the shepherd, these, so to say, are the implements of their husbandry. . . . Idyllic scenes that have come down to us of the tranquil labour of the monks in the field seem less far off than anything else connected with the life of the monasteries. We can still picture to ourselves, in spite of all change, their work with the spade and the plough and the axe, the watching of the shepherd, the work in the shearing time, and the milking at night. Some brief, simple record, though written so long ago that the hand that wrote it has been dust for centuries, brings it all back to us. Take one such case: we read how one Julian had been sent to visit the monastery of St Œquitius, and he

---

[1] *See* also ST JEROME, "Epistles," 18.

tells us: 'I found there some old men, writing. I asked them where was the abbot, and they replied, "In the valley beneath the monastery; he is cutting grass." Folios of description might fail to give the life to the past that is given in those few straight words: "He is in the valley beneath the monastery, cutting grass."'

"Or take this description that William of Jumiège gives of the monks who founded the great monastery of Bec: 'You would have seen them after the office of the Church, going into the fields to spend the day in agricultural labours, the abbot carrying the seeds on his head, and holding tools in his hand; some clearing the ground, others carrying manure on their heads and spreading it on the ground, no one eating his bread in idleness, all returning to the church at the hour of divine office, and then sitting down to a meal of oaten bread and herbs with salt and water."

What does Europe not owe to the monks? The Benedictines were not only the thinkers, the writers, the artists, and schoolmasters, but also the farmers— the agriculturalists of Europe, the pioneers of a golden age of husbandry.

Of a truth there have been no workers like those workers of old—workers without wage, and for the pure love of that peace and satisfaction which true labour alone can bring. The old chroniclers constantly speak of the monks as the leaders of husbandry, William of Jumiège using the words "monk" and "agriculturist" as though they were synonymous.

Guizot says: "The Benedictine monks were the agriculturists of Europe; they cleared it on a large scale, associating agriculture with preaching." Hallam bears a similar testimony that we owe the restoration of a great part of Europe to the devoted energy of the monks, and explains how, if the monasteries *were* endowed with tracts of land which seem to us enormous, it was simply because there was no other way of getting them reclaimed.

The monks became possessed of the, to us moderns, *vast* estates in several ways.[1] On the founding of a monastery the monks invariably, in accordance with ancient precedent, settled in a desert or waste place— places chosen *because* they were waste and solitary, often unhealthy, and such as could be reclaimed only by a vast amount of incessant labour by those willing to work hard and live hard, great tracts of land often given, not being worth the keeping—forests, swamps, barren heaths. Lands which for a long period made no return, leaving their cultivators half-starved and dependent on the charity of admiring benefactors.

Thus was the great mother house of Citeaux founded with its, in after years, 3000 affiliated monasteries. The first monks of Rievaulx (Yorkshire) settled there in 1131, "then," says William of Newburgh, "a place *vastæ solitudinis et horroris.*" Ramsey and Croyland were swamps accessible only by boats, "every wain that came thither was shod with silver." The after glory of Westminster was at first the "terrible place called Thorney," often flooded by tides, and Furness (Lancashire) rose in Beckansgill, the Valley of Deadly Nightshade.

The Cistercians, the stern puritans of mediæval days, invariably reared their lonely homes in undrained valleys, unreclaimed wastes, amid the bush of dense forests, full of unhealthy influences and ague-stricken fens, in order, as St Bernard says, they might have the thought of death ever before their eyes, and the hope of a better country to cheer their ascetic life.

That these places of disease and desolation afterwards became very Arcadias of fruitful delights was entirely

---

[1] The rent-roll of Christ Church, Canterbury, fills nearly four columns of contracted pages of Domesday Survey.

due to the years of indefatigable labour spent upon them by the monks. "Give these monks," says Gerald du Barri, "a naked moor, or a wild wood, then let a few years pass away, and you will find not only beautiful churches, but dwellings of men built around them." The monks of Croyland were the recognised guardians of the fens, making it the special service of their lives to build and guard the dykes raised against the waters. So, too, the abbots of Furness erected dykes to prevent the irruption of the sea at high tides and in gales of wind, precautions neglected after the dissolution of the monastery, causing the sea several times to flow over the Walney Island, doing immense damage.

Again, it was no unusual thing for kings and other large landowners—and, in theory, the whole land of a country was the property of the king, who could dispose of it as it pleased him—to come forward and offer to monastic corporations, established or to be established, large tracts of wild and uncultivated land, on condition of its cultivation, or in exchange for other small portions, which by their untiring industry had been rendered profitable and fertile.

Yet again, the endowment of each monastery was frequently made up of property brought into the community by founders, who—like the English Roger de Montgomery, founder of Shrewsbury; Walter Espec, the great Baron of Helmsley and the Battle of the Standard, "tall and large, with black hair, a great beard, and a voice like a trumpet," at Rievaulx; and Turketel, the great chancellor, at Croyland; and kings like Sigbert, brother of Redwald, King of the East Angles (630 A.D.) — themselves became monks, and others who entered it. In the early monastic days, if the novice was an adult, he was obliged to distribute all his belongings to the poor. The Franciscans, in their first fervour, were very strict upon this, and one who had divided his substance amongst his relations and friends, instead of the actual poor, received a stern rebuke from St Francis and the refusal of entrance. In after days permission was acceded for a grant of them to the abbey.

"If he [the new brother] hath any property," says the Rule of St Benedict,[1] "he shall either first bestow it upon the poor, or, by a formal gift, hand it over to the monastery, without any reserve for himself, because, for the future, he must know that he hath not so much as power over his own body. Let him therefore, presently, in the Oratory be stripped of his own garments, and be clothed in those of the monastery.

"With regard to his [the son of a noble] property, they shall . . . promise, under [written] oath, that they will never either give or furnish him with an occasion of having anything, either by themselves or by any other person or means whatsoever. If they will not do this, but wish to offer something as an alms to the monastery, by way of acknowledgment, let them make a donation of whatever they please, and reserve the income of it to themselves during life. Let matters be so managed that no expectation remain with the child, whereby, being deceived, he may perish (which God forbid), as we have learnt by experience in the case of others. Let those who are poorer act in the same way. But such as have nothing whatever shall simply make the promise [in writing], and with the oblation [a host and a chalice with wine, which the child held in his hands during the ceremony of dedication[2]] give up their son, before witnesses."

On the other hand, the income of the lands and property to which the youthful neophyte was entitled, was sometimes ceded by deed of transfer to the monastery receiving him.

---

[1] Chapters LVIII. and LIX. of an old English edition of 1638.
[2] "Constit. : Lafranci," Cap. xviii.

Large gifts of land were also frequently given for special spiritual services rendered, for the support of various charitable works—as the cell established at Holme, on Spalding Moor, by certain members of the great families of Vavasour and Constable, and two monks maintained in it to guide travellers on the way —for the maintenance of the sick and poor in alms-houses and hospitals, in which various departments the monks of England held and utilised, as trustees for the sick and poor, and other works of charity, two-thirds of the whole realm of England. How well and faithfully they fulfilled that trust is abundantly proved by the fact, that, upon the dissolution of the monasteries, in the sixteenth century, when these same lands passed into the hands of a rapacious king and his dissolute courtiers, the country swarmed with beggars, *i.e.* indigent poor and monks, both deprived of their means of subsistence, by the alienation of the abbey lands, notwithstanding that the Bill for their suppression contained a clause, providing that the old hospitality should be kept up as of yore by their new owners, a clause not abrogated until a succeeding reign.[1]

The charters of institution, and the patrimonial titles of the chief abbeys, are both the proof and the reward for the services rendered to civilisation by the monastic establishments. One abbey was bequeathed a donation on condition that certain waste lands were put into cultivation; another received lands on the precise understanding that it opened asylums and places of hospitality for the poor and sick, for pilgrims and strangers. It was a common practice with Charlemagne and his successors to make grants of lands to

---

[1] St Jac. I. c. 28.

individuals on the express ground that they should clear and cultivate them.[1]

Not alone was lasting benefits conferred by the clearance and cultivation of the land by the monks, benefits which were small when compared to those bestowed on mankind in general; among others, the advantages derived from their society, after they had become large proprietors and landlords with more benevolence, and farmers with more intelligence, skill, and capital, than all their compeers.

In the first instance, they themselves created the villages and towns which, in after years, they governed.[2] To take but a few handy examples, Boston, St Botolph's Town, the capital of the Fens, was originally a desert piece of ground given to St Botoloph by Ethelmund, King of the South Angles, for the purpose of building a monastery there.[3] In a similar way, other monastic towns, like St Edmundsbury,[4] sprang into existence. Bodmin was a growth from a solitary hut which St Guron, a Cornish eremite, occupied in the valley there, near a copious spring, at the western end of the present churchyard, at the commencement of the sixth century.

These gifts of lands were in after days the cause of much contention and evil, as the landlords, on whose

---

[1] At the Middle Age, probably quite two-thirds of the lands of Western Europe was uncultivated, and lying in a natural state, more or less.

[2] Just as some Spanish Benedictine monks have done to-day at the settlement of New Norcia, near Perth, Western Australia.

[3] "Saxon Chronicle."

[4] Annually the *Mote Horn*, and the keys of the town of St Edmundsbury were delivered to the Sacrist by the town bailiffs, the former handing them in his turn to the prior, who, in the same way, returned them to the town authorities through the Sacrist. This was done in token that the town altogether belonged to the convent, and that, during a vacancy of the abbacy, the king did not take it into his hands.

lands monasteries were established, often gave to such a monastery the tithes which had hitherto been applied to the support of the parish priest. On the assignment of such tithes, the monastery replaced the parish priest by one of its own community, or some other person, as vicar, who acted for it in the performance of its new duties.

It was to prevent such irregularities as this that the Cistercians, in their early purity, refused to receive gifts of tithes, lest, by so doing, they should impoverish the parish clergy.

For many years after the introduction of Christianity, there had been no general obligation to pay tithes, the clergy being originally supported by oblations and free gifts from those they ministered to. In those days the ownership of the land was distributed among comparatively few persons. Many of these who built churches upon their estates for the benefit of themselves and their dependents, tenants, or vassals, would also build a residence for the priest, attaching to it some portion of arable, or pasture land, as an endowment, for his use. This land was called *glebe*, *i.e.* top earth, that which is turned over by the plough. In addition to this "glebe," some patrons endowed their churches with the tithe of the produce of their estates.

With this assignment of land passed to the priest the obligations which were attached to it, *e.g.* the support of the poor, and the maintenance of the services, and the fabric of the Church.

"Let the priests receive the tithes of the people," says a canon issued by a bishop of York, "and keep a written account of all that have paid them; and divide them, in the presence of such as fear God, according to canonical authority. Let them set apart the first share for the repairs and ornaments of the Church; let them distribute the second to the poor and the stranger with their own hands, in mercy and humility, and reserve the third part for themselves."

The monks, in fact, with their dependents dwelling within the precincts of the house, formed in themselves quite a large village. Gradually around the abbey was gathered a population whose labour was necessary to the inmates and profitable to the material interests of the house. Around the abbot's close were built the shops, stalls, and sheds serving for the sale of the crops, cattle, agricultural and other produce of the monastic domain. On the anniversary of the feast-day of the patron saint of the monastery there was a fair, sometimes several, attracting large crowds.

The territorial domain, called the *leuga*, annexed to Battle Abbey, was a space about a mile and a half, taken roughly, all round it. Whoever came and settled there became virtually subject to the house, a vassal of the abbot, who governed as its lord. To these subjects he dispensed justice in all cases involving forfeiture; and at every vacancy they raised a hundred shillings as a fine to the newly-elected abbot, probably for a renewal of their privileges. He reflected such honour upon them that they claimed rank as burgesses. Besides the priest and clerk, two smiths, a cordwainer, the founder of the abbey bells, two "porchers," three tailors, a gardener, a weaver, three cooks, three bakers, a rush-worker, a writer, a miller, a goldsmith, two carpenters, two neat-herds, a brazier, a scourer, a wax-chandler, a steward, and a sewer, are found on the early burgess-roll.

The *leuga* contained four woods, three mills, three orchards, a vineyard, a quarry, and a fish-pool; and the town had from one hundred to one hundred and twenty houses, two of which were free, the rest paying quit rents of from three to fifteen pence per annum, together with, in some cases, manual service, or the duty of furnishing a horse for abbot or monk to ride. The abbot found at certain times his portion of malt, but appointed a poor person as his deputy to drink the beer made out of it. Among other prerogatives the abbot could pardon a felon on his way to the gallows, claim all whales and sturgeons cast up on the coast within certain limits, also all wrecks and waifs, flotsam and jetsam; and by grant of Henry I. "of holding a weekly fair *on Sundays.*"

Not alone were rich endowments but high immunities received from both kings and nobles, among them exemption from taxes, peculiar manorial rights, the privilege of coining money, as at St Augustine's Monastery at Canterbury, granted by King Ethelbert, or Athelstan, and enjoyed till the reign of Stephen,[1] and also at Reading.

Not only did these monastic communities give to agriculture their labour, but likewise set a valuable example, which of the two was probably of greater worth to mankind. Previous to the coming of the monk, manual labour of every sort was regarded as altogether incompatible with the dignity of freemen, and, tainted as it was with the memory of slavery, deemed only fit for those under the bondage of serfdom. But an abbot, mayhap a great man in the world, "with the seed-bags on his head,"[2] and his monks, not a few of the princes of the earth, "carrying manure

---

[1] The rent-roll of the Abbey of Saints Peter and Paul (St Augustine's), Canterbury, filled nearly four columns of the Domesday Book, and amounted to 11,680 acres.

[2] Like the great Thomas à Becket, who toiled in the fields like an ordinary monk.

on their shoulders," and "going out to their daily labour in the fields," presented a new spectacle to the astonished world, and one which could not be gainsaid—the spectacle of voluntary labour, willingly and cheerfully endured. By their example they removed the stigma of slavery from toil. The slave and the serf were mere mechanical machines, toiling from morning till evening, in obedience to their master's will, without wage or reward, in the performance of work in which they had no interest; but the Church created the necessity for voluntary labour, for which she offered to those who engaged in it a fair remuneration. By these means she not only imparted a dignity to labour, but made it the means by which the country was greatly improved, her own wealth vastly increased, and the people educated in industrious habits. Not only so, but by the creation of centres of labour, the monasteries attracted the population, which, relinquishing their nomadic life, settled around them, receiving in return for their daily work ample means of sustenance for themselves and their families.

The possession of large estates made them also large employers of labour, and their character as masters and landlords is being continually proved to have been both good and generous, extending to their tenants and labourers rights and privileges which were not enjoyed by those in a similar position under the secular lords. And one thing must be said to their everlasting credit, that they were the emancipators of the serfs, who were in that day no better than slaves, bought and sold as chattels with the soil.

"The monks," says MALLET, "softened by their instructions the ferocious manners of the people, and opposed their credit to the tyranny of the nobility, who knew no other occupation than war, and grievously oppressed their neighbours. On this account the government of monks was preferred to theirs. The people sought them for judges. It was an usual saying that it was better to be governed by the bishop's crosier than the monarch's sceptre."[1]

Even at the period when degeneracy from their original single-eyedness had set in as a flood, and the glory of "our house" as against all others was the supreme point to be battled for, and the wretched sinner who had held religion lightly, and even openly scoffed at Holy Church in his heyday, trembled at length on the brink of the great unknown abyss which should land him—where? When his hands, deluged in gore, and surfeited with the plunder of the widow and orphan, or, still more horrible, with the treasures of the sanctuary, relaxed, and with a trembling hope for mercy at that grand last tribunal of strict justice, heartily committed all that he had into the care of Holy Mother Church, to be disposed as she thought fit—for the welfare and peace of his soul. Even then he had not done all, for the monks, charged with the awful power to bless or ban, boldly asked of his serfs: What of them? Were they not to be free—free for ever from the shackles which had bound them to their lord, and those who should come after him?

And evade the question as he would, there was no gainsaying the demand. The Church was determined that they should be free, not alone in the liberty of the one great universal Master, Christ, but also from the tyranny of man.

It was usual to make the manumission of serfs before the altar. Bodmin Priory possessed a copy of the Gospels, written in the ninth century, at the end

---

[1] "History of the Swiss," vol. i. p. 105.

of which are forty-six entries of such manumissions—all before the Conquest, or between the years 941–1043.[1]

Not only did the monks first give and procure personal freedom to the villeins, but they also commuted, for money payments, the often vexatious services exacted of a tenant by his lord. The abbot was non-resident, generally speaking, on his manors, and his tenants were allowed to manage their own affairs; but the secular lord, being on the spot, exacted the uttermost farthing, knowing exactly the best beast on the land owing him a heriot, and when the tenant was *in extremis*, kept a sharp look-out for the fat bullock, or young horse, which upon his death would come to his share.

Thus, with the people, they and their services were extremely popular; and justly so, for there were men among them who had received the best education the greatest European schools could bestow, who, returning to their native shores, or going hence at the command of their superiors, brought the benefit of the wider taste and more liberal views thus acquired to bear upon the locality in which their lot was cast. Their knowledge of surgery, physic, law, scholarship, etc., were thus dispersed for the betterment of their surroundings. At their hands the sons of the nobles and country gentry acquired what little knowledge they ever succeeded in obtaining of grammar and dialectic; and the sons of the soil sufficient to their need; and in sickness the attention and relief each required in the hospital and dispensary under their charge.

In addition to finding profitable labour for the

---

[1] The MS. is now in the British Museum.

freeman, and remunerative employment for the serf, emancipated by the efforts of the monk, or voluntarily set free by his master, the monastery created that class of yeomen, or small tenant farmer, which has done so much towards the making of England.

As the domains of the monastery expanded in many instances to a considerable distance beyond the house itself in the course of its cultivation, it became necessary to have somebody in the shape of a representative on the spot to see after things. This was done by means of granges, or homesteads, erected as centres of labour, subordinate to the monastery itself. In the granges were established certain monks, or lay brothers, or other labourers whose faithfulness, industry, and skill in the duties required of them had been satisfactorily proved, and who acted as superintendents, or overseers, of those working with and under them.[1] In the course of time the overseer, if a secular, or one not actually a member of the order, became a tenant farmer to the religious house to which the land belonged, paying a certain rent in money or produce to the superior of that house as a recognition of his tenancy, and employing his own labourers.

By this means, what had heretofore been wild forest, desolate, uninhabited swamp, and barren unproductive heath, became fruitful by culture and tillage. Thus, we may understand the urgency with which the unscrupulous, grasping courtiers urged on Henry VIII. to appropriate these lands, seeing that they constituted the landed wealth of the country, being by far the best cultivated and planted and most fruitful of the lands of

---

[1] Archbishop Peckham in 1282 endeavoured to prevent monks farming the manors of their convents. They were often abbatial residences with parks annexed.

England, a fact well known and appreciated even in the present day to those who possess them.

Upon the cultivation of the soil the monks brought all their intellectual resources of calculation and of science to bear. Thus, to them we owe experimental farmery and gardening, resulting in the introduction of varieties of new vegetables and fruits, and all this, it must be remembered, upon lands, the greater part of which had been barren and worthless until the indomitable energy of the monks had rescued it from a dry sterility into a fertility until then unknown.

"Who does not know," says VIOLLET-LE-DUC, "that the best woods, the richest harvests, the finest vines, are even to-day produced on those lands once possessed by the monks."

The whole district surrounding the ruins of even such a third-rate convent as the Welsh Abbey, Cum Hir, exhibits still a striking example of the skill of the monks, as applied to the land. The whole district of diversified hill and dale abounds in woods and fertile enclosures, in a more copious proportion of fruitfulness than most of the adjoining districts, clearly proving the superior industry and active application of the old possessors of the soil—the monks.

"It was the spot," says Cobbett, writing in his "English Gardener" of an ancient kitchen garden of the monks, "where I first began to learn to work—or rather where I first began to eat fine fruit in a garden; and although I have now seen and observed upon so many fine gardens as any man in England, I have never seen a garden equal to that of Waverley [Abbey, in Surrey]. . . . The peaches, nectarines, apricots, and plums never failed: and if the workmen had not lent a hand, a fourth part of the produce could never have been got rid of."

At this very Abbey of Waverley, no less than thirty ploughs were constantly kept at work. No one was idle, and although in latter days there came to be a distinction drawn between agricultural and other manual labour, as against the labour of the intellect, it was not so in the earlier days. The venerable Bede, himself a great master worker, tells us of Easterwin, a thegn of King Egfrith's, who, in the heyday of his young manhood, had exchanged his arms for the monk's habit at Wearmouth, which house he afterwards ruled as abbot.

"It was a pleasure to him," the saint assures us, "to be employed along with the rest of the brethren in winnowing and grinding the corn, in milking the ewes and cows, in working in the bakehouse, the garden, and the kitchen, and in every other occupation of the monastery, working with plough, forge hammer, or winnowing fan.[1]

Owini, a head thegn of the household of the same Egfrith's queen, came to Hastingham "clad only in a plain garment, and carrying an axe and mattock in his hand, thereby intimating that he did not go to the monastery to live idle . . . but to labour," and, being less capable of meditating on Holy Scripture, he more earnestly applied himself to manual labour.[2]

And this manual labour, in theory, practically remained the same until the days when King Henry VIII. brought the reign of the monk to an abrupt end; and men, great in the history of Monasticism as of the world, such as Bernard, monk and Abbot of Clairvaux, and Becket, monk and Archbishop of Canterbury, toiled in the kitchen or the harvest-field as zealously as any ordinary monk, living by the labour of their hands as their "Fathers and the Apostles did" before them.[3]

The Rule of the great legislator for monks had

---

[1] *Vit Abbatum*, Hussey's "Bœda," p. 322.
[2] "Bœda," *H. E.* lib. iv. c. iii.
[3] "Rule of St Benedict," chap. xlviii. p. 203.

placed the noble and the serf, entering any monastery of his, upon an absolute equality, and to this primitive observance the Cluniac, Cistercian, and other reforms of the Benedictine order had again and again returned. But as repeatedly again as the culture of the intellect and the pre-eminence of the house had demanded it, the less capable and uncultured had gradually the exterior work of the monastery shifted upon their shoulders, the working brethren, or lay brothers, as they came to be called, being distinguished from the "monachi," or "quire religious," wholly confined to the observance of religious offices and meditation.[1]

No portion of their lands was neglected. Corn was even grown on the hill-sides, and cut in stairs, a thing never now done. On the high lands of Dorsetshire and Hampshire, a large number of acres together still bear the marks of the plough. The culture of the mulberry [2] and vine—the latter never now attempted—was brought by them to a remarkable success. A vineyard, or wine-garth, was an usual adjunct to a convent,[3] and British wines attaining a certain creditable repute, the vine was cultivated with profit.

WILLIAM of MALMESBURY ascribes the first planting

---

[1] In the life of St Hugh of Lincoln it is said: "Omnes interea Hugonem loquebantur sive prior, sive monachus, sive *conversus*, gratiam attolebat collatum Hugoni," p. 46, also glossary to same. Similarly, on the strength perhaps of Chapter LXXIII. of their founder's Rule, that "the highest degree of perfection" is not contained in it, the Benedictines in England invariably neglect the obligation of rising for Nocturns, the non-use of flesh in the refectory, manual labour, and the keeping of enclosure.

[2] *E.g.* the "Wardon Pear" at Wardon (Cistercian) Abbey, Bedfordshire, and the choice grafts from Normandy, to which Devonshire owes the pre-eminence of its cider.

[3] As at St Alban's, St Edmund's, and Glastonbury. Dugdale's "Monasticon," *sub voc*, gives references to vineyards at Abingdon, Gloucester, Hautun for Evesham, Muchelney, Pershore, Rochester, and Thorney (Westminster). At Wardon, Beds., at its dissolution, there was a "great vineyard" and a "little vineyard."

of a vineyard at Malmesbury to a Greek, Constantine by name, who, somehow or other, found himself in Wiltshire in the early part of the eleventh century. "*Hic primus auctor vineæ fuit quæ in colle monasterio ad aquilonem vicino sita, plures duravit annos.*"[1] He also speaks in glowing terms of the excellence of the wine produced from the vineyards in the rich vale of Gloucester, which he compares with English wine in general, which was usually so sour as to twist the mouth of the drinkers. Cider is said to have been introduced into Devonshire by the Cistercians, but there is abundant evidence of its being the ordinary drink of labourers on the Manor of Axmouth (then the property of Benedictines) as early as 1286.

As manufacturers of special liqueurs, the Benedictines, the Carmelites, the Carthusians, and the Trappists are each and all renowned, that of "La Grande Chartreuse" being especially famous. All these distillations are said to have had their origin in the addictedness of the mediæval monastics "to alchemy, and to researches into the possibilities of the Magnum Opus, the Quintessence, the Grand Arcanum, and the Elixir of Long Life." With the hopeless failure of these, the monks turned their attention to the production of those liqueurs in the composition of which they have become so celebrated.

"It was a most happy thing," says Mr MAITLAND, in his "Dark Ages," "for the world that they did not confine themselves to the possession of such small estates as they could cultivate with their own hands. The extraordinary benefit which they conferred on society by colonising waste places —places chosen because they were waste and solitary, and such as could be reclaimed only by the incessant labour of those who were willing to work hard and live hard."

---

[1] "Gesta Pontif," p. 415.

Some of the great abbeys, as Furness in England, and St Germain des Prés in France, acquired by reason of their territorial possessions, as also by lavish concessions ceded to them by their monarchs, the exercise, on their account, of feudal rights as mesne lords. Thus, the whole surrounding population was in a state of vassalage—a vassalage, it is true, under somewhat different conditions to that exercised under the purely secular lords—to the abbot and convent, by which they provided their contingents for the service of the convent, every tenant being bound to furnish a man and a horse fully equipped for military service—as at Furness, for the perpetual wars of the border and the protection of the coast[1]—keeping courts of justice, and supporting a mint: the gold pieces of the Abbey of St Germain going as far as the fleur-de-lys of the Louvre.

The Prior of Bermondsey, as lord of the manor, erected a gallows for the execution of criminals at this place. Even the gentle nun, Amiccia, Abbess of Romsey, in 1262, successfully petitioned King Henry III. for the restitution of the privilege of trying and hanging criminals, a privilege which had been conferred on the nunnery by King Edgar, but which had become obsolete!

Not even abbesses were exempt from military service, but had to supply their quota of knights, together with their full complement of soldiers, for the king's service.[2] In 1251 Agnes Ferrar, Abbess of Shaftesbury, was summoned to Chester to take part in the military proceedings against Llewellin; and a successor of hers,

---

[1] A body of these troops, commanded by Sir Edward Stanley, was present at the Battle of Flodden Field.
[2] *Cf.* Dugdale, ii. 473.

Juliana Bauceyn, twenty years later, had a similar call made upon her.[1]

It was not at all an unusual thing for monks to figure in the strength of a battle array, or upon occasion having a battle royal on their own special account, as when in the year 673 the rival monasteries of Clonmacnois and Durrow contended for the mastery, the latter being vanquished, and leaving two hundred dead men upon the field.

At the coming of the conquering William, numbers of monks were found in the ranks of both armies.[2] Abbot Leofric of Petersborough, the Abbot of Hyde, near Winchester, with twelve monks and twenty men at-arms, joined Harold in the fatal battle which brought the reign of the Saxons to a close, thirteen cowled and frocked bodies being found close beside the fallen king at the conclusion of the battle. On the conqueror's side Bishop Odo himself led the cavalry. Even as late as the sixteenth century, monks are found engaging in the pursuit of war. James Stewart, Abbot of Dryburgh, 1545, more than once exchanged the cowl for the helmet in the border wars, as did Abbot Litlington of Westminster at the rumour of an invasion from France.

The ships of the Spanish Pope-blessed Armada contained numbers of monks and friars, whose presence there was perhaps not so much on the war-path as, in the event of the certain victory, to bring England again into the fold of Rome.

Strange as it may seem, the Spanish "regulars"[3] often appeared in battle. Cardinal Ximenes, at the

---

[1] The abbesses of Shaftesbury ranked as *baronesses*.
[2] In William's army was William, monk of Marmoutiers, near Tours, a man famous as an arrow-maker.
[3] Members of religious orders as against the secular or parish priests.

head of an army of monks, was present at the taking of Oran, and they seem to have been armed with swords. Yet still earlier than this, the monasteries not only sold their treasures, and mortgaged their estates to provide funds for the Crusades, but also sent vast numbers of monks to the ranks.

Then, again, in those days when right was might, and every man had to be prepared to fight for his own, it was an absolute necessity that the monasteries should not only be in a position to look after themselves and their property, but also to be ever ready to lend a hand in protecting those who could not protect themselves.

The mediæval monuments, wills, and similar documents only show us the better side of mediæval human nature. The great war or land lord of that day was not always, and at all times, the meek and gentle creature which the pious legend, or humble attitude, his tomb, or his last testamentary disposition would have us believe.

How could he be when he had been almost nursed in slaughter, and his blithe young boyhood spent in the midst of the carnage of battle? Chroniclers have ransacked their choicest vocabulary to fittingly designate some of these men. Fierce, ferocious tyrants, who like wild beasts found their greatest delight in ravaging the flock of innocent, peace-loving and God-fearing men. Monsters who smiled at the ban of the Church, and laughed at the terrors of hell; but who, when they came face to face with the awful realities of both, trembled like the aspen leaves, and returned to the fold with even more than the average meekness of the lamb.

But then the pen was ever mightier than the sword,

and a few well-disposed strokes of an expert mediæval chronicler could accomplish almost as much as a charge of artillery. If any man knew how to write down the enemy of his house, that man was the mediæval chronicler.

Alas! it was also only too true that even patrons could sometimes prove unkind, proceeding to the length of cruel words, and, still further, should necessity arise, to hard blows. Thus, it is not at all a surprise to know that mediæval monasteries, as well as castles, were fortified so as to be capable of enduring a siege; the whole settlement, courts, gardens, etc., being surrounded by a crenelated wall, many feet high, with occasional towers. The boundary wall of Furness Abbey enclosed an area of sixty-five acres, in which were bakeries, breweries, malt-kilns, granaries, gardens, fish-ponds, and other appurtenances of a large establishment; the walled close of Fountains, twelve acres, the buildings occupying over two acres.

In or about the year 1093, Peter de Valoines, a nephew of William the Conqueror, and Albreda, his wife, founded the Priory of Binham. By the deed of endowment, the heirs or successors of the founder were to remain patrons, the house being made a cell to the great Abbey of St Alban.

The tide of affairs flowed pretty smoothly for over a hundred years, when, in the reign of King John, and about the year 1212, a certain Robert FitzWalter put in a claim as patron of the house, and it is added, in a sort of casual way, that he was very friendly with Thomas, the then reigning prior. This was sufficient for my Lord Abbot of St Alban's, who promptly removed Prior Thomas from his office. Such an arbitrary act somewhat naturally raised the ire of FitzWalter, who thereupon produced an alleged deed of patronage, which showed that the Prior of Binham could not be removed without the patron's consent, and it is presumed, without waiting for a reply, forthwith besieged the priory, causing the monks great hardships, compelling them to eat bread made of bran, and to find their drink in the water which flowed from the rain-water pipes.

Now, in those days, wise men did one of two things. They either carried their cause to the king, or, failing satisfaction there, proceeded a little further to the Court of Rome, where it was ten to one the victory would be theirs.

So my Lord of St Alban's got the king by the ear, and John, quite contrary to his usual behaviour, swore in his usual manner: "Ho! by God's feet, either I or FitzWalter must be king in England. Ho! by God's feet, who ever heard of such things in peaceable times in a Christian land?" and sent off an armed force at once to relieve the priory and to raise the siege.

In the *mêlée* the valiant FitzWalter disappeared. He had fled for his life.

Occasionally, as occurred at Norwich (1272), St Edmundsbury, St Alban's (1314), Canterbury, and other places, there would be what we should term to-day a grand town-and-gown row, when the whole city population, being at issue with the monastery, would turn out and besiege it, threatening the monks with dreadful things, and not infrequently breaking in and making havoc of all they could get hold of.

At Vale Royal, the people held the monastery so that none of the monks dared to cross the threshold, and one John Boddeworth, who ventured to do so, was instantly murdered, and a game of football played with his head!

Sometimes the matter in dispute would be settled by more peaceable means, as when the Abbot of Meaux claimed a right of fishing in a part of Hornsea Mere, a proceeding against which the Abbot of St Mary's, York, protested. To dispose of the matter it was decided to settle it by combat. Accordingly, both abbots provided their champions, more than one apparently on either side. A horse was then made to swim across the Mere, and stakes were fixed to mark the boundary of the portion claimed by the Abbot of Meaux. From morning to night the fight lasted, when the champions of Meaux were beaten, and the indisputed right to the Mere remained with his Lordship of St Mary's.

The mayor and corporation of Bristol at one time imprisoned the retainers of the monastery, and the abbot, "with a ryotous company," attempted to force the prison, but were repulsed. In the thirteenth century, in a collision between the citizens of London and the Westminster monks, the mob broke into the monastery, and the abbot only escaped their intentions by taking to a boat on the Thames. The latter event occurred in this wise. In a wrestling match, on St James' Day (July 25th), 1222, between the London and Westminster citizens, the latter were beaten, and especially their great champion, the steward of the abbey. Another day was fixed for a return match, during the excitement of which the steward fell upon the Londoners with a body of armed men, beating and driving them back into the city. At the instigation, however, of one Constantine, the Londoners returned in great force, and pulled down the house of the steward and others. For this the ringleaders were given up by the Lord Mayor, and Constantine and two others, in spite of their offer of fifteen thousand marks, were hanged on the spot! .

In the year 1423, early in the morning of 3rd November, certain armed men, who afterwards confessed themselves of the household of the Earl of Northumberland, scaled the walls of the Abbey of Fountains, forced the doors of the church, cloister, dormitory, and other places, and breaking open numerous chests and lockers, seized and carried off the more valuable of the contents, masers, spoons, and other silver plate. Having appropriated this, they terrified the abbot and monks, and finally broke open the prison, and liberated a certain brother of the monastery, who for theft and other crimes was incarcerated there in chains.

"That in the case of monasteries dedicated to God," says Article III. of Archbishop Theodore, summoning to the Council of Hertford in 673, "no bishop is to disturb them in any matter, nor to take away by force any part of their property."

Nevertheless, the monks were constantly at variance with their bishops. The exemption of the houses from the control of the Episcopate was the cause of it all.[1] The bishops were continually wanting to have a finger in the monks' pie, but the monks, as a rule, would have none of it. Hugh de Nonant, in 1189, so irritated the monks of Coventry, that whilst he was holding a synod in their church, they rushed upon him, and broke his head with a cross, and spilled his blood before the altar.

---

[1] The Monastery of Fulda, at the instance of St Boniface, in 751, is believed to have been the first monastery exempted by Papal grant from all Episcopal control.

Sometimes they had little affairs among themselves, as when the retainers of the great Neville family, being refused their usual refection for insolence, on the occasion of the annual offering of that family, by the monks of Durham, cuffed the monks, who, in return, attacked their assailants with the candles from off the altar. At others the quarrels yet nearer home were worked off in the very calm, matter-of-fact manner by the precentor stopping the music to spite the treasurer, and the treasurer putting out the lights to be even with the precentor.

Another little monastic diversion again was a suit-at-law. How intensely the mediæval monk loved a lawsuit the chronicles bear ample witness. A monastery that had never engaged in such a diversion was esteemed a poor specimen indeed of its kind. And bear in mind a mediæval issue at law was not by any means the tame affair which we of later birth, or even those with the memory of a long weary suit in Chancery, may think. Sometimes a cause would go on for years stimulated in the interval by a stout personal encounter, and as neither side ever thought of giving way, the decision only brought a renewal of the legal contest in a different aspect.

Failing to find justice in the English courts, or by special reference to the English king, the appeal was carried to Rome, often only to end, after years of excitement, wrangling, and enormous expense, in the position at which the litigants first started.

At times, an affair of this kind would be settled in quite an unexpected way. Richard de Parco was Prior of Binham seventeen years (1227-44), years spent in the able management of his house. To this end he was naturally involved in many lawsuits. One was an action against the Prior of Walsingham, in the matter of the presentation to the living of St Peter, Great Walsingham. It happened that the bishopric was at that time vacant, and the cause of complaint before it could be tried was settled by the Archdeacon of Norwich, in whom the administration of the diocese lay, for the time being, instituting his own nephew, "*per fraudem et collusionem*," frankly says the chronicle.

Enriched by the economical management of abbots, and the annual produce and commercial labour of their own hands, the monks were enabled to turn their energies to works in other than the agricultural department. Not a few who threw in their lot with them would bring into the monastery the learning they had acquired in the world, and which, unlike property and lands, could not be disposed of so easily. These acquirements were, in the course of time, not only recognised, but utilised to the advantage of the house. Thus, while the majority were engaged in the labours of the fields, others were cultivating and exercising their talents in the workshops and cloisters of the monastery, producing those wonderful treatises and marvellous, illuminated volumes which are to-day the wonder of all who behold them.

Attached to every monastery were schools where gratuitous instruction was given to the children of rich and poor alike. There were also large workshops in which they followed and taught every branch of trade; carving in wood, ivory, and the inferior and precious metals; painting on vellum, glass, wood, and metal; tapestry weaving and ecclesiastical embroidery; damask work, and the enamelling of shrines, tabernacles, and triptychs, church furniture, and book covers;

the cutting of precious stones, the manufacture of arms and musical instruments; the illumination and engrossment of manuscripts and church books, and many another handicraft. The whole life of a monk was passed in the exercise of one description of art, in the execution of a *single* volume. Among many other works, Thomas à Kempis engrossed a Bible in four volumes, commencing the work in 1417, and bringing it to a conclusion in 1459. Maurus Lapi is said to have copied a thousand volumes in less than fifty years, and another monk so much that a waggon with six horses would hardly suffice to draw all that he had written—conspicuous examples of patient industry and loving care brought to bear upon their task. Some abbeys spun and wove their own silk; others were expert in the dispensing of drugs, practising medicine, surgery, and the veterinary art. All were places of security for money valuables and documents; the chiefest records of the kingdom being preserved in them; and also places of rest and safe shelter for travellers of every degree. In short, the monks were the farmers and merchants, the lawyers and doctors, the librarians and record keepers, the teachers, the hospitalers, the guardians, and protectors of the poor and defenceless throughout Europe, as well as religious.[1]

---

[1] The ancient monks of Egypt worked in masonry, agriculture, basket-making, braziery, carpentry, cloth-making, dressing and colouring the papyrus, fulling, masonry, rope and net-making, shoe-making, tanning, upholstery, and fine writing, indeed, every employment, agricultural and mechanical, necessary for the use of life.

To the Cistercian abbots the Pope (1246) applied for the choicest specimens of vestments of cloth of gold—*Opus Anglicum*, for which England was famous. "In truth," says he, "England is our pleasant garden, a well-spring that cannot be exhausted, a land of rich abundance, and where much is, much may be taken."

Under the auspices of the monks of Bath, the woollen manufacture was introduced into England about the year 1330, employing the shuttle and loom to such perfection that the city became renowned as one of the most considerable in the West of England for manufacture—a fame the West country still enjoys. They likewise had a bath-house, near St Peter's Gate, for strangers who sought the healing waters.

The Cistercian monks were all wool traders—a green path over the moors towards Brent, known to-day as "The Abbot's Way," is said to have been a "post road" for the conveyance of the wool of that community. The monks of Melrose sent wool to the Netherlands.

"Buckfastleigh" (now again rising from its desolation towards something of its former usefulness) says Mr Brooking Rowe, "owes what prosperity it has to the monks of Buckfast, for the Cistercians were the great wool traders of the times in which they lived, and the owners of the large mills, some of which are built up with the materials of the abbey and its belongings, are but carrying out in the same locality, in the same ways, the work of former years."

Weaving was engaged in many places, the monks of Canterbury, in 1595, manufacturing a hanging in tapestry for the walls of the quire of their Cathedral.[1] Embroidery, though forbidden in the Rule of Cæsarius, was a common employment for monks. A Bill with the royal sign manual prayed that the king would grant to Dom Robert Essex his frames "ordeigned and made for the making of sylkes," with their instruments which now "stondith unoccupyed within your monas-

---

[1] It is now at Aix, in Provence.

tery of Westminster," and that he will ordain workmen to use them.¹ At the dissolution of the monasteries, Cromwell, the Vicegerent's Commissioners, reported of Wolstrope, Lincolnshire, that "Not one religious person there but that he can, and doth use either imbrothering, writing bokis with very fair hand, making their own garments, carving, painting, or graving, etc."

The monks of Coverham had a fame for the breed of their horses, and the Commissioners of 1537 recommended the place to the king on this account. Their fame as architects and builders is well known; monk-architects, like those at Gloucester who first devised that beautiful and peculiarly English form of ceiling decoration, known as "fan tracery," splendid examples of which remain at Gloucester (in the cloisters), at St George's Chapel, Windsor, and Westminster Abbey, in the Chapel of Henry VII.; or a mere handful of fervent pioneer monks with little more skill than that of a village artificer, yet who could erect buildings which are the despair of modern architects.²

Not infrequently they engaged in the smelting of iron ore. The iron mines in Furness were extensively worked, and mention is made of iron ore found on Walney Island, for the smelting of which the monks

---

[1] *Temp.* Edward IV. Hist. MSS. Com. iv. 177.

[2] For the admission of a stone-mason in the lay order of the Benedictines, as distinct from the quire religious, an innovation upon the original ordinance of their founder, *see* Findel, "History of a MS. in the British Museum." The *monachi cœmentarii*, as they are called by Ivo of Chartres, a contemporary of Lanfranc, had by that time acquired some form of a distinct guild. "Ivonis Carnot," Ep. 266 :—Ascivit quosdam monachus cæmentarios ; Goffridus Vindoc in Ep. ad Ildebert Ceno. Mann. Ep., "Johannem cœmentarium Ecclesiæ Nostræ."

erected a couple of furnaces. Flaxley Abbey, Gloucestershire, possessed a forge, by grant from Henry II., and was allowed two oaks weekly for the supply of it—a privilege commuted in 1258 for the Abbots' Wood, of 872 acres, which was held by the abbey till the dissolution. At Rievaulx, Yorkshire, near the bridge at the lower end of the village, a place is still called the "Forge"; and, judging from the large heaps of slag mixed with charcoal that are still visible in the neighbourhood of the abbey, there clearly was extensive iron works here, and without doubt carried on under the monks' superintendence. The Benedictine monks of D'Orval, Florenville, Belgium, were famous as locksmiths, carrying on useful and extensive iron works. To furnish motive power, they dammed up the stream which traverses the enclosure and fills the fish-pond, thus forming a tank half a mile long, and filling up the valley from side to side.

Others, again, excelled in the goldsmith's craft; others worked in their tanyards and kilns for the manufacture of those encaustic tiles, which are to-day the admiration of the archæologist. Within two hundred yards of the church and gate of Malvern Priory, Worcestershire, the kiln has been found, and also pieces of tile which correspond in pattern with specimens in the Malvern churches, as well as the material used in the manufacture.

They likewise excelled as road-makers. It was to their own advantage, in the conveyance of their merchandise and trading that they should be so. The earliest roads in Scotland, that deserved the name, were the work of the monks and their dependents, and the object was to connect the religious houses, as trading stations, together, and with the capital, or nearest seaport, depôts being scattered in the burghs for the storage of the produce of farm and workshop, as well as booths for its sale. Thus the establishment of a monastery in the days of violence, tyranny, and perpetual unrest was a perfect blessing to the peaceful dwellers in its adjacent surroundings, where robbers and outlaws of every kind abounded.

About the commencement of the twelfth century was founded an order of "religious"[1] who, living in the world, devoted themselves to providing protection, shelter, and such other necessary assistance to travellers. They were called *Pontifices*—that is, builders of bridges, they especially charging themselves with the construction of bridges, roads, hydraulic works, embankments, and similar things appertaining to the safety of travellers in passing over rivers. From this they came to be called *Frates Pontes*, or "Brethren of the Bridge," *Pontifices Hospitalariorum*, and *Factores Pontium*. They wore a white habit, with a cloth badge upon the breast, embroidered with a cross and a bridge. Other monks, like the good Abbot of Aberbrothock, anxious for the safety of those whose business lay in the deep waters, maintained lighthouses, as did the Benedictines of St Matthew's Abbey, in the bay of Aber Benignet, on the coast of Finisterre, Brittany.

In the court of the king and the castle of the noble, the culture of the intellect was completely out of the question, even when all the land was resting from the pursuit of chivalry or the quest of the Crusade. In the monastic buildings lying along the banks of rivers flowing in the sheltered valleys alone could that opportunity be found. Here, in the calm studious cloisters throughout

---

[1] To be "religious" in mediæval days was to be a member of a monastic order, bound by vows.

all that restless age the sacred flame of liberal culture, of polite learning, of a humane civilisation, was carefully tended and encouraged to burn. The abbey church of Haddington has been called the "Lamp of Lothian," and from age to age, all up and down the continent of Europe, such lamps were continually lit for the moral, spiritual, and intellectual illumination of the people.

"The monks," says Mr Thorold Rogers, "were the men of letters of the Middle Ages, the historians, the jurists, the philosophers, the physicians, the students of Nature, the founders of schools, authors of chronicles, teachers of agriculture, fairly indulgent landlords, and advocates of genuine dealing towards the peasantry."

The institution of public education was also due to them, for they established schools in each diocese, and were among the very first to assist in laying the foundations of those great universities which are the pride of our land to-day.[1] Neither did they confine their scholastic training to the intellect alone, but included also tuition in almost every department of science and of art. Thus it is that the annals, particularly of the twelfth and thirteenth centuries, sparkle with the lustre shed upon them by the names of their eminent men. Painters, architects (and they were the fathers of the Gothic style), sculptors, musicians and metal-workers, mechanicians and savants came forth as giants from their industrial hives.

As artists the monks of the Benedictine Order were the precursors of all that has been achieved in Christian art, jealously guarding and handing down

---

[1] Of the nearly three hundred halls and private schools in Oxford, besides colleges, not above eight remained in the middle of the seventeenth century, about one hundred years after the Reformation.

those traditions of treatment of sacred subjects which were preserved from age to age, pure and untainted with worldly sentiment which afterwards came in with scholastics and academic competition. Without exception, the monastic orders were one and all great patrons, always on a princely scale, of the fine arts. Under their wise, patronising care, the painters they encouraged covered the walls of their churches and cloisters with those precious heirlooms of the best period of art, the wonder and emulation of artists of the present day. Every order had its own special painter, and it was by the Franciscans that the great genius of Murillo was first recognised and supported.

Being the sole depositaries of medical and chemical knowledge and compounders of drugs, we owe to them the discovery and preparation of some of the finest of our colours, as well as the invention and improvement of the implements used in painting, in that they prepared their own colours, and, when employing secular painters to decorate their churches and houses, supplied them with all necessary materials from their own laboratories of the best and most durable kind.

Shakespeare has drawn for us such a picture when he depicts Friar Lawrence gathering simples for medicinal use,[1] and many were the deadly poisons and marvellous cures distilled from herbs and flowers blossoming in the herbary and garden of the monastery.

"All over Britain," says a modern writer, "we have much to thank the monks and nuns; for, wherever was a religious house, they planted daffodils; and now when all trace of monastery and convent has passed away, and the hands

---

[1] In "Romeo and Juliet."

that scattered the floral gold have long since crumbled into dust, great clumps of golden daffodils, growing wild in rich profusion, mark the site of the old church lands.

Love of gain eventually led monastery leeches too far afield after patients, and they were wholly interdicted from meddling with physic and surgery by decrees of Pope Innocent II. (1139) and the Council of Tours (1163). As an example, William de Somerton, appointed Prior of Binham by Abbot Hugh of St Alban's in 1317, under the auspices of a certain mendicant friar, spent immense sums in the pursuit of alchemy to the impoverishment of the priory, which, with other exactions by the parent house of St Alban's, rendered it difficult at times to procure even food for the monks.

As missionaries, they carried the Gospel light, with all its attendant peace, good-will, and civilising power into the dark wilds of the countries of the barbarians. In this noble work they not only traversed Britain, Gaul, Saxony, and Belgium, but also the whole of Northern Europe, and, dispelling the gross rites of Paganism, became the friends of the serfs, the slaves, the poor, and the oppressed, shielding them against the feudal tyrant and the pitiless, heartless spoiler who abounded in those rude times.

And all this had the Saxon monks accomplished long before the Roman Gregory saw the "Angels" in the market-place, and, moved with pity, sent Augustine, the Benedictine, to re-evangelise those districts of Britain devastated by the invasions of those hordes of Pagans who had again and again swept over the country. Even at the very time when Augustine and his monks were landing upon the shores of the South, these indefatigable pioneers were forcing their way from the North, valiantly re-conquering the land by the power of the Cross to the service of Christ.

Sufficient has been adduced to show that the monks were no mere drones in the world, and their monasteries far from being the abodes of idleness, or vast empty halls given up exclusively to the practice of devotion, as is generally supposed, but, quite on the contrary, busy hives of active and intelligent industry, where ample scope was provided for every taste, and the employment to its very best advantage of every talent;[1] and thus it came about that each order, each community very often excelled in one particular branch of art or science, divinity or medicine, music or literature.

The Benedictines were famed throughout Europe for their academies and schools of learning; the Augustines for their magnificent buildings and almost royal hospital foundations. The Carthusians were remarkable for their fine libraries and horticultural skill, being the first and greatest horticulturists in Europe, making the deserts of their settlements to blossom as the rose.

The monks of Monte Oliveto were famous for the great skill in the beautiful inlaid work called "tarsia." The Benedictines of Monte Cassino invented the art of painting on glass. A community of the Jeronimite Order, known as the Jesuati, in their now suppressed convent of San Guisto, near Florence, also carried on an extensive manufactory of painted glass, employing Perugino, and other celebrated artists, to make designs, and it is even said that that great painter himself gained from them the art of preparing colours. This

---

[1] The one great principle of the Rule of St Benedict was the distribution of the offices and duties of the house as widely as possible.

community had also distilleries, furnaces, and laboratories, and largely cultivated herbs for medicinal purposes. The Carthusian monks of Paular were breeders of sheep and paper-makers on a large scale, and it is recorded that they returned a rich present of plate to the Count de Nevers as valueless to them, but received a quantity of parchment and leather for their books from him very gladly.

In the monasteries of Great Britain, things were very similar to those abroad, as we have already noticed. The monasteries of Cupar and Arbroath cultivated polite literature; that of Glasgow, solid learning; of St Colm's, historical learning. Some houses were famous for their chronicles, as St Alban's; others, like Buckfast, for their wool. The Abbey of Furness sent ships of considerable burden to trade with foreign countries.

The Priory of Norwich made an income out of its garden in the days of the third Edward; and the method of pisciculture used by monks in general is still to-day a mystery unsolved, while their skill in the management of water power is a wonder.

Indeed, the Tironensis, or monks of the elder St Bernard, were brought to Scotland for the chief object that their Rules enacted that every monk should be an adept at some mechanical art, as painters, carvers, carpenters, masons, smiths, and gardeners, in the perfection of which arts they are said to have been second to none.

Neither should it be forgotten that to the monk the institution of the religious trade guilds, those great amalgamations of labour which played so extensive and important a part in the town life of mediæval days, was due.

In studying the, what appears to us moderns, enormous incomes of the great abbeys of mediæval days, the time of their prime, we must take into consideration the vast outgo in expenditure which was prevalent at the same time.

The religious houses, it must be remembered, had the sole charge of, and undertook the entire duties of all that to-day the heavily-taxed ratepayer pays for so grudgingly, and all which the monk did *gratuitously*. In the monastery was concentrated many separate institutions, which to-day are huge departments in themselves—the public school, the almshouse, the hotel, the hospital and dispensary, the workhouse, and the central bureau for employment and general information and advice.

From the very first, monks appear to have been the transcribers, makers, and collectors of books, and that at times when a copy of the Bible was literally worth a king's ransom. Long before the invention of printing, every Benedictine abbey had its library, or whatever passed as a library in those days,[1] and its scriptorium, or writing-chamber, where monks were constantly employed in making transcripts of valuable works, principally the Scriptures, which were either disposed of for the benefit of the convent, or bestowed as precious gifts.

Not only is posterity indebted to them for the preservation, multiplication, and diffusion of the Scriptures, but also for many classical remains of inestimable

---

[1] When speaking of libraries it must be borne in mind that a library in those days was not quite what it is in our own. At that period a library of 500 books would have been deemed an important collection, and it was not till many years after that we find the great English abbeys stored with such priceless treasures as the antiquary, Leland, beheld at Glastonbury on the eve of its spoilation.

value, as for instance the whole or the greater portion of the works of Pliny, Sallust, and Cicero. The great Benedictine, Montfauçon, gave the first hint that recovered from the obliterated palimpsests some of the most priceless works of the old poets and philosophers —a hint which the incessant labour of the accomplished Angelo Mai has brought to such perfection.

Previously to the invention of printing, copies of the Sacred Scriptures, of the Church Office, and music books, and every other kind of literature, had thus been produced by the tedious process of hand labour. On the invention of printing, the monks were among the very first to patronise the new invention, and to practise it themselves.

Colard Mausion, a clerk belonging to a community at Bruges, who (1414-73) was specially entrusted to copy manuscripts, conceived the idea of substituting the rapidity of movable types and screw printing-presses in lieu of the tedious process of the pen and the engraving pencil. At Subiaco, near Rome, Sweynheym and Pannartz, two printers from Mayence, guests of the monks, published the first edition of "Lactantius," following it up by several other valuable works of ecclesiastical authors (1465-67).[1] In the Monastery of St Eusebius, within the walls of Rome, George Lever of Würzburg printed many publications about 1470. The Brothers of the Common Life, in their houses at Rhingan, Mayence, at Val St Marie, Nuremburg, at Cologne and Rostock, followed quickly in the wake, and became from mere calligraphists, master-printers (1474-79).

---

[1] This was probably the first printing-press set up in Italy, in the Monastery of St Scholastica (1465), the productions of which are eagerly sought after by bibliopolists and antiquarians on account of the remarkable beauty of the printing.

Caxton has been accredited with the introduction of the printing-press into England, in 1472, setting up within the precincts of the Abbey of Westminster, but it is certain that many books were printed at St Alban's Abbey before his time. Another of the earliest printing-presses was that set up by the monks of Tavistock, who, by it, produced the first printed copy of the ancient "Stannary Laws," and also the first printed copy of Walton's "Boke of Comfort," and other works. A copy of "Boethius," printed here in 1525 by "Thomas Rycharde, monke," is preserved in the library of Exeter College, Oxford.

About the same period of the introduction of printing into England, the Dominicans, Carthusians, and Carmelites established large printing workshops at Pisa, Parma, Genoa, and Metz (1476-82); the Franciscans surnamed *Frères Conférenciers*, likewise opened a printing office at Gaude, Holland, and the Abbeys of Cluny and Citeaux sent for workmen to their houses in Burgundy, at Clairvaux, in Champagne, and Mont Serrat, in Catalonia, to print their principal liturgical books.

All this, and very much more, every single religious house, in a greater or lesser degree, according to its financial circumstances, was throughout the length and breadth of the land. And, moreover, all the various duties was performed in a manner altogether more efficient than such are performed to-day by our well-paid and by no means tender-hearted officials.

It is no matter for wonder, then, that the monks were beloved by the poor and unfortunate in their only too often hard fight for a mere existence; and by the suppressed and down-trodden slaves of a hard-hearted and merciless lord, who worked them as very galley slaves, to the enrichment of himself. When that greater tyrant than they all, a tyrant king, in his insatiate greed for land and gold robbed them of their all, even to the miserable crocks of the scullery, the *vox populi* vociferously called " to arms " to save their uninterested and magnanimous benefactors, and had to be quelled by the same king's armies as rebels.

Have the nineteenth-century poor ever so loved the workhouse as those of the sixteenth century did the monastery ? Would the poor of to-day stir one finger to save the wholesale destruction of the workhouses, or raise an arm to protect the Bumbles, their rulers ?

Nay, for it is an ever-increasingly demonstrated fact that the respectable poor of England abhor and detest the workhouse, and would rather die of starvation, and have actually so died, rather than enter within its dreaded portals.

The hospitality of the monks in the relief of the poor was carried on on a large and extensive scale, and in addition to the by no means meagre dispensation of charity by royal and other noble hands.

Udalric speaks thus of the charity dispensed at the Abbey of Cluny :—

"Every day eighteen *prebends*, or portions, allotted to the poor of the place were distributed, consisting of portions of bread with beans four days a week, and vegetables the remaining three. On great solemnities, and twenty-five times a year, meat instead of beans. At Easter nine cubits of woollen stuff each person, and at Christmas a pair of shoes. Other extraordinary benefactions on anniversaries of illustrious personages. Each week the Almoner washed the feet of three poor men (with warm water in winter), giving to each a pound of bread, and the usual *pittance* described above. Besides all this, each day was distributed twelve pasties (tarts), each weighing three pounds, to widows, orphans, the blind and lame, the aged and sick who might present themselves. Twice a week the Almoner had also to traverse the abbey domain, in order to seek out the sick, and to carry them bread, wine, and provisions of the best."

The author of the above adds that the very year in which he was writing his book, 250 hams had been distributed, doles being bestowed upon 17,000 poor persons.

Such a system of charitable relief was initiated and administered by every religious house all over the land, according to the means at its command. In times of special distress and of famine, the huge monastic barns provided a ready sustenance for populations who would otherwise have starved. The great St Bernard thus provided for 2,000 people from one harvest to another.

Right royally lived the Abbot of Glastonbury, entertaining at one time 500 persons of condition at his table, and feeding all the poor of the neighbourhood on Wednesdays and Fridays in each week, and all this charity was administered not in the coldly officious, unsympathetic way of our modern union workhouses and delectable casual wards, where one asking for bread is given a hundred of stones to give him a relish for his breakfast, but with a kindly sympathy accompanied with the consolation of comforting words and the kindly offices of religion. Alas! that we of to-day know nothing of such hospitality save in the name; it being left to the marvellous ingenuity of the superb civilisation of the three centuries following the Reformation to produce "THE PAUPER," and establish the cult of his "ism," a thing and a name unknown before in Christian England!

At Christchurch-on-Avon, Hants, 1,354 loaves, 467 lagenæ of ale, and 934 dishes of meat were dispensed to the poor daily in one year. The Cluniacs fed eighteen poor daily, in Lent "an amazing number." The Prior of Durham constantly maintained four aged women. William, Abbot of St Alban's, whenever he returned from a journey, had all the poor brought to the monastery gate to receive refection.

In addition to many ordinary every-day hospitalities given by the convent, or individual members thereof, there were the greater hospitalities on the feast and other days of rejoicing. Thus, in 1293, a banquet was given on the Feast of St Augustine, at that monastery at Canterbury, to 4,500 persons.[1] Again, at the election, in 1309, of Abbot Ralph Bourne, an enormous banquet was given, at which among others the following articles were consumed: Eleven tuns of wine (£24); thirty oxen (£27); thirty-four swans (£7); five hundred capons (£6); one thousand geese (£16); two hundred sucking pigs (100s.); nine thousand six hundred eggs (£4, 10s.); seventeen rolls of brawn (65s.); coals (48s.); wages of cooks and servants (£6):—Total expense £287, 5s. Six thousand guests sitting down to three thousand dishes.

The Abbot of Glastonbury, we have seen, entertained 500 persons of rank at one time at his table. This entertainment of the great and noble, in spite of their often magnificent donations to the house, was a great and constant drain on the resources of a convent. They gave, it is true, but it was pretty often with the sprat which should land the mackerel. Patrons and donors were as keenly alive in those days as now to the benefit to be derived from a judicious investment of land or capital.

They would come when it pleased them to enjoy the

---

[1] "Chronologia Augustiniensis."

"hospitality" of a monastery—to which their ancestors had given largely but they themselves not a groat—it may be with one or a hundred followers, all who had to be entertained suitably, and would not be put off with a Lenten diet. An abbot would visit a dependent cell of his house for eight days annually with *only* thirteen horses in his train! And this was only a flea-bite. So exorbitant had been the demands of abbots and patrons and founders upon their foundations and cells to their houses that special restrictions had to be inserted in the deeds and charters of foundation to hold them in check. To a small priory, such as Binham, with its eight monks, in its early days, the payment of a mark of silver annually to St Alban's, its great parent monastery, and the reception of its abbot and train of thirteen followers for eight days, must have been a strain upon its slender resources.

In addition to all this there were the corodies, or privilege of foisting all the poor relations of a founder, patron, or benefactor of the house upon that establishment for support, which became at times a grievance hard indeed to be borne.

Or again, the abbot would receive a royal summons to the effect that the king would keep Easter or Christmas (they seem always to have carefully avoided a visit in Lent) at such and such an abbey. The poor abbot would tremble as he obeyed. Alas! he knew what this "honour" would entail. For a month, two, three, the whole period of from Christmas to the beginning of Lent—the whole of Pasch till Whitsuntide, had he to feed and entertain and provide delectation in hunting, hawking, and other amusements for the monarch and his little army of "the Court," and, in the hope of despair, began to borrow the wherewithal by mortgaging his plate and lands, a proceeding which only too frequently plunged himself and his house in hopeless insolvency. At St Edmundsbury the Jews, those financiers of the Middle Ages, actually took possession of the place on such an account, dwelling therein with their wives and families, going in and out as it pleased them. A sight enough to make the angels weep!

And all this was above and beyond the every-day entertainment of travellers and roamers who made use of the monastery as we moderns do the hotel, only with this very precious difference that there was nothing *whatever* to pay. True, one could give "an alms," and probably most did, the majority not unlikely in the coin of the day equivalent to the modern threepenny piece—human nature all the world over! But the monastic Rule was strictly emphatic on this point—of hospitality—to all and every. None were to be refused, lest an angel should be denied unawares.

Upon occasion they did, however, strain a little, as the 1258 *Annales Burtonensis* bears witness.

"It is permitted to give food to actors because they are poor, not because they are actors; but their plays must not be seen nor heard, nor permitted to be acted before the abbot or the monks."[1]

There had been abuses, but there were to be no more.

Thus the great orders themselves, and particular houses of those orders, have become famous with a wide reputation, and individual members of those convents and order have gained celebrity for themselves, and glory and fame for their "house" and their "order."

To no order in particular have the names of these

---

[1] Minstrels were maintained in some houses.

great ones been limited. The rolls of them all are blazoned with the names of these illustrious workers, all admirable and gifted men, who, although individually and by name forgotten or unknown to the world at large, are only so because they worked with a single eye, and solely for the honour of God and the welfare of their community, and for no earthly praise, profit, or reputation.

First among the more eminent of these men, comes that great versatility of genius, Friar Bacon, the Franciscan, who, as a scholar and an exemplar of learning, may be said to have held the keys of all the then known arts. Born in the thirteenth century, he is only to be compared to his great prototypes of the fifteenth, Leonardo da Vinci; or to that other monk, Tutilo, who flourished in the tenth.

Although a voluminous writer, the fame of Roger Bacon, in popular estimation, has always rested on his inventions and mechanical discoveries, the famous oracular "brazen head" being chief among them. Of the rest of his powers, let him speak for himself.[1]

In his quaint treatise "Of Admirable Artificial Instruments," Bacon says:—

"That I may the better demonstrate the inferiority and indignity of Magical power, to that of Nature and Art, I shall a while discourse on such admirable operations of Art and Nature as have not the least Magick in them; and afterwards assign their causes and Frames. And first of such Engines as are purely artificial.

"(1) It's possible to make Engines to sail withall, as that either fresh or salt water vessels may be guided by the help of one man, and made sail with a greater swiftness than others will which are full of men to help them. (2) It is

---

[1] Three of his manuscripts are preserved in the Library of Exeter Cathedral.

possible to make a chariot move with an inestimable swiftness (such as the Corrus falcati were, wherein our forefathers of old fought), and his motion to be without the help of any living creature.

(3) It's possible to make Engines for flying, a man sitting in the midst whereof, by burning only about an Instrument which moves artificiall wings made to beat the Aire, much after the fashion of a Bird's flight. (4) It's possible to invent an Engine of a little bulk, yet of great efficacy, either to the depressing or elevation of the very greatest weight, which would be of much consequence in severall Accidents; for hereby a man may either ascend or descend any walls, delivering himself or comrads from prison, and this Engine is only three fingers high, and four broad. (5) A man may easily make an Instrument whereby one man may in despight of all opposition, draw a thousand men to himself, or any other thing which is tractable. (6) A man may make an Engine whereby without any corporal danger he may walk in the bottom of the sea or other water.

"Such Engines as these were of old, and are made even in our days.

"These, all of them (excepting only that instrument of flying, which I never saw, or know of any who hath seen it, though I am exceedingly acquainted with a very prudent man, who hath invented the whole artifice), with infinite such-like inventions, Engines and devices are feasible, as making of Bridges over Rivers without pillars or supporters."

He is accredited also with the invention of such minor accessories as spectacles and gunpowder, the latter, however, but little known till Barthod Schwartz, a monk of Cologne, brought it into use in 1330.

Leonardo da Vinci himself, also, in a somewhat similar document, it may be remembered, offered to undertake the construction of similar marvels.

Naturally, few were giants of such dimensions or equal to such amazing capabilities. However, Alexander of Hales, the "Irrefragable Doctor," was a friar of this order.

Under their fostering care, architecture made vast

progress. Fra Sisto, Fra Ristoro, and Fra Giovanni (Dominicans), built the Church of Santa Maria Novella, at Florence, where Michael Angelo was daily wont to pray. Fra Gioconde superintended with Raphael the construction of St Peter's. Fra Guglielmo was likewise an architect and sculptor in the thirteenth century.

In England, Alan of Walsingham, Thomas de Northwick, of Evesham, and Ednoth of Ramsey, monks, worked at the same art. Walter of Colchester, the Sacrist of St Alban's, excelled as a painter and sculptor.

For monkish painters we must necessarily go abroad, where Fra Canesole was the early instructor of Raphael and Dom Lorenzo Monaco,[1] and Dom Guilio Clovis, Benedictines; and Fra Antonio da Negro Ponto, Friar Minor;[2] Fra Filippo Lippi, the Carmelite, and Fra "Beato" Angelico da Fiesole; Fra Bartolommeo (styled *par excellence*, Il Frate—"The Friar"), and the Della Robbia (sculptors) shine out from a whole host of Dominican painters, in company with their brother, the eloquent advocate for the purity of art, Fra Jerome (Savonarola). Many Spanish painters wore the habit of their respective orders, and brought their art to such a pitch of perfection that, crude though it sometimes be, is still the profound admiration of the painter and connoisseur.[3]

Among mosaic workers, Fra Giacopo Turrita (Torriti) was the most celebrated, and, according to Lanzi, surpassed all the contemporary Greek and Roman crafts-

---

[1] The painter of the beautiful "Annunciation," hanging in the Gallery at Florence.
[2] Painter of the dignified Madonna in the Frari, Venice.
[3] A deep and real sympathy always existed between painters and the religious orders. Among the Franciscans of St Maria degli Angioli, Bernardino Luini breathed his last.

men in that art. The Benedictine monk, Theophilus, between the twelfth and thirteenth centuries, wrote the very first art treatise, entitled "Diversarum Artium Schedula," or, "The Schedule of Different Arts," a work lately re-published in England and France.

Our own St Dunstan, himself a Benedictine, enriched the monasteries of his diocese with metal work, the result of the labour of his own hands, and Thomas de Bamburgh, monk of Durham, was employed to make two great warlike engines for the defence of the town of Berwick. Richard of Wallingford, son of a blacksmith at St Alban's, and afterwards abbot of the abbey there, constructed a clock for that house in 1326, which is said to have surpassed any hitherto made in England. About the same time a monk of Glastonbury, in Somerset, Peter Lightfoot by name, designed and constructed a similar great clock for that abbey. This work he achieved entirely single-handed, and with the crudest and most primitive appliances. It has been thus described :—

"It will give an idea of the labour involved, when it is stated that the mechanism of the clock occupies a space of about 5 feet cube (125 cubic feet), that the structure is wholly of forged iron, that the numerous wrought-iron wheels, some of which are nearly 2 feet in diameter, and about half an inch thick, besides having to be made truly circular and concentric, had all their teeth cut out and trimmed to workable shape by hand, and that the heavy wrought-iron frames, etc. are fastened entirely by means of mortise, tenon, and cotter, no screws being used in the whole structure. The pinions are of the lantern form, with octagonal check-plates on square spindles, and the pendulum, of modern form, beats seconds.

"It is a curious feature in this remarkable clock that the striking movement is arranged with the axes of its wheels, etc., at right angles to those of the going mechanism; the releasing gear for striking, connecting the two systems, is original and ingenious."

After going continuously for about two hundred and fifty years in the home of its birth, it was removed to the Cathedral of Wells, where it continued its course for a similar further period, to be finally rescued from the crypt, and dust, and oblivion, and restored and re-erected at the Museum at South Kensington, where it continues working—"surely the oldest piece of working mechanism extant?"[1]

St Iltyd of Llancarvan, although chiefly known as a theologian and monastic pioneer, was also no contemptible handicraftsman. The kind of plough invented by him, and called after his name, may still be seen in some of the remoter districts of Wales.

Among the Cistercians, poets superabounded; men like Bernard of Clairvaux and his namesake of Morlaix, and Giacopo dei Beneditti, the author of the "Stabat Mater," and other gems of spiritual poetry, shines among the Franciscans. In the first quarter of the eleventh century, Guy, a Benedictine monk of Arezzio, invented the "gamut," or scale of musical rotation, which, perfected three hundred years after, is still in use. Regino, Abbot of Prüm, was an excellent musician, and author of a treatise on "Harmony." The monastic orders were all great patrons and cultivators of music; the great Benedictine, St Gregory, surnamed the Great, being the pioneer of that grand especial music of the Church known as the Gregorian Chant, which to-day

---

[1] There was a "clokehouse and a clok therein complete" in the south transept of Rievaulx Abbey. In a visitation of the Benedictine abbey at Carrow, Norfolk, in 1514, Richard Nykke, Bishop of Norwich, found that they did not possess a clock, and ordered the prioress to get one, and keep it in order. From the "Paston Letters" (vol. ii. p. 80), it appears the monks took in repairs, as Sir John Paston requests Harcort of the Abbey (Durham?) "to send him a little clokke which was sent him to be mended."

is cultivated with such perfection by the Benedictines, and especially those of the Abbey of Solesmes, and its daughter house of St Michael, Farnborough, Hants.

It was not an unknown thing for monks to write for minstrels. One of the earliest ballads now remaining in the English language is the work of a monk of Reading, in the thirteenth century,[1] the latter part of the reign of Henry III. This interesting scrap of mediæval literature is preserved among the Harleian Manuscripts in the British Museum, being written upon six red lines in square and lozenge black notes of three kinds. It is entitled:—

A Cuckow Song.

Sumer is icumen in,
Lhudè sing cuccu;
Groweth sed and bloweth med,
And spingeth the wdè nu.
Sing cuccu.
Awe beteth after lamb,
Llouth after calvè cu.
Bullue sterteth,
Buckè verteth,
Murie sing cuccu.
Cuccu, cuccu,
Wel singes thou, cuccu,
Ne swik thou never nu.

Among historical writers, our own venerable Bede takes a high place, not alone in the annals of his own country, but also in those of Europe, Pope Boniface calling him in one of his Epistles, "The candle of the English Church." His "Ecclesiastical History of the Nations of the Angles" is his chief work, and was

---

[1] 1226.

undertaken at the request of Ceolwulph, King of Northumbria, who himself became a monk at Lindisfarne three years after Bede's death. The work is in five books, and was translated into Saxon by King Alfred.

Bede was a voluminous writer, having spent his whole life in the writing and transcribing of books, among them the most important being the "Life of St Cuthbert"; various other lives of saints, "Hymns," "Epigrams," and "A Treatise on the Art of Poetry." In the chapter library of Durham are copies of the "Vulgate," the New Testament, and of "Cassiodorus on the Psalms," in his handwriting.

Asser, monk of St David's; Eadmer, Osbern (the English Jubal), Cœdmon of Whitby, Ernulph of Rochester, Benedict of Burgh, Odo, FitzStephen, Thorn, D'Avesbury, and Gervase, monks of Canterbury; Symeon, monk of Durham; Rishanger, Matthew Paris, and Thomas of Walsingham, monks of St Alban's; Richard of Devizes, John of Exeter, and Rudborne, monks of Winchester; Higden (author of "Polychronicon"), monk of Chester, and Lydgate, monk of Bury, were all eminent as historians, annalists, or chroniclers. Robert de Brunne, monk of Bourne, has been styled "The Father of the English Language."

The great Abbey of Monte Cassino, the parent house of the great Benedictine Order, produced a large number of men of letters, as did its daughter house of St Maur—Autpert and Theophanus, Hilderic and the heroic St Bertarius. Paul, the Deacon, abandoning the highest post his king could bestow, became a monk, poet, historian, linguist, and familiar friend of Charlemagne. Desiderius set to work at the age of forty to study letters and music, to write books and compose chants. He erected a new library, where, besides other works, could be found Virgil, Horace, Terence, Cicero, and the voluminous writings of Justinian, and among numerous others the profound Erasmus, Constantine Africanus, Leo of Ostia, and Amatus of Salerno.

The Benedictine Remigius of Auxerre started the first really public school in Paris, and another monk, Antoninus, wrote the first complete history of the world. Gilbert, Abbot of Westminster, a contemporary of Anselm, wrote a "Disputatio Judæi cum Christiano," the report of an actual discussion, which converted Jews on the spot. Authors in those days were compelled to publish authoritative editions of their works, because so many copies from notes of their lectures were in circulation, which facts show that books on popular subjects were even in those times eagerly looked after and anxiously read.

In the thirteenth century the Dominican, Jacobus de Voragine, collected together the pious legends of his own and earlier times under the title of "The Golden Legend," a work which has been translated into every language of the West. Another friar of the same order, Robert Holcot, in the year 1200, wrote a book on the game of chess.

One of the very first, if not the earliest, of encyclopædias was the handiwork of Dom Vincent de Beauvais, who flourished in the thirteenth century. He styled his work "Speculum Majus," because it briefly contained almost everything he could collect from innumerable works that was worthy of speculation. This great work is divided into more than ten thousand chapters, several of which (as that on botany) are sub-divided alphabetically. There was also the De

Proprietatibus Rerum" (On the Properties of Things) of our own countryman, the Franciscan, Bartholomew de Glanville, written about 1360.

About twenty years after the appearance of this work, John Mirfield, a canon of the Priory of St Bartholomew, Smithfield, put forth his treatise on medicine called "Breviarium Bartholemei," a standard mediæval work on medicine, and probably to be found in the medical department of every large monastery.[1]

Religious ladies like Dame Juliana Berners, Prioress of Sopwell, near St Alban's, did not disdain to use the pen, curiously enough, not in the cause of the Church, or even the protection of birds and animals, as their gentle nature would presuppose, but in "Treatyses Pertayninge to Hawkynge, Huntynge, and Fysshynge with an Angle : and also a Right Noble Treatyse of the Lynage of Col Armours, Endynge with a Treatyse which Specyfyeth of Blasynge of Armys." Other nuns, as the Prioress of Kirklees (Yorkshire), "a woman very skilful in physic and surgery," experimented in the healing art. This lady, legend has named aunt to that flower of archery, Robin Hood, and credited to have terminated his life in her priory by bleeding him to death.

Talking of bleeding reminds us that to the Servite, Fra Paolo Sarpi, is ascribed the discovery of the circulation of the blood and valvular action of the veins. Baldwin, Abbot of St Edmundsbury, towards the close of the eleventh century, had a wide reputation for skill in medicine, being esteemed one of the greatest physicians of his time.

Bernard Barlaam, a monk of Calabria, taught Greek

---

[1] The handsomest known copy, in the library of Pembroke College, Oxford, bears the arms of the Benedictine Abbey of Abingdon.

to Petrarch and Leontius Silatus. Galfridus "Grammaticus" (Dominican) compiled the first printed English and Latin dictionary, at King's Lynn, Norfolk.

As early as the opening of the sixth century, Cosmas, an Egyptian monk, otherwise called Cosmas Indicopleustes, from the presumed fact of his having travelled into India, had compiled a treatise on geography, entitled "The Christian Topography of the World," and early in the ninth century, Dicuil, an Irish monk in France, another called "De Mensura Orbis." Adelard, monk of Bath, was also a learned traveller, and another, Athelard (perhaps the same), revived in the twelfth century the knowledge of geometry, and translated the books of Euclid from the Arabic into Latin.

In the fifteenth century, Nicholas of Lynn, a friar of Oxford, an astronomer, made a voyage of discovery towards the North Pole; and Elmer, or Oliver, monk of Malmesbury, anticipating the attempts of modern aeronauts by contriving a pair of wings for sailing through the air, sprang from the top of a lofty tower, and—fractured his limbs!

The monks were from the first great makers of libraries, as well as of books. The Kalendars, a fraternity of religious laymen at Bristol, to whom was committed the custody of the archives of the town, and whose office it was to keep a monthly register of local events and public acts, and whose church also contained a library, with apartments for the librarian, who was identical with the prior of the order, were pioneers in the Free Library movement. On every festival day—and such days were far more numerous than they are now—free access was granted to all who sought instruction, from seven to eleven o'clock in the morning. Books were not allowed to be taken home, as in those days they were so very precious.

To the diligence of a monk named Piaggio, the method of unrolling the Greek manuscripts unearthed at Herculaneum was discovered, and his process is employed at the present day. About the middle of the sixth century Dionysius Exiguus, a Roman abbot, born in Scythia, introduced the method of dating the years from the birth of Christ, placing its date in the eighth year of the one hundred and ninety-fourth Olympiad, 753, from the foundation of Rome.[1]

Being appointed to the post of cellarer at St Peter's (Benedictine) Abbey, Hautvilliers-on-the-Marne, Dom Perignon, in 1688, conceived the idea of "marrying" various wines, and thus produced "Champagne," and though vast improvements have taken place, the principles he introduced have never been abandoned.

This production of choice wines was one of the results consequent upon the attention paid by the monks to agriculture, by which they arrived at the capabilities of the soil, and, coupled with a studied and careful grafting and zealous tending, taught them how the wine might best be made and stored so as to mellow it to perfection. The decline in the cultivation of the vine may be said to be due to the dissolution of the monasteries. From the name "Vine Street," the Abbot of Westminster must have possessed a vineyard, as of the orchard in Orchard Street. At the dissolution of religious houses, a vineyard of five acres was scheduled as part of the possessions of Barking nunnery.

---

[1] It is believed that he placed it about four years too late.

# BOOK III

### CONVENTUAL CONSTITUTION

THE corporation or convent, *i.e.* the corporate body of religious persons living and working together under one roof or block of buildings, called a monastery, was under the care and guidance of a head or chief officer named the "abbot."

The abbot was himself a member of the community, society, or order electing him to the post of father and protector of his fellows. Having been once elected, the care and government of the whole house and its members involved upon him. Yet, although thus invested with a power absolutely monarchial, he, in theory at least, could absolutely do nothing without the publicly (in chapter) given consent of every individual member of the convent who had elected him to the honour of being its head.

From the monastic annals an interesting account is gained of the method employed in creating a new fraternity—a daughter to a mother house.

All the brethren being assembled in chapter, after the usual business, and a period of silence, the abbot arose, and, after a slight introduction relative to the matter in hand, said: "In the name of the Father, and of the Son, and of the Holy Ghost, Amen. I ordain and constitute magister [so-and-so] Abbot." The person thus named was immediately carried in the arms of the monks to the high altar, with the exclamation: "Thou art Abbot of ——." Returning to the chapter house, the abbot elect was taken by the right hand by his superior, and placed in the principal seat with these words: "I confirm thee Abbot, and to thee commit cure of souls, and the rule over —— Abbey, and all its substance, its persons, and possessions, present and future, as well in temporals as spirituals, as —— Abbot of —— [the parent house] gave it to us." He then placed a copy of the Rule of St Benedict and a small bag of relics in his hands, and proceeded to name the twelve monks of the convent who had been selected to accompany the new abbot. Having absolved them from their obedience to himself, they immediately professed the same to their new superior, and both he and they a short time after departed to their new house after a benediction from the abbot.

Neither in its original idea was it even necessary that the abbot of a monastery should be an ecclesiastic, or a monastery itself an ecclesiastical institution. As a matter of fact, many abbots were laymen,[1] and it was not until recent days that the majority of monks were in holy orders.[2] About the eighth century in France many lay-abbots were intruded into the abbacies, usurping the revenues, but Hugh Capet again restored the election of the monks.[3] About the

---

[1] *See* "Answ. of Ecgbriht," 734, a. xii.; Cuthbert, "Canons," 747, c. 7.

[2] Generally speaking, to-day a monk is a cleric, and those out of holy orders, the lay brethren, are not considered as "monks" proper.

[3] In England the Crown frequently interfered in the election of abbots, either by forcing its own nominee, or withholding its assent to the elect of the convent.

same period some presidents of secular colleges under a variety of names, all signifying jurisdiction, were called abbots.

Among the Egyptians, as we have seen, the superior of a community was called "David."

All the abbots of branch houses were subject to the head or superior of the mother house, as all the affiliated Benedictine houses to Monte Cassino, the Cluniacs to Cluny, and the Cistercian to Citeaux. The Abbot of Melrose (Mael or Mul-ros—the bare promontory), and other associated houses were subject to the superior authority of the Abbot of Hü or Hy. Thus his rule sometimes extended over a very wide tract of country, and even passed beyond the seas to other countries, where minor houses or "cells" had been affiliated to the great parent house, under the name of alien priories, the heads of which were called "priors." Sometimes these lesser houses disassociated themselves from their central house, and became themselves abbeys, or independent monasteries. Thus, all the Cistercian monasteries in England were abbeys ruled by their allied abbots, in supreme and complete jurisdiction, independently of their recognised over-lord, the Abbot of Citeaux; whereas, on the other hand, all the Cluniac houses were virtually alien priories, completely subject to the jurisdiction of specially appointed prior representatives, and paying heavy tribute to their parent house of Cluny, in France.

In those places where the monastic church was also the cathedral, the bishop was treated as the abbot, occupying (as at Ely), his stall in quire, the real abbot being called the prior. Were he a mitred abbot (as at Gloucester), he assumed the habit and ornaments (the mitre originally of materials less costly, and the crook of the staff turned inwards, to mark the internal jurisdiction exercised over his house) of a bishop.

The privileges attached to the dignity of an abbot were many and great. Not only was he over-lord of his house, a spiritual lord of the realm, frequently the equal, sometimes even the superior of his bishop, but a great and important personage in the secular world as well.

When Abbot Whiting of Glastonbury, a good man and a true, went abroad, which he seldom did, save to attend synods, chapters, and Parliaments, he was attended by upwards of a hundred persons.

Independent of the jurisdiction of the Episcopate, they were frequently at issue with the bishops at any encroachment on or curtailment of their prerogatives. Thus arose the antagonism between the bishops and those houses struggling to gain for themselves exemption from the prying and interference, as they called it, of their ecclesiastical superiors.

Besides sitting in Parliament, they were frequently chosen as sponsors for children of the blood-royal, exercised the privilege of making knights and of coining. Bells rang in their honour in their progresses, not infrequently with a retinue little less than that of a monarch, whilst at home they were served by the children of nobles as pages. In the ecclesiastical province they gave the benediction wherever they chose, conferred the lesser orders, consecrated churches, and performed other similar rites.

Apart and within the monastic precincts, a separate and independent residence was assigned to him, with a like estate to provide for the maintenance of his proper dignity. In the convent the patronage of every office was in his hands, and his officers were numerous. They were called obedientiaries—that is, officers under the abbot, told off to superintend or fulfil certain duties, being under a special obligation of obedience to his representative, the prior.

First, there were his own personal or domestic attendants, his chaplain, barber, and cook. These two latter, it would appear, were not necessarily monks, as an instance occurs of such a barber receiving ten shillings a year as wages. The cook would upon occasion ride before the abbot, when upon a journey, to prepare refreshment, for which purpose he was allowed the use of a horse.[1] Next the officers of the house: The prior, or representative of the abbot, the sub-prior, the third and even the fourth, and perhaps a claustral prior, wardens of order under him, all of whom held chapters, and were presidents in hall. Then came, in varying order, the cellarer, treasurer, chamberlain, and sub-chamberlain, seneschal, kitchener, refectioner, pittancier, almoner, hostillar or hospitaler, infirmarer, terrier of house (inner hostillar or terrar), granetarius, master of the common house, orcharder, porter, and an infinity of smaller offices, the object being to distribute the offices and work as widely as possible, in order that all might fully recognise the responsibility accruing to each as a part of the whole house, and to create a personal interest in its welfare.[2]

In addition to the above were the heads of departments connected with the purely religious side of the convent as apart from the domestic. Thus the pre-

---

[1] *See* full description of an abbot's household, as at St Augustine's, Canterbury, "Consuetudinary," Cotton MS. Faustina, c. xii.

[2] The forensic or out-door officers, by reason of their duties or exterior business, were not always under obligation to attend the quire offices.

centor, or chantor, assisted by a sub-chantor, looked after the choral section; in the sacristan and his helpers was reposed the care of the church, its ornaments and vestments, and in the penitentiary, the spiritual condition of the house generally, whilst the master of the novices devoted himself to the care and instruction of that section of the community.

These offices, as well as officers, varied very considerably of necessity in almost every house, very few being identical or discharging the same duties. In the larger houses, of course, offices and officers were as much multiplied as in the smaller they were curtailed; and whereas, in the former a single department had a series of assistants, in the latter several offices would be administered by a single monk.

At Abingdon the abbot had his abbey proctor, who acted also as his bursar, and further, alternately with the seneschal, his court-holder and man of business; his keeper of courts, who was also granarer and larderer, and receiver of guests; his chaplain, who was also one of his hebdomadarii,[1] or weekly celebrants, and his constant companion. At Durham the chaplain was the abbot's chamberlain and comptroller. At Gloucester he could have as many as five esquires; one to be seneschal, the second marshal, to regulate the expenses as comptroller of the household, and regulate the fare in hall and number of guests, the third cook, the fourth chamberlain, and the fifth usher of the table. Of these one only was to have a horse. In addition to the esquires he could have a sub-chamberlain, a pantryman, a butler, a cook as drysalter, a farrier and a messenger, also four grooms of the robes, another groom, and a couple of pages. For the use of himself

---

[1] The officers (priests) in charge of the services for a week.

and his chaplains, four palfreys and a long chariot, eight dogs of the chase and four harriers, but the hounds were to be driven forth of the hall at mealtime by the ushers.[1]

The prior,[2] sometimes called the major, or greater prior, was a kind of prime minister of his lord, the abbot, his chief of the executive of the convent, his representative in his absence. In this latter degree he had liberty to perform all the duties of his master, save those of appointing and disposing obedientiaries,[3] and consecrating novices upon their admission to the order.

In the presence or absence of the abbot he it was who struck the cymbalum, beat upon the table for the commencement of work, and *monitum* in the dormitory, and corrected the faults of the readers in church and chapter. He could call a chapter of servants at any time, and punish delinquents at pleasure.

In quire, chapter, and refectory the first place next the abbot was assigned him, and in the execution of his office he had for assistant a sub-prior, and sometimes others.

In the absence or illness of the abbot he could hold chapters, visit the infirmary and the school of the novices, hear their lessons, hold a chapter of them, and punish them; after Compline he inspected the monks, and made the *circa* (grand rounds or patrol) of the monastery after nightfall. When the abbot was abroad or away for a lengthened period, he could, according to the fault, extend discipline to the prison,

---

[1] WALCOTT, "Sacred Archæology," p. 3.
[2] "Dean" was an old appellation of prior, for to every ten monks there was a prior.
[3] In some places it would appear he had power to depose servants and others corrupting their office by fraud.

and in a vacancy of the abbacy could profess monks, and discharge similar abbatial duties.

As in the case of the abbot, the convent provided the prior with a separate establishment; and (as St Alban's) with horses, retinue, and equipage; or (as at St Edmundsbury) with a chaplain, two servants, and five horses, of which two were palfreys and one a baggage horse; or (as at Abingdon) with one man who had a corody[1] in the hall, and maintenance for a horse, with the use of others, but these the abbot might take for his own business. When he sat at table he had the further privilege of sending his cup to the cellarer to be twice filled, but the cup was to be without a cover.

As he himself was a spy upon the abbot, others were appointed to spy upon him, for he could go nowhere without one or two monks; when sitting in office one of the novices was to attend him, and when clerks or laymen were dining in the refectory, he was to stay for company's sake, asking two or three monks to do so likewise.

Sometimes, as at Abingdon, the abbot had two monks, one called proctor, the other curiarius—to ease him of his burden. In the hands of the former was the management of the revenues, in those of the latter the whole care of the house was reposed. The admittance of visitors, whose arrival had been announced to him by the porter, was to be according to their difference in rank. Particular attention was to be paid by him to the parents of monks, who were to announce their arrival to him only.

The abbot's hall or house at Fountains—171 feet by 70 feet—must have been one of the noblest in the kingdom. Its central space was divided from the aisle

---

[1] Maintenance—bed and board in the house.

which surrounded it by eighteen marble columns. The abbot's chapel, with the altar mound, from which the slab has disappeared, was east of the hall, and north of it a crypt, cellar, and storehouse in which, tradition says, the six white horses of the abbey were kept.[1] The garden and orchard appertaining to the abbot's house extended eastward of the church.

The prior's lodge at the Cluniac Priory of Wenlock (Shropshire), about middle fifteenth-century date, presents an unique example of the domestic arrangements of the abode of that officer, who in houses of that order took the place of an abbot in others. Although one side only now remains, the buildings seem to have occupied a quadrangle at the south-east angle of the great cloister court. It is a building of two storeys, surmounted by a very high roof, the whole length about 100 feet. A light and elegant cloister corridor or gallery, unglazed, extends throughout, communicating with the rooms on either floor. Large buttresses divide it into compartments at regular intervals, and these, in their turn, are sub-divided into a couple of compartments by smaller buttresses, the space between being filled in with two trefoil-headed lights, divided horizontally by a transom, the water drains from the upper rooms being carved with heads of lions and other grotesque figures.

On the ground floor is a kitchen, now utilised as a brew-house, and opening into it that peculiar structure which so frequently is found in mediæval buildings, and called a *garde-robe*. Next is the bakehouse, which is succeeded by a small room, modernised out of its original proportions. At the north end is a small

---

[1] This tradition is supported by the fact that at the time of the Dissolution the abbot really possessed *sex equi ad bigam*.

chapel, or private oratory, still retaining in its projecting window recess its ancient stone altar, panelled in front, and in the south wall its piscina.[1]

By a flight of steps a narrow corridor, with window-openings of open and closed panel-work divisions, similar to that on the ground floor, gives access to what was in all probability the prior's hall, a fine, triple-bayed apartment, with a high-pitched roof of oak of great beauty, and a flowered cornice running round the top of the wall. On the east, four windows of two lights each, recessed in the wall, give light to the room. Within the recesses are stone shelves, and on the south wall traces of mural painting.

South of this hall is another chamber, also entered from the corridor, and which formed perhaps the parlour of the prior. A fireplace is set in the south wall, on either side of which is a window which, with two others, light the apartment. In the north-east angle is a perforated stone basin or drain, ending in a lion's head. A staircase in the east wall leads down to a closet, and another in the north wall at the south-west corner connects the upper rooms with the offices below.

In some instances it would appear that the prior was under the thumb of the abbot's chaplain.[2] The chaplain, we are told, was to receive at the "Bowcers," or bursar's, hands all such sums of money as were payable by him to the lord prior's use for his maintenance, expense of his whole household, and other necessaries. Among other things, he was to provide the lord prior's apparel, to see that all things were in

---

[1] In a charter of Finchale Priory, dated 1474, the private chapel of the prior is described: "Capella Sancti Nicholai juxta cameram domini Prioris situata."

[2] The writer is probably speaking of a prior, the superior of a priory, and not of a prior under an abbot.

good order in the hall, that the furniture of his table was sweet and clean, that every man executed his office diligently as he ought to do, and that no debate or strife should be within the house. The plate and treasure of the lord prior was in his custody, to be delivered out for use and received again when done with. He paid the wages of all the gentlemen, yeomen, and all other servants and officers of the lord prior's house, and discharged all other debts whatsoever. His chamber adjoined the prior's chamber, he never sleeping in the dormitory save in the absence of the abbot. Although separate habitations for abbots are mentioned as early as the reign of Alfred the Great, Æthelstan, Abbot of Ramsey, is described as dining with his monks in the common refectory, and the Synod of London, held in the reign of Henry I., ordered abbots to eat and sleep in the same house with the monks, unless any necessity prevented. In later times such an order if imposed, or still binding, was utterly ignored. The abbot's house at Westminster is now the Deanery, that at Buildwas, recently restored, contains a large hall or reception room, with a thirteenth-century ceiling of oak and Spanish chestnut, lighted by beautifully moulded Norman windows, one on either side of the door, also of good Norman work, a chapel and ambulatory. Other chambers for noble guests, a kitchen, cellars, etc., were generally attached to the abbot's lodgings. Not unfrequently there was a painted chamber for councils, or the reception of important personages and guests, called "pictoria," or "Jerusalem" and "Jericho" chambers (from the hangings representing those places), as at Westminster.

At the Priory of Bridlington, the prior superior's lodgings consisted of a hall approached by two-and-twenty steps, a great dining chamber, a little sleeping chamber with a garret over, a little chapel with a closet adjoining, the kitchen, cellarer's chamber, buttery and pantry, the chamber of the auditor, a parlour with a chamber above, and three little chambers for servants.

Sometimes the "lodgings," as they were called, of the abbot or prior, as the case may be, was part of the conventual buildings; at others they formed a distinct building or dwelling apart, being formed of a second court as at Durham and Finchale, parallel with the quire of the church, and forming the southern side of a second court.

A prior under an abbot also had his separate "lodge," or suite of apartments, usually adjacent to the great cloister, detached to it by a short passage. At St Alban's he had a chamber over the dormitory, abutting on the hostry chapel. At other places the sub-prior slept in such a chamber, nigh to or over the dormitory door, in order that he might hear if any stirred or went out.

### Novices

"Let not an easy entance be granted to one who cometh newly to religious life," says St Benedict,[1] "but, as the Apostle saith : 'Try the spirits if they be of God.'[2] If, therefore, the new-comer persevere knocking, and continue for four or five days patiently to endure both the injuries offered to him, and the difficulty made about his entrance, and persist in his petition, leave to enter shall then be granted him, and he shall be in the Guest Hall for a few days.[3] Afterwards he shall be in the Novitiate, where he shall meditate, and eat, and sleep."

---

[1] "Rule of St Benedict," chap. lviii. p. 237, edit. 1638.
[2] 1 St John iv. 1.
[3] Sometimes called the *Pulsatorium* (from "Knock and it shall be opened to you"). Here they stayed and waited upon the strangers in the hostrey.

Further, he was to be watched with the utmost care, by a senior "who has the address of winning souls to God," in order to see if he was sincere in his application. All "the rigour and austerity" by which a monk walked towards God, was to be laid before him, and if he promised stability and perseverance at the end of two months, the whole Rule was to be read through to him, with the addition of the words: "Behold the law under which thou desirest to fight; if thou canst observe it, enter in; if thou canst not, freely depart."

If he stood firm, he was to be taken back to the cell of the novices for further trial "in all patience," and after a further space of six months, the Rule was again read to him, "that he may know unto what he has come." Still persevering, the Rule was read yet a third time, and if he then promised, "after due deliberation," to keep and observe all things commanded him "he was received into the community, knowing that he is from that time forward under the law of the Rule, so that he can neither leave the monastery nor shake off the yoke of the Rule, which, after so long a deliberation, he might have accepted or refused."

When admitted to profession in the presence of all, and before God and His Saints, he was to make a promise of "stability, amendment of manners, and obedience."

The form of this promise was to be drawn up in his own writing "in the name of the Saints whose relics are on the altar, and of the Abbot there present." If he could not write, another, at his request, was to write it out for him, and, having put his mark to it, he[1] with

---

[1] In a case in the chapter house of Westminster are preserved many such slips of parchment, vows of monks, signed by them with a cross.

his own hand laid it upon the altar. Then, after a verse by himself, and a response by the monks, the new brother cast himself at the feet of all, that they might pray for him, from which hour he was counted as one of the community.

Such was the plain and simple order "of receiving Brothers to Religion" as directed by St Benedict himself, and although after legislators added much to the primitive simplicity of the great patriarch's Rule, in substance it remained the same.

By the "Norman Institutes" persons coming to conversion,[1] were not to have an easy admission, but to be mocked and proved in various ways, according to the above text of the Apostle, an instance being given in true mediæval style of a parent, who was ordered to throw his son into a river, in order to test his obedience, but was restrained, however, by the monk, and received in a manner very similar to the above. But, after his admission, the novice, kissing the feet of the president of the chapter who had proclaimed his admission, withdrew to the church, and sat down before one of the altars, out of the quire, till the chapter was finished. The shaving of the head and the benediction of the tonsure,[2] and the robing in the monastic habit having been accomplished, he was then led through the quire for all the monks to kiss him, and was placed last. For three days he took the sacrament, and on the third the hood was removed from his head. Up to this time he had preserved a constant silence, departed from the chapter after the

---

[1] Converts, or novices, were so called from the words of their profession, *Promitto conversionem morum*, meaning that they had abandoned the secular life for ever.

[2] The tonsure seems to have been performed out of the church, though the shorn hair was sometimes burnt in the censer.

customary opening sentence of the Rule had been read, went in no procession, and slept in hood. On the third day after profession, he took his first seat in chapter and was allowed to speak, read, and sing, by his master's solicitation, in the convent like the others. Assent having been given, he could then perform all the offices, saving the celebration of Mass, which, except he receive special permission, he could not do till a year after.[1]

Some abbots, on the contrary, allowed their novices to stay in chapter, lest, taking disgust at the disciplines, they should decline profession, and disclose the secrets of the house. The friars, however, never allowed their novices to attend chapter at all.

The Emperor Charlemagne, in the "Capitularies," added the following excellent amendments to the rules of monastic institutions. That young men destined to the monastic life must first pass their novitiate, and then remain in the monastery to learn the rules before they are sent forth to fill their duties outside. Those who give up the world in order to avoid the king's service should be compelled to serve God in good faith, or else to resume their former occupation, and all clerks were required to make their choice between clerical life in conformity with the regulations. The abbeys were not to receive too large a number of serfs, lest the villages should be depopulated, and no community was to have more members than could be properly looked after by one superior. Young women were not to take the veil until they were of an age to choose their own career in life. Laymen were to be dis-

---

[1] At St Augustine's, Canterbury, the newly received swore to the utmost of their power not to suffer the house to be bound for the debts of others, or to reveal its secrets.

qualified from governing the interior of a monastery, nor shall they fill the post of archdeacon.

The period spent in the novitiate of a religious house was none too pleasant. The Rule said new-comers were to be "tried," and tried they were in every way. Any bit of pride the aspirant may have had was quickly knocked out of him. From the very commencement he never had a moment to himself. Under the eye of the master, he slept in the chamber of novices, or the dormitory, and sat in the place appointed for novices in the cloister. He never read in the convent, or sung alone, never offered at Mass, nor received the peace (*pax*). Without his master's leave no one spoke or even made a sign (the monastic equivalent of speaking in solemn silence times) to him; but any monk conversing in the cloister, and wishing to reprove or advise him, by the master's leave could do so.

Accused of a fault he was immediately to rise, soliciting pardon, and dared not sit till the master bade him. He made frequent confessions of faults committed both before and after he took the habit, to the abbot, prior, or other person deputed by him. For greater faults he was either chidden or beaten in chapter or the novice chamber.

After enduring all these severities with a cheerful and undaunted spirit, he was at length recommended to the abbot and convent in chapter assembled for profession, and, upon their consent, was received into the fellowship of the house. Professions of monks were entered in a book called "Pactum," at Ensham, and after profession monks were named from the places they came from, as Abbot John Islip (in Oxfordshire) of Westminster, and Abbot Wheathampstead (in Hertfordshire) of Saint Alban's; or Walter de Colchester,

Sacrist of Saint Alban's, and Thomas de Bamburgh, monk of Durham.[1]

In a convent the monks were divided in three classes. The first, or elder monks, were called "seniors," or wisefolk (*Sempectæ senes-sapientes*). They were monks who had passed their fiftieth year of profession, and were thus excused the obligations of the house, save that perhaps of saying Mass. They were also accorded special privileges, as a chamber in the infirmary, with a junior monk for company, and a boy to wait upon them. They were treated with much respect, never told anything unpleasant, or given any offence. Perfect liberty was likewise accorded them, and they went in, out, and about any part of the house without restriction. Properly speaking, those called "seniors" were monks who had not yet reached their fiftieth year of profession, but, being near to it, were excused the more arduous duties attaching to the cellarer's, almoner's, and kitchener's offices.

The second class comprised those of the middle period, from twenty-four to forty years' advancement. These, being exonerated from the petty offices and labours of the house, undertook the more important business of the convent, and the choral and cloistral duties.

The third and last class was that of the "juniors," who, up to the twenty-fourth year of their profession, bore all burdens of the quire, cloister, and refectory, as gospellers and epistollers, incense (*thurifers*) and taper bearers (*cerofers*), readers in church, chapter, and refectory, serving in the hall and similar labours.

---

[1] The fashion of wholly repudiating the secular name, both Christian and surname, for a fanciful one after some saint or sacred mystery, is of late date, and probably a foreign importation.

"Let the Juniors," says the author of the Benedictine Rule, "therefore, honour their Seniors, and the Seniors love the Juniors. But in addressing each other by name, no one shall call another by his simple name; let the Seniors call the Juniors Brothers,[1] and let the Juniors call the Seniors 'Revered Fathers.' But because the Abbot represented the person of Christ, he shall be called *'Domnus'* [Lord], and 'abbot,' not as if he took this title upon himself, but out of honour and love for Christ. Let him remember to conduct himself in such a way as to be worthy of so great honour.[2]

Persons in priestly orders were not to be admitted too speedily, but, if such an one persisted in his request, it was to be made known to him that he would have to keep all the discipline appointed by the Rule, and that no relaxation would be made in his favour.[3] St Benedict had, previously to the drawing up of his Rule, experienced a period of trial at the hands of a false priest, hence his caution in respect to the admission of that order into the houses of his Order.

That it was not the original intention of the saint that the majority of the members of the communities observing his Rule should be in priests' orders, is proved by Chapter LXII. of the same, where he directs that if any abbot should desire to have a priest or deacon ordained for his monastery, he was to choose from his monks one worthy to fill such an office. Such a selected one, however, it is strictly laid down, was to beware of haughtiness and pride, presuming to do nothing except as ordered by the abbot, and to be well aware that he was now much more subject to the discipline of the Rule. Acting contrariwise, he was to be judged "not as a priest, but as a

---

[1] *Nonnos*—Latinised Egyptian.
[2] "Rule of St Benedict," chap. lxiii. pp. 263, 264.
[3] *Ibid.* chap. lx. p. 249.

rebel," and if after frequent admonitions he did not amend, the bishop was to be informed of his behaviour. If this was ineffectual, and his faults became notorious, he was to be "thrust out of the monastery, provided his disobedience be such that he will not submit and obey the Rule.[1]

St Benedict, by his Rule (Chapter LIX.) provides for the admittance of children, both of nobles and the poor, without distinction of class, into the houses of his Order. Children thus dedicated from infancy to the life of the cloister were called *oblates*, a term also applied to those assuming the cowl on their death-beds, and to lay persons who offered themselves with a rope or a bell round the neck, or four coins in their hands, or else laid their heads on the altar, there engaging themselves, resigning all their property. The hands of boys were wrapped in the cloth of the altar, with a petition for their admittance.[2]

Some Rules ordained that boys should not be offered under ten years of age. By Cluniac Rules they might be professed at fifteen. Boys under this latter age were not to be admitted as monks, because abbots, for fear or interest, had admitted children to the habit— children who had scarcely left the breast.

Pope Alexander III. forbade any profession of virginity until the candidate had reached the age of fourteen; the Council of Trent extended the period two years further, but more ancient Councils had set the proper age at five-and-twenty. Bellamine put it at the age of puberty—fourteen in males, twelve in females; while Pope Gregory I. postponed the age till sixty.

---

[1] "Rule of St Benedict," chap. lxii. pp. 257, 259.
[2] The Benedictine Oblates was an order founded at Rome by St Frances Romana, who died in 1443, the members of which were neither cloistered nor bound by vows.

In 1191 Pope Celestine III. freed children who had taken such vows.

Strictly speaking, there was no hard and fast rule in regard to age, which differed considerably according to time and place. St Gregory the Great, because of "the hardness of monastic life" in islands, fixed the age of admission at eighteen, and such was the English Rule in 1222 in Benedictine houses; in other countries it was fourteen.[1]

The same applies to the extent of the novitiate, which similarly varied. Matthew Paris mentions a three years' novitiate; Allan, a Canon of Beneventum, was five years a novice at Canterbury (St Augustine's); and one year's probation is mentioned in Cistercian abbeys. The Cluniacs remitted a part of the time, some early, others as late as forty years, and others were never professed, owing probably to their having to cross the sea for that purpose.

In early days no distinction whatever was made in admittance to the order in accordance with the express Rule of the great patriarch. There were relaxations in this respect, as also to that of receiving property or gifts from those admitted. Instances are on record of lands being frequently given as the price of admission, and of the rejection of the postulant upon the record of the property being found upon examination insufficient. The preference given to the reception of nobles and those of the higher classes was also complained of. Our own Richard I. complained that the monks of his time associated to themselves low persons such as tanners and shoemakers.

As the great houses grew in wealth and importance,

---

[1] Those who had been brought up in the house as children were called *Nutriti;* those who became monks late in life *Conversi.*

favoured of kings and nobles, they became strictly inclusive and conservative, so that the privilege hitherto open to all became the exclusive prerogative of kings and prelates, the former sending letters requesting the admission of certain persons, requests not to be denied. Founders and benefactors frequently reserved the right to appoint a monk or nun of their own choice in the houses of their foundation.

John, the twenty-first Abbot of St Alban's, made a statute that the number of monks should never exceed one hundred, unless any person famous for rank of science, or a powerful man, whom it might be dangerous to offend, should request his admission. It was at this same Abbey of St Alban's that the only Englishman who ever attained to the honour of the pontifical throne—Nicholas Breakspear—was refused admission to the novitiate.

The number constituting the communities of the English religious (Benedictine) houses of course were never the same at any period, as they fluctuated up and down, according to the religious fervour or lukewarmness of the different periods of history.

The monks of Gloucester Abbey, in the eleventh century, reckoned at *eighty-six;* at the opening of the following century *one hundred;* in the middle of the fourteenth *fifty-four,* with two hundred officers and servants; in the opening years of the sixteenth *forty-eight;* and at the dissolution *thirty-six,* with one hundred assistants, and two hundred more in the country.

The thirteenth and fourteenth centuries were undoubtedly the golden days of English Monachism—days when the abbeys were all filled with the full complement of monks. Peterborough with a roll of *one hundred and ten;* Westminster with *eighty;* and St

Edmundsbury a like number. When we read of the large numbers of inmates of religious houses, it must be remembered that the major portion were but servants and others employed within the walls, and added to the minor number of actual monks.

Gloucester, we have seen, had as many as two hundred officers and servants in 1330; and St Edmundsbury, in the previous century, could count its *one hundred and eleven* servants and fifteen chaplains in addition to its eighty monks.

In addition to the monks living in the cloister, there was another class of brethren associated with them, yet living in the world. Kings, prelates, and nobles were thus frequently enrolled as members of religious orders, as were also founders and benefactors of all kinds, who participated in the privileges of the order, and shared the devotions of the monks. Thus, under the title of "Conscript Brothers," both Charlemagne and Louis the Good-Natured became members of the royal monastery of St Denis, and the Emperor Lothair was similarly invested with this title by the Monastery of St Martin-lez-Metz. William the Conqueror was a confrater of Cluny and Battle, and Henry VI. of Croyland.

Not unfrequently such brethren were formally admitted to the order in their last hours, and buried in the habit so assumed. King Sebbi is said to have been the first unprofessed layman to be buried in the monastic habit. Burial in a friar's habit was not uncommon in late mediæval days.

## HABIT

"Let clothing be given to the brethren," says St Benedict, in Chapter LV of his Rule, "suitable to the place where they live, and to the temperature of the air; because in cold countries more is needed, and in warm, less."

The decision was to be with the abbot of each monastery, but it was suggested that for temperate climates a cowl and a tunic should suffice for each monk; the former garment to be of a thick material in winter, but in summer something "finer, and worn thin"; there was also to be a scapular for work, and shoes and stockings were to cover the feet. With the colour or coarseness of the garment supplied, the monk was not to find fault, and they were to be, it is added, such as can be procured in the country where they live, or bought at the cheapest rate.

Further, it was to be the abbot's care that the garments were to be of a size and length suitable for those who were to wear them. Two tunics and two cowls, "as well for change at nights as for the convenience of washing," were to be considered as sufficient. On receiving new clothes the old ones were to be given up "at once," to be laid by in the wardrobe for the poor. In the same way they were to give back their shoes, and whatever else was worn out, when they receive anything new.

When sent on a journey they were to receive drawers from the wardrobe, which, upon their return, were to be replaced in the wardrobe, "washed clean." Cowls and tunics, somewhat better than those ordinarily worn, were to be given out upon such occasions, and similarly restored upon their return.

One of the principal obligations of the monastic life

was that of poverty; no one was to have anything, or even to call anything, his own.[1] The abbot was to supply all that was necessary — a cowl, a tunic, a girdle, shoes, stockings, a handkerchief, tablets, a knife, a pen, and a needle—that all pretence of necessity might be taken away. In order to obviate any evasion of this rule, it was the abbot's duty to frequently examine the beds to see if any private property be discovered therein, and in the event of anything being found which had not been received from the abbot, the culprit was to be subjected to the severest correction.

The eremetical life began, as we have seen, in Egypt and the countries of the East. In such a climate the clothing worn would naturally be of the scantiest. In the lives of the desert fathers, we read that when the clothing in which they had first arrived failed them, they resorted to the primitive use of leaves and rushes, plaited in a kind of matting, for a covering.[2] The skins of animals in their natural condition, or tanned into a kind of rough leather,[3] was an improvement on the primitive use of the fruits of the earth, and by the time of St Benedict something more civilised in the shape of cloth garments had become usual, as we find the monk, Romanus, presenting the boy eremite with his first habit, whilst he still dwelt in his cave alone.

The "habit" of the Egyptian monks has been described as follows—(i.) the *lebitus*, a long-sleeved linen

---

[1] "Be naked, in imitation of Christ, and in obedience to the precepts of the Gospel."—"Rule of St Columba."
[2] Legend tells that both Saints Mary Magdalene and Mary of Egypt had no other covering than their own luxuriant growth of hair.
[3] Compare St Paul's Epistle to the Hebrews (chap. xi. 37), and the clothing of Elijah, the Tishbite (2 Kings i. 8); of the (false) prophets (Zech. xiii. 4); and of St John the Baptist (St Matt. iii. 4).

garment, open at the hands, and sometimes up to the wrist; it was also known as the *colobium*; (ii.) the *pera* or *melote*, a kind of jacket of goat-skin; (iii.) the *cuculla*, a kind of hood covering the head, and coming half-way over the shoulders.

Although always coarse and simple, the habit of monks and friars varied in shape and colour, according to the different statutes of the orders.[1]

St Benedict undoubtedly borrowed his habit from that of the Eastern monks, altering it so far as to make it compatible with his intention. Thus, for instance, he lengthened the cuculla so as to envelop the whole body, but finding that in this shape it was anything but convenient in manual labour, transferred it from general use to ceremonials only. In its place he adopted the scapulary (*scapulum*), which covered the front of the body, the head, and the back.

According to Sulpicius Severus, the Western monks also wore a short mantle, or kind of cope, called a *maforte*. The Greeks and Orientals adopted the *pallium*.

In warm countries only one tunic would be necessary, but in the colder, an extra garment or two. Thus the under-tunics, or shirts (*staminia*), would be of wool and linen (linsey-woolsey), confined by a linen girdle or belt. The undermost appears to have reached to the knees, the outer to the ankles. Over these

---

[1] At various periods of monastic history, and especially during the Middle Ages, some of the religious orders became affected with the ridiculous foppery and taste for extravagant dress of the times in which they lived. The Grandmontines of the thirteenth century are an example of this, painting their cheeks, washing and covering up their beards at night that they might have a handsome and glittering appearance the following day.

Anglo-Saxon monks wore the cowl. Hose (*socks*) or stockings and breeches (*braccæ femoralia*), tied with laces (*poynts*), and leggings (*caligæ*) were also worn. Socks (of white cloth or felt) were of two kinds, called from their use *diurnal* (day), and *nocturnal* (night) socks. Some think them a large and thick kind of shoe, of sufficient size to receive the foot with the ordinary shoe upon it. Probably they were a kind of soft shoe, or slipper, for indoor wear. A combination garment of stockings and breeches in one piece occurs amongst the habit of the Anglo-Saxon monk, and the Highland *campestre*, or fillibeg, is thought to have been a probable dress of British monks.

The monks of the Orient appear to have gone generally barefoot, but this, if we are to judge from St Benedict's Rule, was not a custom amongst their brethren of the West.[1] Monks were to be given, he says, among other things *pedules* and *caligæ*, and when we consider the strict injunction of the patriarch as to manual (frequently agricultural and similar) labour, feet coverings of light make or texture would be worse than nothing.

Probably the first kind of boot wear was a kind of leathern stocking, fastened with thongs, or fastened up the side with buttons, very similar to the modern gaiters. From the mention of grease (oil or hog's-lard), soap, and other unctuous matters for the cleansing of the *bota*, or round-toed boots of monks, we may infer that the feet covering worn in the fields, etc., was of a hard and rough description, and, we are told, hob-nailed, very much as they are to day. The cleaning of shoes

---

[1] With the Franciscan and Carmelite (discalced) friars, however, bare (sandalled) feet was *de rigeur*.

was strictly enjoined, a man, called *Frico*, washing them and applying the softening matter.[1]

The night shoes (*nocturnals*) were of a lighter make, warm for winter (*pedules*), says Mr Mackenzie Walcot, and light in summer (*sotulares*) ;[2] but one Rule orders wooden clogs, lest the bed-clothes should be soiled by dirty feet.[3] Over the tunic or tunics (the upper furred in winter)[4] was worn the frock, a long ample-sleeved gown, reaching to and covering the feet, and over this again, at the time of manual labour, the scapular, or sleeveless tunic. The head was covered with a hood, split with pointed ends in front, attached either to the tunic or scapular.[5] The cowl, originally a hood, afterwards became, as we have seen, a wide, flowing garment, with large, loose sleeves worn exclusively by professed monks at ceremonials and quire duty as a kind of overall garment, or *pallium*.

For outdoor wear would be added the mantle, or cloak pelisse (*pylche*), sometimes with hood attached.[6]

In addition to his actual clothing, each monk would, according to the direction in his Rule, have his own little property, or rather that portion of the corporate belongings which the abbot for the time being thought good to commit to his care, *i.e.* a handkerchief (*lineum*

---

[1] Blacking is first mentioned in the sixteenth century, when, "cleanly blakt with soot," boots shone "like a shoeing horn."
[2] "English Minsters."
[3] Pattens, or ironed socks, were forbidden to certain canons from the noise their use occasioned. Bishop Jewel also speaks of some monks and friars who stalked about upon pattens.
[4] Pope Honorius allowed monks to wear black furred caps in quire from Michaelmas to Easter, the winter season of the year.
[5] A white night-cap is mentioned, which was probably the hood, as monks were to cover the head when lying down. At night the frock was discarded, and an old suit of clothes generally worn.
[6] No monk was to travel without his hood close, and breviary (*portvoise, porthose*).— "Const. Benedict XII."; "Nigr. Monach. Concil.," vol. ii. p. 608.

*pannum*), and a pocket to keep it in; a knife[1] (*cultellus*), a comb, writing tablets (*tabulæ*) for noting the offices, a bodkin, needle and thread, and such-like necessaries. These small articles would seem to have been kept in a pocket, or pouch, worn at the side, or, on the other hand, attached to the girdle. The handkerchief is mentioned as worn on the left side. Breviaries were likewise carried at one period suspended to the girdles of monks, to facilitate a constant study at all intervals of leisure. Relics also enclosed in little boxes (*reliquaries*) were distributed by the sacrist among certain of the brethren, and worn by them suspended from the neck.

The names of the monks were to be sewn upon all garments, which were to be carefully preserved from moth, and not mended too much, in the wardrobe (*vestiary*),[2] and, when old, to be given to the poor, or sold, should the convent be in debt. A new habit was generally given once a year.

To the novice the habit was given in quire, to the monk in the chapter house, after it had been blessed and sprinkled with holy water by the abbot. "The Lord take away from you the old man with his deeds," said the abbot, and, drawing on the hood, bade him be clothed with the *new man*, all the convent assembled answering *Amen*.[3]

Prayer was to be said at the assumption of the day habit; sometimes a short prayer was said at putting on each separate garment, just as in late mediæval days a symbolical interpretation was placed upon them.

---

[1] Grandmontines were to wear it with a steel and without ornament.
[2] Probably very similar to that for church robes in the transept of Gloucester Cathedral.
[3] At one period novices did not wear hoods at St Alban's.

By this mystic application the hood and tunic were said to represent the six wings of the cherubim, two in the hood, two in the sleeves, and two in the body part; the scapulary signified the armour assumed against the Devil, perhaps in relation to idleness overcome by manual labour; and the frock, covering all, the all-surrounding protection of God.

As a member of the monastic community, the dress of the abbot was not one whit better than that of the lowest monk, but when he stood up, or went forth as the chief representative of the convent in the Councils and Parliaments of the realm and the Church, he was attired with all the insignia of his rank and office.

As early as the beginning of the eleventh century Pope John XX. had allowed abbots to assume pontificals, or the habit of bishops, much against the will of the latter, and in the following century, notwithstanding the opposition coming from the same quarter, the abbots received the further grant to wear the mitre, ring, and sandals, and in some instances gloves.[1] In regard to the mitre worn by an abbot, a distinction was drawn in that, unlike that of a bishop (except in the case of exempt abbots), it was to be plain and garnished (embroidered) with orphreys.

The use of the pastoral staff, or abbatial crook (*ferula*) was a conventional right of abbots and abbesses as significant of their office, of spiritual authority, charge, and jurisdiction over the houses in which they ruled. It would appear that, contrary to the crooks of bishops, the heads of the crooks of the abbots were inverted or turned (or held) inwards to signify that they held a limited and internal jurisdiction *only* over their convent,

---

[1] In 1055 Pope Leo granted the privilege of wearing mitre, sandals, and gloves to the Abbot of St Augustine's, Canterbury.

as the bishops did an outward and more expansive authority over their dioceses.

It has also been stated that the attachment of a veil-banner, or *sudarium*, to the crooks of abbots not only distinguished them from the crosiers of prelates, but also betokened subjection to the occupant of the see in which the monastery was placed, except, of course, in the case of exempt abbots. Such a statement is not, however, borne out by the testimony of illuminations and monumental effigies, which show these *vexillums*, or veil-banners, attached indiscriminately to the crosiers of both prelates of the Episcopal order and abbots. Probably the veil on the abbot's staff was removed or covered in the presence of the diocesan. At Worcester the mitred prior was allowed to carry only a blue and white staff in the presence of the bishop.

Two kinds of crooks seem to have been in use by abbots, one a plain, unadorned staff of wood, such as is frequently found in the tombs of abbots; the other of precious metal and rich decoration, for use on ceremonial occasions. Such a wooden staff, once the property of Abbot Sebroke of Gloucester, who died in 1450, nearly five feet in length, is preserved at Newcastle.

When he sat in Parliament, the abbot assumed a special robe of white, furred with a fur of a similar colour called lettice, and when he rode forth to take his pleasure, he went on a mule, held by a gilt bridle, with a saddle and cloth of blood colour, and a hawk on his fist, followed by a retinue equalling, if it did not surpass, that of a bishop.

The superiors of the following monastic houses sat as "mitred abbots" in the English Parliament, prior to the dissolution of the religious houses in the sixteenth century:—Abingdon (St Mary); Alban's, St

Bardney (St Oswald); Battle (St Martin); Bury (St Edmunds); Canterbury (St Augustine); Colchester (St John); Crowland (St Guthlac); Evesham (St Mary); Glastonbury (St Mary); Gloucester (St Peter); Hulme St Benet (Benedict); Hyde (Saints Peter and Paul); Malmesbury (St Aldhelm); Peterborough (St Peter); Ramsey (Saints Mary and Benet); Reading (St James); Selby (St German); Shrewsbury (Saints Peter and Paul); Tavistock (St Mary); Thorney (St Mary); Westminster (St Peter); Winchcomb (St Mary); and York (St Mary).

Of these, the Abbot of St Alban's long claimed the precedency against the Abbot of St Peter's, Westminster, but the latter eventually succeeded in securing the first place. In general councils, the Abbot of St Augustine's, Canterbury, sat next to the Abbot of Monte Cassino, the head of the Benedictine Order; and at Rome the nine mitred Abbots General, viz.: Benedictines of Monte Cassino, Basilians, Canons Regular of St John Lateran, the Camaldoli (reformed Benedictines), Vallambrosians, Cistercians, Olivetans, Sylvestrinians, and Jeromites sit on the left of non-assistant bishops.

The chief first and foremost duties of monks was the discipline of the cloister. "To pray, groan, and weep for their faults; to subdue their flesh; to watch and abstain from pleasures; to bridle their tongues, and shut their ears from vanities; to guard their eyes, and keep their feet from wandering; to labour with their hands, exult with their lips, and rejoice at heart in the praises of God; to bare the head, bow down, and bend the knees at the feet of the Crucifix; to obey readily, never to contradict their superiors; to serve willingly, and assist speedily the sick brethren, to throw away the cares of the world, and attend to celestial concerns with their utmost endeavours; not to be overcome by the arts of Satan, and to do everything with prudence."

They were to be imitators of Christ, strictly keep to enclosure, love holy poverty, be ready in obedience, observe silence, have a mutual love for the brethren, and an upright performance of the appointed duties. Upon rising for Matins, they were to meditate upon their actions; to bear patiently the injuries of others; to him that struck upon one cheek to turn the other, so that such a change of character would be produced— "that they who were prone to quarrels, and passionate, would now bravely endure the curses of others; not to be broken by contempt or injury, but bear all things with a resolute heart, and preserve their peace of mind, and rest amidst reproaches"; to converse of, and meditate the last judgment, wait for the Lord, and dread the anger of the judge; never to laugh, because, being charged with the sins of the people as their own, constant lamentation was their duty; to have no' private friendships, because such would prejudice the concord of the community by generating parties, and causing distraction; to be silent and solitary, because dead to the world; to use private prayer when under a vicious impulse, because such prayer reminded them of their crimes, and made them think themselves more guilty; to have respect for their habit in act, speech, and thought; not to be querulous, angry, slanderous; not to regard rashly the lives of their superiors, nor to become rebellious by beholding their faults, and to walk with their heads down.

In short, monks were to

> "Imitare Sanctum Benedictum,
> Serva verbum tibi dictum,
> Bonum est laborare manibus,
> Melius orare cum fletibus."

and their whole lives to be spent in labour and prayer—*orare et laborare*.

Quire duty occupied the major portion of their time. Soon after midnight,[1] the little bells (*parvulum signum*) rang to Matins, and the monks left the dormitory for the first service of the day. In Benedictine houses it was the custom to call the brethren individually at the door of the dormitory or cell, after the manner of the ancient monastics, and those of modern Greece, by striking upon the door with a wooden mallet with the ejaculation, "*Benedicamus Domino*," the occupant of the cell answering from within, "*Deo Gratias*."

Matins over, they either retired again to the dormitory, or stayed before so retiring to recite the Office of Lauds. St Benedict's Rule, however, appears to provide for no return to the dormitory. In Chapter VIII. on "The Divine Office at Night Time," he says that the time that remained after Matins[2] was to be spent in study by those brethren who were somewhat behind-hand in the Psalter and lessons. This was in winter-time (*i.e.* from the first of the month of November until Easter). In summer (*i.e.* from Easter to the first day of November), the hour for Matins was to be so arranged that, after a short interval, during which the brethren might go forth

---

[1] "*Octava hora*," says St Benedict, *i.e.* 2 A.M., but it would necessarily vary with the different seasons.
[2] Matins were called *Vigiliæ*, because they were said during the night watches.

for the necessities of nature, Lauds[1] might presently follow about the break of day.[2]

Prime, or the first day office, followed at 6 A.M., after which, on a signal from the smallest bell (*skilla*), the brethren went to the lavatory, having put on the day habit. After the Matin Mass, which followed, Tierce was said at 9 A.M., for which the sacristan rang the great bell. Here, or earlier, a pittance or breakfast (*mixtum*), was partaken of, generally consisting of bread and wine. About noon dinner was served, a cymbal ringing for the brethren to wash themselves at the lavatory before entering the refectory.

In earlier and stricter days dinner was served much later, at Nones, or 3 P.M., High Mass following the Office of Sext, said at 12 (mid-day); when the dinner was set back, mid-day was called *Nones*, or noon.

After dinner all adjourned to the church for the midday service of Sext; thence they proceeded to the cemetery, where they prayed bareheaded for their brethren departed, amongst the graves. In summer, the *meridian*, or mid-day sleep—a remnant of Oriental practice—was indulged in, followed by labour or study until Nones (3 P.M.), and resumed again after the office until 5 P.M.

After Evensong an hour was passed in collation, prayer, and devotion, and the Salvi at 6 P.M. Then recreation before Compline, the last day office; after which all the doors in the cloister were locked until 7 A.M. the next day, the keys being handed to the superior, and the community, retiring to the dormitory, brought their busy day to a close.

---

[1] Called also *Matutini* because said in the early morning. Matins and Lauds were thus the Night Office, or *Nocturns*.

[2] "Rule of St Benedict," chap. viii. p. 75, *et seq.*

At these services the whole convent was supposed to be present. Those working at a distance from the monastery, or travelling, were alone excused, and were permitted to use a short prayer, as an equivalent, in the fields or other places where they happened to be at the time. At one period it seems that the monks took their Psalters with them to their field labour, but this was afterwards forbidden. Generally speaking, as among the Cistercians, the lay brethren and monastery servants, and those convent officials whose business required their presence, were excused attendance at the nocturnal service.

In others, neglect of or late attendance at the church services was not allowed to pass without punishment. St Benedict in his Chapter on the celebration of Matins, orders the lessons or responsories to be "somewhat shortened," if " perchance " the brethren rose too late. All care was to be taken to prevent this, but should it so happen, he, through whose negligence it came to pass, was to make satisfaction for it in the oratory.[1]

Behaviour at the services, or in quire, as it was called, was strictly looked after by an officer appointed to that duty. Clear and distinct pronunciation was insisted upon; the song-school was responsible for a decent, if not a perfect vocal harmony, and lapses in the night offices into indiscernible slumber were rigidly provided against.

" Care must be taken," says one of these monastic Custumals, " that the lessons in the reading be not so abbreviated as not to allow sufficient time for the brother who goes the round, both within and without the quire, with his lantern, with its light so enclosed

---

[1] "Rule of St Benedict," chap. ix. p. 87.

as to shine in one direction, or through a single aperture on any particular object or any one who may have gone to sleep during the lesson."

Ulric, writing on the customs at the great Abbey of Cluny, gives still further detail on the matter :—

"If, however," he says, "during the lessons, he who carries round the wooden lantern should come to him, and, supposing him to be asleep, should throw the light on his face, let him, if awake, bow reverently. But, if he was asleep, and the lantern shall have been placed before him, as soon as he is waked, he must take it up and first examine the right side of the quire, and then, returning through the middle, do the same in the outer quire, and lastly the left side; should he find any one asleep, he must throw the light in his eyes three times; if on the third time he does not wake, he must place the lantern before him, that when he is awaked, he may take it up, and carry it in like manner."

Every hour of the monk's day was allotted to some distinct occupation. Study and labour filled up every interval between the time spent in sleep, meals, and the service of the sanctuary—a perpetual alternation of work (manual or mental) and prayer. No one was idle, for there was ample work for all. Everything that was or could be required—food, raiment, and the thousand and one things necessary, even in a monastery—were, with few exceptions, produced on the spot.

Their mills ground the corn which their own fields had produced, and their clothes, through the hands of weavers and tailors, came from the wool of their own sheep. And so on through every department—shoemakers, carpenters, blacksmiths, down to the apiarist and orcharder. The culture of fish, so necessary in those days of consistent fasting, they brought to a fine art—an art, alas! lost to us moderns. Vast fish-ponds are found attached to every monastery of consequence, where fish were reared for the service of the house.

Every morning the day's work was distributed by the prior, to each individual his share, in the chapter house. Thence the brethren, shouldering the necessary tools, set off two and two to accomplish their allotted task in the fields and orchards.

While these were engaged on the lands without, the remainder were employed in study or the work of the house within.

Although under primitive observance secular education had been in a manner tabooed, yet, in after-time, this became an important factor in the routine of a great house. Children of all classes were sent to the monasteries to be educated, without charge, in the arts and sciences, and often in agriculture and mechanics.[1] When the monasteries were destroyed, the education of youth had to be provided for by charitably disposed persons in the foundation of grammar schools. King Edward VI. thus distributed some of the ill-gotten wealth to this purpose.

The chief part of the education of a monk was the learning of the services of the Church and his Rule. Psalmody was a great feature, and the novice, studying in the cloister, was expected to make himself perfect in his Psalter, so as to be able to say it by heart to a word. Latin also, and French[2] and singing, writing by means of *Breviales Tabulæ*, or copy-books, and arithmetic by *Compotus*, or counters.[3] Embroidery was largely practised in monasteries.

---

[1] Schools were attached to religious houses as early as the seventh century.
[2] From the Conquest till the fourteenth century.
[3] A piece of metal, etc., used as a means of reckoning.

The nuns were of equal ability with the monks, teaching writing, drawing, needlework, confectionery, physic, and surgery. Fuller says: "Nuns with their needles wrote histories also: that of Christ, His passion, for their altar-cloths, and other Scripture (and more legend) stories in hangings to adorn their houses." "Old Jacques," adds Aubrey (writing of Kington, St Michael, Wilts), "who lived on the other side, hath seen forty or fifty nunnes in a morning spinning with their wheels and bobbins."

The novitiate was a department in itself. It was in the sole charge, under the abbot, of a master, called of the novices. Lyndwood says he was to be an old man.[1] By Lanfranc's "Decretals" he was to wake the children in the morning, and by the "Norman Institutes" to shave the boys, and the boys him (!), and to wash the heads of boys too small to shave themselves. His duty was to instruct the neophytes in the Rule and observances of the order, and to regulate their behaviour at all times and places. He was wholly responsible for their conduct, until they passed out of his care.

Monastic recreations were few and monotonous, and consisted chiefly of a sober walk in the cloister garth, garden, or cemetery, or a game of bowls upon a green. Gardening was also a favourite pastime. Abbot Feckenham, Westminster's last abbot, was planting saplings when the news was brought him that his house, having been dissolved, existed no more.

In the stone benches of Westminster, Gloucester, Canterbury, Durham, and other monastic cloisters, the novices have left traces of their games in the

---

[1] Oxford Edition, p. 144.

repeated holes, sometimes arranged in nines together thus :—

WESTMINSTER       GLOUCESTER

o   o   o

o   o   o

o   o   o

in which they amused themselves in the now forgotten games of "Fox and Geese," "Nine Men's Morris," "Knockings In and Out," etc.

In some monasteries, and even nunneries, more lively amusements, as tumbling, playing, and dancing, were indulged in at seasons of festivity. From the letters of Archbishop Peckham, we learn that other, to him objectionable, diversions were indulged in. At the Priory of Coxford, in Norfolk, the prior played chess with his canons;[1] in others the monks actually hunted, and kept dogs, birds, and strange animals as pets—apes, peacocks, falcons, cranes, and even tame bears — in the cloister. The Archbishop denounces such breaches of decorum as grave offences, not to be passed over, but the consuetudinary of St Swithin's, Winchester, appoints the care of these "*animalia a diversis fratribus per multa tempora acquisita*" to the cellarer of that house, and yet again, in 1515, Abbot Parker forbade the use of hounds, falcons, or showy dresses to his monks at Gloucester. By a charter granted in 1168 to the Abbot and Canons of St Osyth's

---

[1] In some excavations at Kirkstall, in 1856, a chess piece of the twelfth century, carved from the tusk of a walrus, was found. *See* description of a figure, *Archæological Journal*, vol. vi.

Priory, Essex, permission is given to keep four fox-hounds and two harriers for hunting purposes. In the reign of Richard II. an abbot of this priory was imprisoned at Colchester for poaching on the king's preserves and killing his venison.[1] Whistling was a fashion and an amusement in the Middle Ages, and was actually asked for by an archbishop.

Annually the parents, relatives, and friends of monks were allowed to visit them with a companion. The Festival of the Nativity of the Blessed Virgin Mary was a usual day. At Canterbury all received four times a year, from the sub-cellarer, an *exennium*—a gift of eatables or drinkables, in honour of friends visiting them, it being sent to them.

Although in theory a monk was bound to enclosure, *i.e.* the extent of the monastic domain, necessity urged a not infrequent extension beyond it. When a monk travelled he was sent on his way with a special service of prayer.[2] On his way he said his proper offices as he would had he been at home. At night he slept in the granges of his own or other monasteries, but never without a light. Farm-houses, we learn, were used as inns, annual rents being paid to some by some houses to find a *hospitium* for travelling monks passing that way. William, Abbot of St Alban's, acquired a house in London to accommodate his monks tarrying there, with a chapel, numerous beds, orchard, stable, kitchen, court, garden, and well, and a perpetual servant to reside there and keep it.

Everything possible was done, in short, to facilitate

---

[1] According to Mr J. Y. Watson, a local historian, this is the first recorded notice of fox-hunting in England.
[2] Liberty to travel was rarely granted, at St Alban's only with difficulty obtained, even after a continuance for three years in the novitiate.

his journey. Generally he went with a companion, or at least an attendant to carry his luggage, in the shape of bedding, a cresset, candles, two loaves, and a flask of wine or ale.

Whilst the traveller was away he was not forgotten, a commemoration of all the absent being made at the close of each day at the last prayer; and when he returned he went into a kind of retreat to shake off, as it were, all the contamination he had taken in his short or long contact with the world. Strict account was likewise taken of the time he had taken to accomplish his journey, and if he had exceeded the time allotted, he was to carry half-naked (in his shirt, carrying his clothes) a ferula from the "parletory door," through the cloister to the chapter (house), and there be beaten.[1]

"When they" (the brethren sent on a journey) "come back," says the Rule of St Benedict, "they shall, on the very day of their return, lie prostrate on the ground of the oratory during all the canonical hours, while the work of God is being fulfilled, and beg the prayers of all on account of the faults they may have committed on the way by sight or hearing, or by idle discourse. Let no one presume to relate unto others what he has seen or heard outside the monastery, because therefrom arise many evil consequences. If any one shall presume to do so, let him be liable to the penalty [punishment] prescribed by the Rule. In like manner shall he be punished who shall presume to break the enclosure of the monastery, or go anywhere, or do anything, how trifling soever, without leave of the abbot."[2]

The keeping of silence, "the key of the whole order," was a principal duty of a monk, not only during Divine

---

[1] "Const. Benedict," XII.; "Nigr. Monach. Concil.," vol. ii. p. 608.
[2] "Rule of St Benedict," chap. lxvii. pp. 283-285.

service and at meals,[1] but during the whole day, except at recreation, when a general permission to speak was given, as the "parliaments"[2] allowed at certain times and places, as at Ely in the west alley of the cloister. A particular officer, called the explorator, was told off to see that silence was observed in the cloister; when searching, he made signs, and was answered in a similar way.

"Let leave to speak be seldom given," says St Benedict, "even to perfect disciples."[3] To duly observe this injunction, stones were wont to be carried in the mouth.

"Agathon," says "The Golden Legend," "bare thre yere a stone in hiss mowthe tyll that he had lerned to kepe scylence."[4]

From certain officers, by reason of their duty, the restriction was relaxed or removed, but to speak after Compline, that is to break the solemn or greater silence, was subject to the severest punishment. In some places, according to St Bernard of Clairvaux, this law was so strictly observed that a person labouring under blame was not allowed to excuse himself, or one entertaining suspicious to divulge them.

Hence, to facilitate a perfect observance or evasion of this rule, a system of sign-language, as among modern deaf mutes, was introduced. These signs were probably only permitted during simple silence times, and when the solemn silence commenced were prohibited. Du Cange gives a catalogue of such signs, *e.g.*

---

[1] The Essenes kept silence at meals.
[2] "Parliaments" at St Alban's were read in the constitution and customs of the order by junior monks in the cloister.
[3] In accordance with Scriptural precept (Psalms xxxviii. 2, 3; Prov. x. 19; xviii. 21).
[4] *Legenda Aurea*, ccxxxv. 6.

for a fish, a wave of the hand, like the motion of a fish's tail in water; a book, an extension of the hand, with a motion as of turning a leaf; for milk, the little finger on the lips, as an infant sucks milk.[1]

Signs were not only used for persons and things, but likewise for actions and qualities, as seeing, hearing, good, evil, etc.

### DISCIPLINE

Infringement of discipline, or breach of conventual rule or regulation, was strictly visited upon the offender. A guilty monk, on declaring his guilt, and on his knees promising amendment, was publicly absolved by the abbot, who assigned him a penance for his fault. These penances were frequently enjoined, and for grave offences were rigid and severe.

It is related of Robert de Stichill, afterwards Bishop of Winchester (?), that when a young monk, he was thoughtless and rebellious, and on a certain Sunday, when he was ordered to sit in the midst of the quire upon a stool, he was so ashamed at his position that he took it by the leg and threw it into the nave among the people.[2]

In his "Custumal," Abbot Ware says of the chapter house:—

"It is the house of confession, the house of obedience, mercy, and forgiveness; the house of unity, peace, and tranquillity, where the brethren make satisfaction for their faults."

In the chapter house was not only public confession

---

[1] *See* Aungier, "Hist. of Hounslow and Syon Monastery" (8vo., 1840), for signs used in Syon Nunnery.
[2] "Rob. de Graystanes," vii. 45.

made, and mercy and forgiveness dispensed, but discipline in all its harshness administered. To its central pillar, or other convenient position, would the trembling culprit be bound, while a selected number of his brethren laid on (in love) with scourges, after he had been stripped of his clothes at the *spoliatorium* (in the chapter).

This was in accord with the holy Rule of the Blessed Father Benedict, who ordained (Chapter XXIV.) that "the measure of excommunication or punishment [chastisement] should be meted out according to the quality of the faults," the estimation of the gravity of which was to be left to the judgment of the abbot.

A brother guilty of small faults was to be excluded from the common table; in the oratory he was neither to intone Psalm nor Antiphon, nor read a lesson until he had made satisfaction. The abbot was to decide when he was to take his portion of food, and in what quantity. Thus, for example, if the brethren ate at the sixth hour, he was to take his refection at the ninth, and so on, until by proper satisfaction he had obtained pardon.

For graver faults (Chapter XXV.) he was to be excluded from the table and the oratory; no brother was to consort or speak to him;[1] nor were any to bless him as he passed by,[2] nor the food given him to eat alone, in such measure and at such time as the abbot thought best. He was to work alone, and continue in penance and sorrow, remembering that terrible sentence of the Apostle: "That such a one is delivered over to Satan

---

[1] Any brother, without the command or leave of the abbot, holding any intercourse whatever, or speaking, or sending a message to any excommunicated brother was to incur the same penalty of excommunication (Chapter XXVI.).

[2] To be deprived of the benediction was to be sent to Coventry.

for the destruction of the flesh, that his spirit may be saved in the day of the Lord."[1]

The brother thus excommunicated was to be in the special care of the abbot, who, as a wise physician, was to use every means in his power, especially by sending mature and wise brethren—secretly, as it were—to comfort and console the wavering one, and win him to make humble satisfaction. In this work the abbot was bound to exercise the greatest care for the offender, with all prudence and zeal so as not to loose one of the sheep committed to his charge, imitating the loving example of the "Good Shepherd" who left the ninety and nine sheep to seek the one which had gone astray.[2]

Should all his endeavours for the reclamation of his erring charge have been in vain, and the brother often corrected, or even excommunicated, still proving obstreperous, the "sharper correction"—the punishment of stripes—was to be administered to him (Chapter XXVIII.), and, should even this be without avail, he was to add that which was still more powerful—his own prayers and that of all the brethren for him, that the all-powerful Lord would vouchsafe to work a cure upon the unruly. But if he would not be healed and corrected by this means, then at length the abbot was to use the sword of separation, according to the saying of the Apostle: "Put away the evil one from among you."[3] And again: "If the faithless one depart, let him depart,[4] lest one diseased sheep should infect the whole flock."

Yet even in the administration of the strict discipline of a religious house the quality of mercy was not strained. "For," continues Chapter XXIX. of the

---

[1] 1 Cor. v. 5.   [2] St Luke xv. 4.
[3] 1 Cor. v. 13.   [4] *Ibid.* vii. 15.

saint's Rule, "any brother leaving the monastery through his own fault, or who had been cast out on the promise of amendment, was to be received back again 'into the lowest rank' even unto the third time, but after this all entrance was to be denied him."

Monastic penance in the eleventh and two following centuries varied with the gravity of the offence. For a common fault the offender was separated from the common table; for a greater a triple scourging in the chapter, put on short commons, had head cowled, put in solitary confinement, and at the recitation of the canonical hours, lay prostrate before the quire door.

St Benedict (Chapter XXX. of his Rule) ordains that boys or others under age who commit faults, and by reason of their age being incapable of understanding the greatness of the punishment of excommunication, were to be punished by severe fasting, or sharp stripes, that so they may be corrected.

Great care was taken in the exercise of this discipline, and the boys and younger novices were not permitted to witness the humiliation of their elders. The latter were always disciplined in the chapter-house, while the former received their meed of chastisement in another apartment, sometimes in the infirmary chapel, or the common house or room. In the latter the rod of discipline sometimes hung over the fireplace. Eckhard "being tied to a pillar of the *Pyralis*,[1] he was severely beaten with rods." Against the south wall (near the south-west door) of the Priory Church of Bridlington, Yorks, is an iron "joug," or collar, for punishment.

Sometimes an incorrigible monk was sent for punishment to a neighbouring convent, which had to spend two pence a day on his maintenance. Prisons

---

[1] Du Cange calls *Pyrale* the conventual hypocaust, or fireplace.

were attached to most monasteries, and monks guilty of the gravest offences were hand-cuffed, fettered, and chained. These prisons were known by various names, frequently indicative of their capabilities of discomfort and pain. The "Little Ease," in which the prisoner could neither sit, lie, nor stand; "Bocardo," as at Oxford, over the gate near St Michael's; "Hell," as at Ely; the "Lying House," as at Durham; the "Lantern,"[1] as at Lewes, and the "Gate House." At some houses the prisons were underground vaults, at others (as at Durham and Norwich), they adjoined the chapter house, or were over the gate, as at Binham, Hexham, Malling, and Tewkesbury. At Durham the confinement sometimes lasted a year, food being supplied to the prisoner through a trap-door by means of a rope.

"Underneath the Master of the Fermyre's (the infirmary) chamber," says the author of the "Rites of Durham," "was a strong prison called the Lynghouse, which was ordained for all such as were greate offenders ... for the space of one hole year in cheynes." No one was to have access to this dungeon save the aforesaid master, "who did let downe there meate through a trap-door, on a corde, being a greate distance from them."[2]

In some extraordinary cases the guilty were immured,

---

[1] From *latere*, to lie hid. Archbishop Arundel tells William Thorpe he shall be made as sure as any thief that is in the prison of Lantern.

[2] At Todmarton, Gloucester, anciently the seat of the Rivers family, a dungeon, 13 or 14 ft. deep, and about 14 ft. high, has iron rings fastened in the wall, intended probably for securing offending villeins, all lords of manors, in common with the heads of religious houses, having this power over their villeins, or socage tenants, whom they ruled like petty kings in their country seats, convents, castles, and boroughs, having all kinds of cognisance of their own men, the right of gallows within their liberties, where they could judge, condemn, and execute. At Canterbury the monastic courts were held in the conventual church.

after the pronunciation of the sentence, *Vade in pace*— "Go in peace."

William le Bachelor, Grand Preceptor of the Knights Templar in Ireland, died imprisoned in such a cell, with a loop looking towards the high altar of the Temple Church, London; and at Thornton, the skeleton of Abbot de Multon (about 1445) was found built up in a similar cell, in which were a candlestick, chair, and table.[1]

The prison was under the charge of the master of the infirmary.

### THE GATE-HOUSE

Entrance was gained to the *close*, or walled enclosure, within which the whole group of the monastic buildings were surrounded by gates set in certain positions. The principal entrance was through the gate-house, a fine massive structure, with chambers above the entrance gate for the accommodation of the gate-keeper and his assistants. The gateway, generally groined in the lower storey, was arranged in two or three arched entrances—a great arch for waggons, horsemen, etc., and a smaller postern for passengers on foot.[2] In some places the porter's lodge was built on one side of it, or a gate hall to

---

[1] Instances of the immurement of monks and nuns must be received with considerable caution, as some of these so-called immurements were quite possibly freaks or eccentricities of heart, or other upright modes of burial so prevalent in the Middle Ages. The treatment of lunatics at this period was also peculiarly cruel. *See* the case of Alexander de Langley, p. 233.

Mediæval bishops were also required to have one or more prisons for their criminous clerks, and that of the Bishop of Chichester remains over his palace gate, and the Bishop of London's stood at the west side of Westminster Abbey. Criminous priests were imprisoned in England as early as 740 A.D., and in 1351 their meagre fare was prescribed.

[2] An example remains at St Alban's. Walley (Cistercian) Abbey, Yorkshire, preserves one of the finest monastic gate-houses in England.

serve for persons waiting. At Bridlington, a part of the gate-house served as a prison. At Evesham an almonry adjoined, and sometimes a chapel was here annexed for the use of the labourers and monastic servants.

### THE PORTER

At the principal gate of the monastery was stationed the porter—a man mature in age, and of life unblamable.[1]

"At the gate of the monastery," says St Benedict, "let there be stationed a wise, old man, who knows how to receive and to give an answer, and whose ripeness of age will not suffer him to wander from his post. He ought to have a cell near the gate, that such as come may always find him at hand, ready to give them an answer. As soon as any one shall knock, or a poor man cry for aid, let him presently answer: 'Thanks be to God,' or invoke a blessing; and with all mildness of the fear of God, let him reply speedily in the fervour of charity. If he need help, he shall have a junior brother with him."[2]

This rule was strictly followed in Benedictine houses, where the porter had a deputy to take his place at the gate while he was absent on a message. He had sometimes also a boy who lay at the gate at night with the sub-porter, and took the key, after curfew, to the cellarer's bed, fetching it thence again in the morning when he required it. In some houses the porter locked the gates at the ringing of the bell for Compline, and carried the keys to the abbot.

The porter himself generally lay at night in the gate-house, and was allowed a horse that, upon the summons of the abbot or cellarer, he might ride with

---

[1] Mention is made of deaf and dumb porters and blind ringers.
[2] "Rule of St Benedict," chap. lxvi. p. 279.

them. In a large convent there was, of necessity, several porters, as, for instance, of the almonry gate, where the poor made application for alms; of the court, and of the cloister, to prevent the entrance of all unauthorised persons.[1]

### THE CLOISTER

The cloister (from *claustrum*, an enclosure) was the heart of the convent, for here the greater part of the time of the monk was spent—cells, as we understand the term, not being known in England until King Henry II. founded the Carthusian Abbey of Witham in 1178. Separate apartments for the religious was the peculiar introduction of the Carthusian Order, whose members aspired to complete solitude, to effect which each had his separate apartment, or suite of three or more rooms with a garden, each and all converging from the great cloister.

The great cloister of a monastery—sometimes there was a second or little cloister, and perhaps even a third, attached to the infirmary [2]—was formed of a large quadrangle enclosed on all sides, by the high walls of the church on the one hand, and of the other monastic buildings and appurtenances on the other, to which it served as a communication from one part to another by means of *slypes*, or passages.

Its usual position was to the south of the church, in order to gain as much sun as possible, and also to insure protection from the northerly and early winds of the inclement season of the year. In hot climates this arrangement is found to be reversed, the cloister

---

[1] JOHN DE NORTHWOLDE, in his tract on the minor officers, mentions a portership of the refectory. *See* also DU CANGE.

[2] As at *Canterbury, Gloucester,* and *Westminster.*

being found upon the north side of the church as a protection against the heat;[1] or again, as at Canterbury, Gloucester, Tintern, and other places, for the better supply of water, and the more effective disposal of the drainage.

All around the central open space ran a paved and covered arcade, the roof leaning against the wall on the one side, and being supported on the outer by open "panes," or bays, of trellis-work in stone, frequently of great beauty both in design and craftsmanship, through which light and air were admitted to the arcade.

The roof of the arcade was either vaulted with stone or open timber work. The cloister of Gloucester (1370-1412) is a magnificent example in stone, in which the superb fan-tracery work has been cunningly employed, the first, it is said, of this kind of work. Wood-work was as effectively employed at Durham, Fountains, and Kirkstall.

The cloister walks at Westminster were paved with a patterned way of square stones down the centre, and others set diagonally, it is said, to distinguish them from the rest, a course of square stones running against the walls. Particular mention is made of the "middle tread," a device found also in the naves and ambulatories of monastic churches to keep the processions in order.

All the principal apartments of the monastery were in direct communication with the great cloister; the minor or lesser offices, as chequers or others for the transaction of business, being usually grouped near it. The usual arrangement was for the refectory to be on the side opposite or parallel to the minster, the dormitory on the east or west, the latter site not unfrequently occupied by the guest-house.

---

[1] *Caen, Gerona, Mayance, Pontigny, Toulouse,* etc.

The size of the cloister varied with the size of the convent—that is, according to the number of religious persons for which the house was founded. At Gloucester each walk was 145 feet long, a trifle over 12 feet wide, and about 18 feet high, and at Westminster 135 feet square. In the east alley or walk of the Gloucester cloister there are ten large windows, nine divided by mullions into eight lights; in the other three walks ten six-light windows apiece.

At first these cloister traceries were left open and unglazed, glazing being introduced about the fifteenth century.[1] In stress of wind or weather, mats and thick hangings, fenestrals or window-blinds, were employed to protect the inmates. The monks at Rochester were wont to use blinds when the sun was hot, and Ordericus Vitalis, the monastic historian, at the beginning of one winter in his Normandy cloister, writes that "the weather is so cold that my fingers have become stiff, and I must cease writing until the spring."

In winter time, to promote warmth, the stone floor and benches were strewn thick with hay, straw, or sawdust, in summer with sweet-smelling rushes, with ivy leaves at Easter. Artificial light was provided by means of lanterns, cressets, or mortars, suspended at intervals from the bosses in the roof, or set where most needed, particularly at the four corners of the cloister, and before the church and other doors. The walls covered with paintings in fresco,[2] would in winter have the addition of thick curtains or hangings.

---

[1] Even as late as Queen Elizabeth's reign most of the shops, with the exception of the goldsmith's, were still without glass.

[2] "Nothing learn'd in letter-lore,
　Within my poh-cloister I behold
A painted Heaven, where harps and lutes adore
And eke an Hell whoso damned folk see the full sore."

In the centre of the cloister lay an open court or space called the cloister garth (*pratum claustri*), "Paradise," "Laurel Court," or some similar name.[1] In some instances it was merely a plain grass plot; in others planted with flowers and shrubs, and with a conduit, or fountain, of running water in the centre. At Durham this was surmounted by a dove-house, and at Winchester a chapel in which Masses of Requiem were said for those buried in the garth.[2] It may have been here that the open grave lay as a perpetual *memento mori* of the transience of their mortality, and an antidote to the worldliness which would all too fatally creep into the sacred life of the cloister. Birds and other domestic animals as monastery pets were at times kept in it, particular mention being made of a petulant tame stork, which was the delight of the boy novices at Westminster, who fed and caressed it.

Out of quire and sleeping time, the cloister was the living place of the monks. Here they pursued their various employments, studied, taught school, learned and lived their Rule, and transacted their business. An officer, parliator (*ostiarius*), had charge of the doors, and the whole cloister was under the surveillance of an officer known as the cloistral prior.

The ordinary day of the monk began about 2 A.M., when a bell roused him from his slumbers in the dormitory to take his place in the quire for the Nocturns (Matins and Lauds). Generally these two offices were said together, in order to avoid the necessity of a separate rising from bed for the two offices.

---

[1] The enclosed portion of the forecourt of basilicas was called "Paradise."

[2] The garth does not seem to have been a general burying place, although abbots, and sometimes monks, were interred in it, as also in the cloister alleys.

With the office of Prime, the first day office, the work of the day began. After washing at the latrines, and putting on the day habit, they heard Matin Mass, partook of *mixtum*, a slight breakfast of bread and wine, and adjourned to the chapter for consultation on the affairs of the house. Chapter over, the officials dispersed, each to his special department—the kitchener to his kitchen to arrange for the meals of both convent, and guest, and the poor; the sacrist to the church to clean and arrange for service or function; the precentor to his quire and organ to write and mend his music, or arrange for some ordinary or extraordinary procession in church or without the precincts; the infirmarer to his patients in the hospital; the cellarer to bakehouse and brewhouse, and sometimes even farther afield; each and every to his particular work in its particular department.

Meanwhile, the bulk of the brethren, old and young, had adjourned *en masse* to the cloister, each separating there to his place in the north or south, the east or west cloister, preparatory to taking up the work of the moment. According to seniority, they sat on mats on the bench tables against the wall in their alley, a president at each end, and the abbot or his prior near the lower church, where those seeking him on business communed with him.

In the windows opposite each in his separate pew or carrel[1] sat others [2]—accountants, illuminators, transcribers, writers, etc. Aumbries, or painted cupboards [3] on the wall, held the library—manuscript works—of

---

[1] *Carola*, mediæval Latin—a lattice, railing, inclosure, literally a circle.

[2] "In the cloyster, Item one conduit or lavatory of tynne, with divers coffers and seats there."—"Inventory, Peterborough, (1539).

[3] As at Lilleshall Abbey.

"ancient-written doctors of the Church, as other profane literature, with divers other holy men's works." They sat one behind the other, but sideways when talking was allowed.[1]

In the west alley the novices gathered about their master, sitting in the window-seats, learning the rudiments of the Rule of their great patriarch, and the Psalter, or singing hymns and Antiphons under his direction, "the disciples asking their masters about things they did not know; the masters instructing their pupils, and, above all, teaching them to master the Rule of St Benedict."

Sometimes, in addition to their own schools, many of the great houses maintained free schools in the town, as well as on the various properties held by them in the country, as the school at Beccles, kept up by the Convent of St Alban's.[2] Matthew of Paris attests to the efficiency, in the twelfth century, of the school of St Alban's. "There was hardly a school in all England at that time more fruitful or more famous either for the number or the proficiency of its scholars."[3] Again, it is recorded of the Abbot of Evesham, that he paid £10, a sum equal to £120 of modern money, and "borde and tabelying frely in the monasterie to one schole-master for the keeping of a free schole in the said town of Evesham."[4]

The course of teaching comprised the primitive sciences, grammar, logic, and philosophy. Books were chained for the instruction of less advanced students. "Æsop's Fables" is known to have been one of them.

---

[1] French was the language of every-day life in the monasteries.
[2] Matthew Paris, "Memoirs of St Edmund's Abbey" (Rolls series), vol. iii. p. 182.
[3] *Ibid.* vol. i. p. 296.
[4] H. Cole, "King Henry VIII.'s Scheme of Bishoprics," p. 117.

Pious students kissed the Bible when they opened it for reading. When boys began to read loudly, or show inattention, they were set apart so as not to touch one another either with their hands or clothes.

In this "nursery for students," it was not all sunshine, for the rod (*ferule*) was not spared. Fifty-three stripes at a time is mentioned as being administered. Some, cruel only to be kind, masters were wont to carry pebbles in their pockets to beat them with. Abbot Turketul, of Croyland, was in the habit of visiting his school at least once a day, distributing fruit and sweetmeats to deserving boys as rewards.

An ecclesiastical school in the Middle Ages was known as a *schola studium*, or *studium generale*. The master of the novices was to be chosen for skill in, and love for, teaching. Abler scholars were sent to study at the universities. In 1283, the Abbey of St Peter's, Gloucester, had a "nursery, or mansion place," for thirteen student monks. It was called Gloucester Hall, and is now Worcester College, Oxford.

The east alley (*claustrum capituli*) was reserved to the exclusive use of the abbot, and such ceremonies as the washing of the feet of poor men, "with sundrie solemn rites and signs of great humilitie," at the Maundy on Holy Thursday. The bench whereon they sat still remains at Westminster, and beneath the nosing, the metal eyes to which the carpet used upon that occasion was wont to be attached. The Maundy of the monks was made in chapter.

Off the south alley lay the refectory, or great dining-hall of the monks. The Maundy bench for children sometimes remained in it, and handy the refectory door, a lavatory and almonry, or closet, for hand towels (changed every Sunday) for washing before entering for meals. Feet were washed on Saturday nights, and there was a monthly shaving.[1] Confessions were heard there (at Canterbury), and the brothers sat in penance.

In the north, or it may be the south alley, was the scriptorium, unless a special apartment was set apart for this purpose, as was generally the case in later days. Here were the carrels, or rows of little cells, lying beneath each window, in which the studious brother pursued the even tenor of his way, far removed from the distractions of the world.

Each alley of the cloister quadrangle was under the superintendence of an obedientiary (*guardianus trisantia*), whose chief duty it was to preserve the silence in which all work was prosecuted. To ensure this and the prescribed decorum, these "spies of the cloister" walked up and down, ever on the alert to pounce down upon the transgressor. "Parliaments," or general conversation, was strictly forbidden save at specified times. Conspicuous in some cloisters was a picture of the founder of the order, with his finger laid upon his lips significant of the silence rule. At Westminster, a window still exists in the south cloister walk, from which the appointed person could watch the younger novices at their work or play, and from which also the light which stood on the bracket hard by could be extinguished.

The claustral prior, as the representative of the abbot, always remained in the cloister. To his office many privileges were attached. At Abingdon he was allowed a *corodier*—that is, a man with a corody, or

---

[1] At Canterbury once a fortnight in winter, in summer twice in three weeks. The seniors were to be shaved first, "because in the beginning the razors are sharp and the towels dry." The prior appointed the day.

maintenance in the house, likewise a horse, with its keep. He only could sit in the novices' school, hear their lessons, hold a chapter of them, and beat them if need be. In a lengthened absence of the abbot, he could extend the discipline for a grave fault even to the prison. In the abbot's illness he took his place, and during a vacancy could profess monks. As the abbot had his "spies," or attendants, so had he, for he could go nowhere without one or two monks, or even sit in office without a novice attending him.

When sitting at table, he could claim the privilege of sending his cup (which was to be without a cover) down to the cellarer to be filled twice. When any *externs*[1] or outsiders—clerks or laymen—dined in the refectory, he was to stay with them for company's sake, asking two or three monks to do the same.

At 6 P.M. the abbot, or the prior in his stead, after seeing all to bed in the dormitory, locked the cloister and other doors, and took charge of the keys until the following morning, when, at the proper time, they were delivered into the hands of the proper officers.

Every morning, the day of the month was proclaimed in the cloister, after the office of Prime, by the boys, and a procession made daily through the entire circuit and the church, the whole precinct being encompassed on certain occasions, as the Rogation Days.

In the cloister, or other special apartment—the barber's rastyr-house,[2] or shaving-house (at Canterbury under the chapter-house)—the periodical shaving and clipping of hair and beards[3] took place. The time

---

[1] Externs, properly speaking, were clerics and lay folk affiliated to the order as exterior members.

[2] *Rasturæ*—Rastura in the Gilbertine Rule is shaving the head, but Du Cange renders it bread raspings.

[3] The shaving of the beard began about 1200. Lay brethren frequently retained their beards, and were known as Bearded Brothers.

varied in different places. Usually it was a monthly operation, but sometimes oftener, as once a fortnight in summer and three weeks in winter. The Gilbertine canons were to be shaved seventeen times a year, but the "Inquirenda of King Henry VIII.'s Visitors," asks "Whether ther ye bee wyekely shaven." The razors were kept in an aumbry, close to the entrance to the dormitory.

By the "Norman Institutes," the novice masters were to shave the boys, and the boys them, the latter washing the heads of boys too little to shave themselves. Until 1266 the monks of St Augustine's, Canterbury, shaved one another in the cloister, but in consequence of frequent injuries resulting from the awkwardness of the operators, secular persons were hired and paid by the year, an example soon followed by other houses. The cost of the shaving usually was defrayed out of the chamberlain's exchequer, and the razors kept in the aumbry, close to the entrance of the dormitory.

Archbishop Lanfranc, in his "Decretals," directs that no monk be shaved in his hood, and the shavers to be habited in frocks. They probably also wore aprons, an appendage in frequent use in monasteries. Conversation was generally permitted during the progress of the shaving, and any one who thought it necessary might be shaved with the consent of the abbot or prior. At Christmas and Easter after shaving baths were allowed.

The tonsure of monks is mentioned in England as early as the Dooms of King Withred (696), and the Excerptions of Ecgbriht. It was larger than the tonsure of priests, the entire upper surface of the head being shaved in token of their more entire renunciation of the world, and of their servitude to God, slaves having been anciently shorn. At a monk's initial shearing, the first locks were wont to be cut off by a king, or some other great personage, and in some places afterwards burned in the censer. Anciently, to offer a lock of hair to a monastery was to become a participator in its prayers, good works, etc. In 697, an officer is recorded as having pulled off his shoes, and, advancing to the altar, offered up a lock of his hair. Beards were in like manner consecrated to God when their owners became monks.

In the hands of the CHANTOR or PRECENTOR was the disposal of the choral part of the Church service, and the training of the monks who formed the quire. This he did in the SONG SCHOOL, a convenient room usually adjacent to the church, or in the cloister. He appears also to have taught some of them to play upon the organs, which were used on principal days at High Mass and Evensong.[1] Liberty was accorded him to "lug the ears" and "pull the hair" of boys, and to "chastise with the hand" the novices who told lies, or were negligent in quire. None could leave quire before Mass was over without his leave. As often as he held the quire he had an allowance beyond the commons of the house, and the singers the privilege of repairing to an appointed place to refresh themselves during their choral duty.

In discharging his quire duty he stood in the centre of the quire, directing it from the right-hand side, a sub-chantor (*succentor*) sometimes presiding over the left. He prepared the tablets and the singing-books, and had the custody of the keys of the aumbries in which they were locked. The arrangement of pro-

---

[1] Monks were wont to travel from monastery to monastery to teach music and singing.

cessions was wholly his. On festival days he distributed copes to the monks and staves to his assistant chantors, pairing them in order at the quire door. Another church officer was the SACRIST, or *Secretarius* (churchwarden), who provided all necessaries for the proper celebration of Divine Service. All vestments and ornaments were in his care, the washing of the altar vessels and linen (in vessels of brass kept exclusively for the purpose)—that is, if he happened to be a priest or deacon; the furnishing of the wafers for the Communion of the convent, the lighting, cleaning, and decorating the church on festivals. In his capacity of church guardian he and the sub-sacrist were to sleep in the church in a stall (*pulpitum*), which was allowed to none other without the leave of the abbot or prior. The care of burials and of the churchyard was a part of his duty; the latter he was to see free from nettles and weeds, horses and other animals. In contradistinction, when unoccupied, he was exempted from no weekly office. At Westminster he made the ink used in the High Courts of Justice.

In some houses the sacrist's and precentor's offices were combined; in others held in conjunction with other duties.[1] In the twelfth and thirteenth centuries the sacrist seems to have been the principal TREASURER or bursar in most Benedictine monasteries. As such the rents from lands, offerings, and other monies passed through his hands—all other officers presenting their accounts to him for audit; paid wages and other outgoings. He had a chamber in the infirmary and another for an office (*chequer*), where his meat was served from the great kitchen.

---

[1] As chief librarian, registrar, secretary of the seal, etc.

The treasury house was in his particular care. At Durham it was situated on the west side of the cloister, close to the door leading up to the dormitory, in the midst of which was an iron grate, having a strong iron door of the same work, "with a lock, and great slots of iron," and within a square table covered with green cloth, for telling money. In the treasury all the chief valuables of the house were kept—the best muniments, the relics, the chapter seal, and the evidences and other documents belonging to royal and noble families.

An exterior officer very similar to the treasurer was the steward, or seneschal. He was not unfrequently a layman of rank, with inferior assistants under him, upon whom fell the discharge of the principal part of the duties of holding manorial courts and transacting the other exterior business of the abbot and convent. In return he was the recipient of valuable fees, the privilege of hospitality, servants, horses, clothes, etc.

### THE LIBRARY AND SCRIPTORIUM

Nothing approaching what is to-day termed a library was to be found even in the largest monasteries. In many there were, undoubtedly, collections of a certain number of books, but until the advent of the printing press their number was necessarily small. Yet with an assiduity highly commendable they collected together a large number of most precious manuscripts at a vast expense. At a time when all books had to be produced by sheer hand labour, the cost of transcription was enormous, when compared with the then value of money and the rate of wages. STOW tells us that in the year 1274, a Bible in nine volumes, fairly written, with a gloss, or commentary, sold for fifty marks—equal to thirty-three pounds, six shillings and eightpence. At the same time wheat was selling at three shillings and fourpence a quarter, and a labourer's wage was three half-pence a day. A century and a half later a copy of Wycliffe's New Testament cost four marks and forty pence—two pounds sixteen shillings and eightpence. About the same time the sum of a hundred marks—sixty-six pounds thirteen shillings and fourpence of modern currency—was paid for transcribing a copy of the works of Nicholas de Lyra, in two volumes, which was chained in the library of the Priory of the Gray Friars.

By this time the price of wheat had risen to five shillings and fourpence the quarter, and the wages of a ploughman fallen to a penny a day; and with it, ere the fifteenth century closed, the fall of the pen, when the price of a parchment copy of the Scriptures fell immediately from four or five hundred to sixty, fifty, and forty crowns.

"A monastery (*claustrum*) without a library (*sine armario*)," writes Geoffrey, sub-prior of St Barbara, in Normandy, to Peter Mangot, monk of Baugercy, in 1170, "is like a castle (*castrum*) without an armoury (*sine armamentario*). Our library is our armoury. Thence it is that we bring forth the sentences of the Divine law, like sharp arrows, to attack the enemy."

"There is, in my opinion," adds John of Trittenheim, Abbot of Spanheim, in 1486, "no manual labour more becoming a monk than the writing of ecclesiastical books, and preparing what is needful for others who write them."

The translation, transcription, and diffusion of the Holy Scriptures was their chief task. Nearly one hundred years before the printing-press began its work,

Wycliffe had given the English people their first complete translation in their mother tongue. That nearly two hundred manuscript copies of this, the Lollard's Bible, are still in existence testify to the large number of copies which must have originally been made.

Still earlier Athelstan, King of all England (tenth century), had encouraged the translation of the Bible into the Saxon language, causing a copy to be placed in every church.

Upon the invention of printing the monks were among the first to welcome the new art, and the Bible was one of the first books printed by John of Gutenberg when he set up his printing press in Mayence, in 1456. Edition followed edition, and by the year 1500, it had been published in Latin almost one hundred times.

Neither did they confine their skill to the multiplication of the Scriptures solely. As early as the sixth century, the monks had turned their attention to procuring and copying manuscripts—the choicest production of the intellects of Greece and Rome. Richard Bury, Bishop of Durham, in the thirteenth century, is said to have strewn even the floors of the rooms of his various palaces with books, the work of the small army of copyists and illuminators he maintained. Abbot John Whethamsted of St Alban's was such another. Over eighty books caused he to be transcribed during his tenure of office. Fifty and eight volumes were transcribed by the care of another abbot presiding over Glastonbury.

To their diligent care and handicraft we owe the priceless gatherings of magnificent manuscripts which form the *chef d'œuvres* of our national collections.

So zealous indeed were they, that they often got

lands given and church tithes appropriated to encourage and enable them to carry the work on. With what care they executed their work, such choice examples as the Book of Kells,[1] the Gospels of St Wilfred, St Cuthbert, and St Chad bear ample witness. The exquisite and incomparable beauty of the illuminations, the clear brilliancy and glow of colour, the mathematical precison of the even lines, the perfect form of the perpendicular letters, and the accuracy of the interlacing work, may not be matched with any production of the printing press in the present day, and well may have inspired the legend that they were written by angel hands.

With the art of writing, that of illuminating was closely allied, being largely practised in conjunction therewith, and reaching its highest development in the manuscripts of the thirteenth and fourteenth centuries. So faithfully did they adhere to the traditions of their school, that experts are able to decide beyond dispute that such and such a document was written in this, that, or the other monastic school.

Writing monks were distinguished by the name of *Antiquarii*. They were the elder monks who were employed in the making of the Church and other rare books, the juniors and boys being employed upon the common copying work of the house. But in many of the larger houses skilled writers were hired to despatch the business of the convent. They were known as *Librarii*, or common scriptores, but their employment was forbidden by some orders, as by the Gilbertine, in England.

In a large monastic establishment, possessed of much property the amount of clerical work was simply

---

[1] Now at Trinity College, Dublin.

enormous. For the proper management of its estates, a large number of clerks would find constant employment in what may be termed the legal department—leases, mortgages, conveyances, assignments and a thousand and one transactions, rendered trebly intricate by the numberless parcels into which the tenures were split up. The mere keeping of the accounts of such a house was a perpetual task, the expenses of each brother bearing office, and of each department to which he belonged, being kept with a painfully minute precision unknown in the present day. The rolls were kept from day to day, and presented at regular prescribed intervals for audit.

Next would come the educational department—the production of reading and writing books, of church and music books,[1] their constant replacement and repair.

Last, but by no means least, was the record office, wherein were collected and digested the principal affairs of the particular house, and the occurrences of the kingdom. In the early days, the task of chronicling the events of English history was entirely the work of the monks. Every monastery of any standing had its accredited chronicler, whose business it was to make a record of any affair of the moment taking place within or without the house.

The earliest European chronicles are those of France, which begin in the fifth century. In the twelfth century, Abbot Suga (he died 1152) had them collected, collated, and translated from the Latin into the vernacular prose by the monks of the Abbey of St Denis, near Paris. These chronicles were continued under the name of "Grandes Chroniques de St Denis,"

---

[1] Monks frequently wrote for the minstrels.—WART. vol. 1. p. 87.

up to the fifteenth century, becoming authoritative annals.

A monastic chronicle, which had been regularly entered up for a long period, naturally became a great treasure, and to be regarded as an object of much veneration. When Henry I. came to the throne, the chronicle was still being written in the English tongue by the monks of Worcester, and for some years after his death was still carried on at Peterborough.

In addition to the muniments of the house, there were the memoirs of founders, benefactors, and other persons, an account of whose family concerns was regularly taken — records of their births, deaths, marriages, children, and successors. Thus, recourse was constantly had to them for proving of age or generation. Not only were the clerical constitutions of the national and provincial synods sent to the abbeys to be recorded, but, after the Conquest, even Acts of Parliament. Thus, an exemplification of the charter of liberties, known as *Magna Charta*, granted by King Henry I., was sent to an abbey in every county to be preserved.

It was to the religious houses that King Edward I. sent to search for his title to the Scottish crown, and when his claim to that sovereignty was acknowledged in that country, he caused the fact to be recorded in the chronicles of the Abbey of Winchcomb, and of the Priory of Norwich among other places.

"Yet," says Matthew Paris, monk of St Alban's, last of the great chroniclers (1200-59) "the case of historical writers is hard, for if they tell the truth they provoke men, and if they write what is false they offend God."

In fact, in those days of strife and tumult there was

no other safe depository than the monastery. The documents and valuables of private families were frequently sent to them to be preserved. Upon their deaths, the seals of noblemen were deposited there, just as the seal of King Edward the Confessor was in the safe keeping of the Westminster monks.

To return, the books constituting the library of a religious house were entrusted to the care of a specially appointed officer—generally the precentor or chantor. The book to be read was assigned by the abbot to each monk, to be punctually returned at an appointed period, an inventory (very curious specimens of which exist)[1] of the whole being carefully gone through in chapter every Lent.

Among the directions upon the introduction of the Benedictine Rule into his diocese by Archbishop Lanfranc is one touching the library and studies of the monks. In the first week in Lent, the librarian was to place in the chapter house all the books which had not been delivered to the monks for study during the preceding year. These latter were to be brought in by those to whom they were entrusted, and the librarian read a list of them. They were then returned in regular order, and those who had not fulfilled their year's task by reading them through did penance by prostrating themselves and confessing their fault to obtain pardon. The librarian then delivers another book to each of the brethren, taking a list of those lent and those returned.

Founders not unfrequently gave or collected books,

---

[1] The catalogue of the library of Deeping Priory, Lincolnshire, a cell of Thorney, is headed: "*Isti sunt Libri de Armariolo Monochorum de Est depyng.*" A MS. in the Bodleian Library, containing a list of books formerly belonging to the Nunnery of St Martin, Dover, is styled: "*Præsens hæc matricula bibliothecæ prioratus Dovorræ anno incarnationis Dominicæ*, 1389."

or had them written for their foundations. Others bequeathed them or gave them as donations. William Place, master of St John's Hospital, Bury, St Edmund's, by his will, dated 1504, bequeathes to the Monastery of Seynt Edmund ... "My book of the dowts of Holy Scryptur to ly and remain in the cloyster."

From this it may be gathered that what books formed the library at that house were kept in the cloister; which was the case at Durham, where certain aumbries or closets, contained the books forming the library there.

However, from the "Durham Rites," we learn that "there was a Lybrarie in the south angle of the Lantren, which is now above the clock, standing betwixt the chapter-house and the *Te Deum* wyndowe, being well replenished with ould written doctors and other histories and ecclesiastical writers."

The library of the Irish Cistercian House of Newry, County Down, with all its effects, is recorded as having been destroyed by fire in 1162, and the library attached to the White Friar's Priory.

London is mentioned as being granted, with other parts of the house, to Richard Moresyne in the thirty-second year of King Henry VIII. (1541). The library founded by the renowned Richard Whittington for the London Grey Friars, in 1429, is described as being 129 feet long and 31 broad. It was all wainscotted about, with 28 desks, and 8 double settles of wainscot. In the year following, it was furnished with books at the expense of £556, 10s., whereof the aforesaid Richard Whittington gave £400, and Dr Thomas Winchelsey, a friar there, the other £156, 10s.

The custom of lending out books was early in vogue, although the restrictions laid upon borrowers were harsh and severe. Before a book could be taken away, a bond had to be given, or a pledge of something of equal or greater value to insure its return, failing which, he was anathematised here and hereafter.[1]

One of the earliest lending libraries on record was that of the Kalendars of Bristol; another, that known two centuries after Bodley's day as the Bodleian Library, at Oxford. Here the books were kept in boxes, and given out under pledges. To Bishop Thomas Cobham of Worcester belongs the honour of founder, manuscripts being the first contributions to it. Among the early donors appears the names of Humphrey, Duke of Gloucester, Richard of Bury, Bishop of Durham, and Thomas Kempe, Bishop of London.

Museums were sometimes attached to monastic libraries, where stuffed crocodiles, ostrich eggs, and similar wonders were displayed to the gaze of the curious.

In the earlier mediæval days, the monks were accustomed to study or write in "pewes" or carrels, a term corrupted from *quadril* through the Norman *carole*, signifying something square. These carrels were small, enclosed closets of wainscot, erected in one of the alleys of the cloisters. At Durham, in the cloister, "there were carrels fynely wainscotted and verie close, all but the forepart, which had carved worke to give light in at their carrel doores, and on every carrel was a deske [*Scriptoria*] to lye their bookes on, and the carrel was no greater than from one stanchell (central bar) of the window to another." For the use of the younger monks and novices "over against the said treasury door, was a fair state of wainscot, where the novices were taught, and the master of the novices had a pretty seat of wainscot

---

[1] At the Middle Temple they had only a simple library, which, standing always open, was at last robbed and spoiled of all the books in it.

adjoining to the south side of the treasury door, over against the state where the novices sate, and there he taught the novices both forenoon and afternoon.[1] No strangers or other persons were suffered to molest or trouble the said novices or monks in their carrels, while they were at their books within the cloister. For to the purpose there was a porter appointed to keep the cloister door."[2]

In the cloister of their monastery, as has been observed, the monks lived their daily life. Yet much was done to make the cloisters comfortable, according to the acceptation of such a term in that rough age. The carrels were to this end. The seats, raised about four feet, were each enclosed on all sides by partitions to exclude wind and draughts. Sometimes they were placed against the wall and provided with a wooden back, the floor boarded beneath, and strewn with hay or straw for warmth. Their hoods and fur-lined almuces would afford an additional warmth to their bodies. Then there was the continually burning fire in the common room, to which all could resort upon occasion. At other times, as at Durham, the carrels were set before each window, three in each.[3] It is very questionable whether the now empty traceries were ever filled with glass, and even if they were so provided, they were probably

---

[1] At St Alban's, at the close of the fourteenth century, the Matin Mass was set back from Tierce to Prime to allow continuous study of the monks.

[2] "Rites of Durham."

[3] The "Cottonian MS." Faustina, c. xii. f. 96., in a transcription of the Westminster Customs with adaptations for St Augustine's Monastery, Canterbury, thus speaks of these carrels: "De karulis in claustro habendis hanc considerationem habere debent quibus committitur claustri tutela, ut videlicet celerarius sen alii fratres qui raro in claustro resident suas karulas in claustro non habeant; sed neque aliquif ratres nisi in scribendo vel illuminando, aut tantum notando communitati aut etiam sibimet ipsis proficere sciant."

insertions of a late date. For one thing window-glass, as we know it, was not in everyday use till long after the dissolution of the monasteries. In all probability, to combat the inclement season of the year, rush-mats, shutters, oiled-paper, or other like protection were in use; and for another, we must remember that our ancestors were altogether a hardier race than men reared amid the luxuries of to-day. If the cloisters were comfortless, the castles were no less so. Comfort and privacy were no more looked for in the convent than in the castle. Until King Henry II. founded his Carthusian monastery at Witham, in 1178, there was no such a thing as a *cell* in England. It was a peculiarity of the Carthusian Order, and when introduced was regarded as a novelty.

In the south walk of the Gloucester cloister are some twenty of these carrels remaining, in perfect condition save that the desks and seats have vanished; also the closets, or aumbries, where the books were kept, can still be seen. At Beaulieu, seven carrels filled the north wall of the cloister.

Generally speaking, the carrels were few in number, and reserved for those having special or constant business to transact within the cloister. Nicholas de Clairvaux, the secretary to St Bernard of Clairvaux, has left us a description of his writing-cell, shut in and concealed on every side by the various parts of the monastery.

"Its door opens," he says, "into the apartment of the novices, where commonly a great number of persons, distinguished by rank as well as by literature, put on the new man in newness of life. . . . On the right, the cloister of the monks runs off, in which the more advanced part of the community walk. . . . There, under the strictest discipline, they individually open the books of Divine eloquence, not that they may winnow forth the treasures of knowledge, but that they may elicit love, compunction, and devotion. From the left projects the infirmary and the place of exercise (*deambulatorium*) for the sick, where the bodies, wearied and weakened by the severities of the Rule, are refreshed with better food, until, being cured, or at least in better health, they may rejoin the congregation, who labour and pray, who do violence to the Kingdom of Heaven, and take it by force. And do not suppose that my little tenement is to be despised. First, it is a place to be desired and pleasant to look upon, and comfortable for retirement. It is filled with choice and Divine books, at the delightful view of which I feel contempt for the vanity of this world, considering that 'vanity of vanities, all is vanity,' and that nothing is more vain than vanity itself. The place is assigned to me for reading, and writing, and composing, and meditating, and adoring the Lord of Majesty."

Yet not as a common monastic scribe did Nicholas occupy this cell, but by reason of the dignity of his office as secretary to the lord abbot. MABILLON, in his "Études Monastiques," says that "many of those little cells, where the transcribers and bookbinders worked" at Citeaux, were still to be seen in his time.

Additional studies were sometimes built over alleys (*trisantiæ, deambulatoria*), as at Chester, Norwich, St Alban's, and Sherborne.

The eulogy which Nicholas de Clairvaux passes upon his books will have been noticed. The monks loved learning for its own sake, and the spiritual solace they received from it, chiefly as showing them the vanity of the world and the unrest of its votaries.

"Our Saviour by His own example," writes Richard of Bury, a bishop of Durham in the fifteenth century, in his treatise on books, "Philobiblon," chap. xvii., "precludes all unseemly negligence in the treatment of the books, as we read in Luke iv., for, when He had read over the Scriptural prophecy, written about Himself in a book delivered to Him, He did not return it to the minister till

He had first closed it with His most holy hands, by which act students are most clearly taught that they ought not, in the smallest degree whatever, be negligent about the custody of books."

A last word, on the materials employed in the scriptorium, before this chapter is brought to a conclusion. Paper, on account of its perishable nature, was little used, vellum and parchment, for the providing of which special revenues were assigned, supplying its place. MABILLON says he could find no paper books more ancient than the tenth century. The ink used differed considerably from our own, particularly in its lasting quality, the writing in many cases being as black and brilliant as the day upon which it was first applied. It differed also in its make—gum, soot, or ivory black, being its chief ingredients.

Pens of metal were in use, but quills had become common by the seventh century. Chalk and pumice-stone were in use for rubbing the parchment, penknives to scrape it, a large knife to cut it into the required size, and a leaden plummet, or weight, to keep it in position. A pricker (*punctorium*), or awl, to make dots to ensure evenness of line, a style of bone or iron and an ink-horn, completed the outfit. Counters (kept in purses) were used by the monks to cast accounts with.

### THE KITCHEN

The kitchen in monastic houses generally adjoined the refectory; in the Benedictine houses it was situated behind it; in the Cistercian at the side. This position was convenient for the passing of the food through a "hatch," "turn," "window," or "grille," direct from the kitchen to the refectory. In large houses there were more than one kitchen, the chief being known as the great kitchen (*coquina cœnobii*).

The kitchens of mediæval days were much more important in both size and equipment than they are to-day. The remains of the kitchen at Gloucester Abbey show that apartment to have been 36 by 17 feet 6 inches, and the one at Durham, built by Prior Forcer (1368-70), almost, in its original state, similar, 36 feet $8\frac{1}{2}$ inches in diameter. The kitchen at Canterbury was still larger, being 45 feet.

We read of them as "a large pastery, with five ovens, new built, some of them 14 feet deep." "A great kitchen with four ranges, and a boiling place for small boiled meats." "A boiling house for the great boiler." The great kitchen at Jervaulx Abbey, York, contained three huge fireplaces. A smaller kitchen with offices adjoined the larger kitchen. At Westminster and Chester it had a larder and a tower on the west side. An ewery, or scullery, was also attached.

The most usual shape was four-square, but sometimes it was built as an octagon, as at Durham, or a round, or in a bottle-form, these latter being principally found abroad.

The kitchen of the Cistercian Abbey of Fountains is one of the most perfect specimens remaining. It is constructed in two compartments, each furnished with an immense fire-place, the arches being composed of the somewhat rare masonry termed "juggled."

For the infirmary there was generally a separate kitchen, and another for the exclusive use of the abbot. The abbot's kitchen at Glastonbury is roofed like an octagonal chapter house, with a lantern in the centre. Abbot Chinnock is supposed to have been the builder (1374-1420).

At the London Charterhouse, the kitchen—" Egypte, the fleyshe kychyn "—situated at the entrance gate, was so called from the flesh-pots of Egypt, flesh-eating being unknown in the charter houses.

The kitchen was under the superintendence of the officer known as the kitchener (*coquinarius*), in whose hands was the marketing and purveying of the house. Besides buying the provisions for the use of the kitchen, he overlooked the cooks, butchery, and fish-ponds, and saw that the broken meat was carefully reserved for the poor. At Abingdon he was excused every weekly office with the exception of the Great (high) Mass, and the Mass of Our Lady; but his attendance at chapter was required unless specially engaged. Every morning he visited the sick in the infirmary to take note of what they required, and again attended at their tables to see if they had received what was necessary. The herdsman (*vacarius*) was subject to him. The kitchener at Evesham used to attend the markets, and had a horse allowed him for the purpose.

In some houses, certain lands were set apart to supply this department. At St Alban's no less than fifty-three farms were so devoted, each of the value of forty-six shillings annually. Nine carriers, bringing provisions from London, received a part, the rest going to the cellarers and household. In addition to this, there were allowances from other manors, the proceeds of the odd or fifty-third week being devoted to keeping up the supply of culinary utensils. At Yarmouth, the convent had also a house where fish was laid up, especially herrings, for the use of the convent.[1]

Although the table supply of monasteries was what

---

[1] Large quantities of provisions were salted and laid up at Martinmas for winter use by our mediæval ancestors.

we moderns would have called meagre—consisting as it did of herbs and pulse, spiced fish stews, sauces seasoned with pepper and cumin, cheese-cakes, wafers and rissoles, beans and dripping—the man appointed was expected to be an adept in the culinary art. In some houses, as at Abingdon, two or more cooks were appointed; one to preside over the dietary of the monks, the other over that of the household. In other houses the brethren (monks, not novices) were appointed to the office in turn, week by week, or for longer periods.

This latter method was in accord with Chapter XXXV. of the Benedictine Rule, which treats "Of the Weekly Servers in the Kitchen."[1] From this we learn that the brethren were to wait upon one another in turn, and no one was to be excused from the work of the kitchen, unless prevented by sickness or other more necessary employment. Moreover, to the inexperienced, or weak brethren, assistance was to be given, that they might do their work with alacrity.

Should the community be large, the cellarer was to be excused work in the kitchen, as were others occupied in more urgent business.

The monk ending his weekly turn was to leave all things clean, and wash the towels wherewith the brethren wiped their hands and feet. All the kitchen utensils were to be handed over to the cellarer, clean and whole, and that officer was to deliver the same to the brother entering upon his turn.

One hour before refection the weekly servers were to take a cup of drink and a piece of bread over and above the appointed allowance, as they had to serve their brethren in the refectory, and so could not dine until

---

[1] "Rule St Benedict," pp. 155-57.

after the general refection, but on solemn days they were to forbear this privilege until after Mass.

The kitchen servers were to be admitted to their duty by prayer in the oratory. On Sunday, immediately after Lauds, both the outgoing and the incoming officers for the week were to cast themselves upon their knees before all, and ask to be prayed for. He that had ended his office was to say the verse: "*Benedictus es, Domine Deus, qui adjuvisti me, et consolatus es me;*" after a triple repetition of which he received the blessing; he that began his week immediately following with the "*Deus in adjutorium meum intende: Domine ad adjuvandum me festina,*" which likewise being repeated thrice by all, he also received the blessing, and entered upon his office. Both the outgoing brother and the incoming were to wash the feet of all.

The monk Ælfstan, who was afterwards advanced to the Episcopate, was at one time cook at Abingdon, where it is related that, unassisted, he cooked the viands, gave them out, lighted the fire, fetched the water, washed the dishes and the pavement, which, it is added, he kept scrupulously clean. Even the great St Bernard of Clairvaux participated in these humble duties, washing the dishes in the scullery of his monastery.

In a monastery kitchen, cleanliness was strictly allied to godliness. In Cluniac houses over-sleeves were worn to save those of the habit, aprons were also worn, and gloves to protect the hands from burning when moving the cauldron on the fire. St Benedict devotes Chapter XXXI. in his Rule in directing "What kind of man the cellarer in a monastery ought to be."[1]

He was to be chosen out of the community on

---

[1] "Rule St Benedict," pp. 143-147.

account of his wisdom, mature and temperate character. He was not to be a great eater, nor haughty, nor headstrong, nor arrogant, nor slothful, nor wasteful, a God-fearing man who would act as a father to the whole brotherhood. He was to have the care of everything, but to do nothing without the leave of the abbot. Should a brother ask anything unreasonable, he was not to be treated with contempt, so as to grieve him, but reasonably and with all humility refused.

Of the sick, children, guests, and the poor he was to have a diligent care, and to look upon all the goods of the monastery as though they were consecrated vessels of the altar. He was neither to be neglectful, covetous, nor wasteful of the goods of the house, and on him to whom he had nothing else to bestow he was at least to give a kind answer. All that the abbot should appoint should be under his care, but he was warned not to meddle with forbidden things.

To the brethren he was to distribute their appointed allowance of food "without arrogance or delay, that they be not scandalised,"[1] and in the event of the community being large, helpers were to be given him, by whose aid he might quietly perform the office committed to his charge.

Such things as were necessary were to be asked for and given at suitable hours, "that no one may be troubled or saddened in the House of God."

The cellarer was the principal of the great monastic obedientiaries, the third in command, acting as general of the commissariat, house-steward, manciple, proctor, purveyor, bursar, etc. He presided over the goods, hospital, granaries, cellar, kitchen, and stables. In his hands reposed the care of everything relating to the food

---

[1] *Vide* St Matt. xviii. 6.

of the monks, the vessels of the cellar, the kitchen, and the refectory. He took stock of all provisions, of buttery (*bottelarie*), beer cellars, malthouse, and bread-room, the brew, and the bakehouse; saw the amount of kitchen expenditure, both in regard to the abbot's table and that of the monks, as well as that all arriving strangers were in due time properly served. He waited upon visitors, minutiæ, and monks returning from journeys; saw that no one sat down before the abbot, or prior, supplied bread, wine, or beer to any "weary" monk asking in reason at the turn in the cellarage. In collecting the spoons after dinner, he was to be careful to carry those appertaining to the abbot in his right hand, the remainder in his left.

He, too, appointed the pittances, ordered the daily provisions, weighed the bread daily, and found wine and minstrels for the great festivals, and ale of the best, galls, gum, and copperas for the ink for the use of the precentor, and in the season of Lent, honey to sweeten the hard pulse. He was to be careful of the healthy, and more especially of the sick.

On account of his onerous duties he was excused frequent attendance in church—from ordinary Masses and Hours, expect those of Matins, Prime, and Evensong. After the Gospel had been read at the Great Mass on feast-days, he had permission to leave quire, and every day in Lent, after the verses of the Offertory had been sung.[1] At Canterbury he was "father of the monastery," and kept a court-mote in his hall. At St Edmundsbury he held his court of thieves and robbers, and had such power over highways that none could dig chalk or clay without his leave.

---

[1] If the community was a large one, he was to be excused work in the kitchen.

In the absence of the abbot, he or his agents had the pre-emption of all food for the use of the convent. Sometimes a monastery would have a couple of cellarers —one to manage the internal affairs of the house, and another for the exterior business. In some cases the former, under the name of *Hordarian*, shared with the cellarer and refectorian the labour of providing for the bodily needs of the community, being set over the *board*, or supplies of food required for the refectory, for which purpose certain estates were set apart for his administration.

The cellarer's hall, or cellarage, was usually placed under the dormitory, or refectory, as at Kirkham, Lewes, and Sawley; or over an undercroft (*covert—cellar*), with an upper room forming a guest-house or hall, as at Battle and Beaulieu (where it has a dividing wall from the cloisters), Canterbury, Chester, Sherborne, and Winchester.

A range of pillars commonly divided it longitudinally into two alleys, and further by wooden lateral partitions into separate rooms. At Canterbury, the beer and wine cellars were in the western range of vaults; and at the north end, as at the Charterhouse, the "turn"— an oblique opening with a spout in the wall—through which the cup of wine was passed to the fatigued or thirsty monk as a refresher.[1] At Chester part of this vaulted space was stocked with fish, brought up by the abbey boats from the Dee. At Fountains, one enormous range was stored with the wool for which the Cistercians were famous, and at Durham food was stored in the sub-structure of the refectory, and materials for furniture and clothing in that of the dormitory.

---

[1] The larder gate still marks the entrance to the kitchener's offices at Canterbury.

The refectory, or frater-house, the common dining-hall of a monastery, was usually raised upon a cellarage for the storage of provisions, and according to Benedictine arrangement, lay parallel to the minster, in order to prevent the noise and fumes from reaching the sanctuary. In Cistercian houses, however, it generally stood at right angles to the cloister.

The refectory was usually the finest apartment of all the monastic buildings, its groined or vaulted roof being not unfrequently supported by rows of piers, as at Lanercost and Finchale; and its walls beautifully wainscotted or arcaded, as the remains at Peterborough, or painted in fresco with pictures of sacred story or pious legend — representations of the Doom, or Last Judgment, and of the Last Supper were favourite subjects.[1]

"In the south alley of the cloisters," we read in the "Rites of Durham," "is a fair large hall, called the *frater-house*, finely wainscotted on the north and south sides, as also on the west. And on either part of the frater-house there is a fair long bench of stone mason-work, from the cellar door to the pantry or cover door. Above the bench is wainscot-work two yards and a half in height, finely carved and set with embroidered work; and above the wainscot there was a fair large picture of our Saviour Christ, the Blessed Virgin Mary, and St John, in fine gilt work and excellent colours; with pictures, though washed over with lime, yet do appear through it. This wainscot-work hath engraven on the top of it, '*Thomas Castell, Prior, Anno Domini* 1518, *mensis Julii*.' So that Prior Castell wainscotted the frater-house round about."

---

[1] During the fifteenth century in Florence, the Institution of the Holy Sacrament was a common subject for representation on the walls of convent refectories. Ghirlandajo painted one for the Ognisanti; Leonardo, another for S. Maria delle Grazie, and Andrea del Castagno one for S. Appollonia. The great hall at St Alban's was adorned with tapestry; at Gloucester, with portraits of kings of England in fresco.

The ancient refectories of Durham and Carlisle are now used as libraries; that of Beaulieu (Hampshire) as a church; and those at Chester and Worcester as school-houses.

The kitchen communicated with the refectory by a buttery-hatch[1] through the wall. At Canterbury there was a covered alley, and at Westminster a covered way to the hall, but in smaller houses, a hatch or window formed the means of communication. At Tintern, an almonry-hatch communicates from the refectory with the cloister, to which a ready access was gained by the poor and visitors by way of the water-gate, and use of the adjacent ferry.

The early English refectory of Beaulieu,[2] although the roof has been lowered, and an unsightly buttress erected against the south wall to support the roof, presents us with a fairly good example of a monastic dining-hall. A fine range of triple lancets are set in either wall, and a very fine triplet with intervening shafts in that of the south. The wall space between the two to the west is occupied by the stone pulpit of the reader, ornamented with dog's-tooth or flower moulding. This pulpit is approached by a staircase and passage in the thickness of the wall, lighted by a two-light window and three smaller lancets, with a beautiful open arcade in front, supported by slender shafts of Purbeck marble.

Among the bosses on the roof of royal and ecclesiastical personages are represented King John, the founder, Richard, King of the Romans, and Pope Innocent III.

---

[1] Buttery was a contraction for "bottlery," a place where "bottles" are kept, in the charge of the "bottler," or "butler."
[2] Now the parish church of St Bartholomew.

At the upper part, or eastern end of the hall, was a raised daïs, whereon stood the high table of the abbot. Abbots had separate tables, because, "living in penitence, and using only the common viands, strangers would be no expense to them, and the frugal would there see an example to confirm them in that virtue."

"Let the table of the abbot," says St Benedict (Rule, Chapter LVI. p. 231), "be always with the guests and strangers. But as often as there are few guests, it shall be in his power to invite any of the brethren. Let him take care, however, always to leave one or two seniors with the brethren for the sake of discipline." This was the Cistercian custom.

In the ninth century the Council of Aix, and subsequently St Dunstan, Benedictine monk and archbishop (925-88), decreed that the abbots should dine in the common refectory with their monks. At Croyland, every principal feast three monks were to dine at the abbot's table, every second feast two, and on certain days the prior. It was also enacted that every day in the year two monks should dine in the abbot's hall, whether he was present or not—an invitation which was to extend no further than when he had no other visitors. By the customs of Abingdon it was enjoined that before Easter the abbot should invite, twice or thrice in the week, from custom, twelve, sixteen, or seventeen, to dine alternately at his table, or any other at a different time whom he should chose. By the injunctions of the visitors of King Henry VIII., the abbot's table was "not to be somptious, or full of delicate or forayne dishes, but honestlye furnished with common meate, at which table the said abbot, or some senior in his stede, shall sit to receive the guests."

In the great refectory hall of St Alban's, the abbot's table was set upon a daïs, which was approached by an ascent of fifteen steps, every fifth of which was a landing place, upon which the monks, bringing up the meal in service of plate, stayed to sing a short hymn. In the midst of his table sat the lord abbot, with noblemen, ambassadors, and strangers of eminence and quality placed at the ends, the floor being strewn with hay, rushes, straw, or similar matter.

Down the hall two long side tables were arranged along the walls for the monks, on whom the kitchen officers and novices waited, they taking their repast when the monks' dinner was over.

The "Survey," taken at the suppression of the monasteries, gives the goods or furniture of Pipewell Abbey as follows: "The Frater. It. ther 3 bordes, 1 pulpett, 11 tables, 2 payr of truseulles, 1 forme"; the whole being "sould" for the sum of two shillings.

The monastic dinner hour was usually at or after Nones, or about 3 P.M. Subsequently it was put back to mid-day, together with the name of the later hour, noon, or none.

At the ringing of a small bell (*cymbalum*), or gong, hung in the refectory, the monks were summoned to their chief meals. Leaving the parlour they washed their hands at the lavatory, in the cloister adjacent to the refectory door, and assumed their pinafores, or super-tunics, worn to protect their clothes at dinner,[1] and entered the dining-hall two and two, taking their appointed places at the side tables on the matted benches, according to seniority of entrance to the order the same as at chapter.

---

[1] These pinafores are mentioned by Lyndwood, and occur in foreign Consuetudinals.

At the beginning and end of dinner, the abbot or his deputy, the prior, rang the little gilded hand-bell standing upon the abbot's table at his right hand, called the *squilla*.[1]

Each monk, upon sitting down, drew his cowl down and ate in silence;[2] a silence that was only broken by the voice of the reader sitting in the refectory pulpit. Whilst the *hebdomadaries*, or weekly servers, laid the dishes, the weekly reader began the lection from Holy Writ or "The Lives of the Saints," in the wall pulpit.

"One of the novices," says the "Durham Rites," "at the election and appointment of the master, did read some part of the Old and New Testament, in Latine, at dinner-time, having a convenient place at the south end of the high table, within a fair glass window compassed with iron, and certain steps of stone, with iron rails on the one side to go up to it, to an iron desk thereon which lay the Holy Bible."

This "convenient place" was the refectory pulpit, which was frequently of stone built into the wall, generally on the south, but sometimes, as at Kirkstall and Tintern, on the west. The example at Beaulieu is of the thirteenth century. The Annals of Dunstable Priory, under the date 1483, make mention of a clock "over the pulpitt."

The reading for the edification of the brethren during the repasts would seem not to have been confined to the sacred Scriptures, history (*rotundius*) and sermons (*attractius*) being also mentioned.

This custom of reading at meals was not exclusively monastic, for in castles "Gospels" were read at table,

---

[1] This bell was formed of a hollow ball of metal, with a slit for the sound, and a loose pellet within. It was chiefly used in the refectory.

[2] Anything wanted was asked for by signs.

and histories and stories of deeds of daring, etc. Part of the advice King Edward IV. left behind him for the education of his son, afterwards Edward V., was that at his hour of meat there was to be read before him noble stories, such as behoved a prince to understand.

In Chapter XXXVIII. of his Rule, St Benedict thus writes of "*De Hebdomadario Lectore*" (of the weekly reader): "Reading must not be wanting while the brethren eat at table. Neither ought any one presume to read who shall take up the book at hap-hazard; but let him who is appointed to read for the whole week enter upon his office on Sunday." Like the other servers, he received his duty with prayer and the blessing in the oratory, and the saint goes on to direct that the greatest silence must be kept at table, so that no muttering or voice may be heard there, save the voice of the reader. The brethren were so to minister the one to the other whatever was necessary for meat and drink, so that no one need ask for anything, but should anything be wanted, let it be asked for rather by a sign than by a word.

No question was to be asked about anything that was being read, or about anything else, unless perchance the superior should wish to make some brief exhortation for the edification of the brethren, and lest it should be grievous for the brother who was reader for the week to fast so long, he was to take a little pottage (bread and wine—*mixtum*) before he began to read, "on account of the Holy Communion (*Mixtum . . . . propter Communionem sanctam*)." Afterwards he was to eat with the weekly cooks and other servers of the kitchen. The brethren were not to read or sing in turns, but such only as may edify the hearers.[1]

---

[1] "Rule of St Benedict," chap. xxxviii. pp. 165-67.

It would appear that the task was generally deputed to a novice (*lector mensæ*) of the house.

Beside each plate was laid a neat cover or napkin, containing a "commons" of bread.[1] Usually the number of each mess varied between three and ten persons.

The ordinary fare varied with the period and the strictness, or otherwise, of the several orders. In primitive times, and at the various periods of reform, the fare was hard and meagre in the extreme. Thus the Cluniacs, although they fared sumptuously in their decadence, in their first fervour revelled in rotten eggs, beans with the pods on, and wine of such extraordinary poor quality "that one might drink of it for a month without intoxication."

No monks, it is said, ate meat or blood[2] till Charlemagne obtained the concession from Pope Leo for monks on this side of the Alps to use the fat of bacon, the others having the oil of olives.[3]

St Benedict thought it sufficient for the daily refection that there should be at all seasons two dishes of cooked food, "because of the infirmities of different people; so that he who cannot eat of one, may make his meal of the other." These two dishes of hot food were to suffice for the brethren, but if there were any apples, or young vegetables, they might be added as a third dish. One pound weight of bread was to suffice for the day, whether there be one refection or both dinner and supper. If they were to sup, a third part of the pound

---

[1] A *commons* was a plate to each, a *pittance* (from *pietas*) an allowance in one plate to two. See "Rule of St Benedict," chap. xxxix. A "corody" was a monk's portion of food and drink.

[2] Until Lanfranc's reform (1082), meat was eaten in refectory in this country.

[3] In 1337 meat was not eaten on Wednesdays and Saturdays during Advent, or from Septuagesima to Easter Day.

was to be reserved by the cellarer, and put before them at supper. Should the labour of the monks have been hard, it was in the power of the abbot to make some addition to the prescribed allowance, care being taken "always to avoid excess and surfeiting, that the monks be not overtaken with indigestion."

To children of tender age a less quantity was to be given than that allotted to elders, and every one "except the very weak and the sick," were to abstain altogether from eating the flesh of four-footed beasts.[1]

Monks, and especially those of the Cistercian reform, were great breeders of pigs, and an officer called the PORCARIUS was found in many houses. At St Edmundsbury he had for his profit the *fructus de candâ* (offal, or dung) of every pig fed in the house. Many charters contain clauses as to the number of pigs convents were to have in certain fields. The satirical Archdeacon Walter Mapes, ridiculing the Cistercians for their pretended abstinence from flesh, says: "Pigs they keep many thousands of them, and sell the bacon, perhaps not all of it; the head, legs, and feet, they neither give, nor sell, nor throw away; what becomes of them God knows; likewise there is an account between God and them of fowls that they keep in vast numbers." On the other hand, Nigell Wireker, writing of the Grandmontine hermits, says, "that they sent no fat pigs to the woods."

In the days when relaxations crept into the monastic observance, the monks of Furness (Lancashire) pulled down their old frater and erected a *couple* of new ones, side by side, one of which they called the "lean" frater, where meat was excluded; the other the "fat" frater, where on three days in the week the brethren dined on

---

[1] "Rule St Benedict," chap. xxxix. pp. 169-71.

meat, an evasion of the statutes precluding the use of meat in the refectory.

Thus we find the ordinary fare to have consisted of pulse, fruit, vegetables, bread, fish, eggs, cheese,[1] wine or ale. The mid-day was the only or chief meal of the day, not only in monasteries but in castles likewise. A little bread and wine (*mixtum*), fruit, etc., serving by way of breakfast, and supper was known as the *liberes*,[2] *collation, mixtum, pittance*, or *caritas.*

On festivals and anniversaries various additions were made to the everyday fare, either by the gifts of charitable benefactors or from the profits of lands, etc., left for the purpose. Beef, mutton, pork, sucking-pig, poultry, game, sugar, rice, currants, raisins, dates, almonds, spices, pastry, cakes, and all kinds of bread, wine, ale, and beer, were served on great days at Ely, besides a special capon-feast, and the wild-boar banquet on All Saints' Day—these coming under the names of *pittances*, mandates (by bequest), graces, and liveries.

The fare here on ordinary days appears to have consisted of fish, vegetables, pastry, blanc-mange, fig tarts, fruit, bread, cheese, wine, and milk.

When abbots were installed in their abbacies, or monks promoted to the priesthood or profession, great feasts were given with a large assemblage of seculars. At the installation feast of Abbot Maryns of St Alban's, which took place in 1302, the table literally groaned under its weight of delicacies. Dishes of coneys and peacocks were coloured with (alkanet) bugloss, sauces flavoured with ginger and galingale, blanch powder, amedan, fine flour cakes, grains, cardamon, flaunpayns,

---

[1] The monks of Jervaulx were famous for their cheese.
[2] A slight morning repast or refreshment is still called "bever" in some parts of Buckinghamshire.

honey, ginger, cinnamon, cloves, and mace, appeared as the festive fare.

In the fifteenth century, Abbot Bromsgrove allowed a goose or capon and a pint of wine to every monk of Evesham at Pentecost, whilst at Durham, during the Whitsun week of 1347, the amount of provisions consumed was still more extensive. Dyke thus quotes the cellarer's rolls on this occasion :—

| | |
|---|---|
| 600 salt herrings | 14 calves |
| 400 white herrings | 3 kids, 6 sucking porkers |
| 30 salted salmon | 71 geese, 14 capons, 59 chickens |
| 12 fresh salmon | |
| 14 ling, 55 kelengs, and 4 turbot | 500 pigeons |
| | 5 skins of hogslard |
| 2 horse loads of white fish and a conger, playse, sparlings, seels of white fish | 4 skins of cher (butter milk ?) |
| | 14 pounds of figs and raisins |
| | 13 pounds of almonds |
| 9 carcasses of oxen salted | 8 pounds of rice, pepper, saffron, cinnamon, and other spices |
| 1¼ carcasses fresh | |
| ¼ ox fresh | |
| 7½ swine, in salt | 1300 eggs. |
| 6 swine, fresh | |

the whole supplied at a cost of £11, 4s.

The Diet Rolls of the daily consumption at St Swithin's, Winchester, furnish an example of the *menu* of a great fast-day and a great feast-day. The former is for the Good Friday of 1492, and consists of three items only : 1000 eggs, 3s. 4d.; red herrings, 5s.; figs, as *entrée*, 8d. The latter is the fare supplied on the Feast of the Nativity of St Mary, in the same year : grenelynge, 4s. 4d.; mylwelle, 4s. 8d.; eels, as *entrée*, 3½d.; rice, as pittance, 4d.; plaice for supper, 2s. 8d.; mustard, 1½d.

Three halfpenny-worth of mustard seems to have been a standing dish with the monks on non-fast days, and the daily cost of feeding forty monks at an average of 8s. a day cannot be considered as extravagant.

Fish was used in large quantities, being specially cultivated in the stews attached to the monasteries, where the larderer and his men employed "dragnet," and "trameyll," "flewes," and "bervenettes," or chose eels from the great perforated iron barrels where they were kept for the consumption of the convent. In 1082 Prior Symeon of Winchester induced the monks to eschew meat by introducing delicate fish dinners.

"To every two," at Canterbury on a fish day, "when they had soles, there were 4 soles in a dish; when they had plaice, 2 plaice; when they had herring, 8 herrings; when they had whiting, 8 whiting; when they had mackrell, 2 mackrell; when they had eggs, 10 eggs. If they had anything more allowed them beyond this ordinary fare, it was either cheese, or fruit, or the like."[1]

Beer, cider, and wine, were the principal drink of monks, as it was with us moderns until the introduction of tea, coffee, and similar beverages.

The opinion of St Benedict was that one pint of wine a day was sufficient for each monk, but he added the saving clause, that if the situation of the place, the extraordinary labour, or the heat of summer, created a necessity for more, the superior, in his discretion, could do what to him seemed good.[2]

Altogether, the saint speaks with hesitancy on this matter "of the measure of drink" for monks. "Although we read,"[3] he says further, "that wine is not at all the drink of monks, yet, because in these,

---

[1] Quoted from a Reg. Eccl. Cant. by Battely in his continuation of "The Antiquities of Canterbury" (Somner), Part II. p. 96.
[2] "Rule of St Benedict," chap. xl. pp. 173-75.
[3] "In Vitis Patrum Verba Senior," vol. iv. p. 31.

our times, they will not be so persuaded, let us at least agree to this, not to drink to satiety, but sparingly" (Eccles. xix. 2); adding that where the poverty of the place would not allow the appointed measure, but much less, or perhaps none at all, those who dwelt there were to bless God, and not murmur; and further, that those in more favoured places, upon whom God had bestowed the gift of abstinence, were to know that they should receive their proper reward.

In the face of the statement of the satirists of the monks, of the detracting covetors of their belongings at the dissolution of the religious houses, and even of some modern writers, disinterested research has proved that monks, as a rule, were not given to drunkenness. Their own chroniclers tell us very little about it, and even where it is mentioned, it is always spoken of with sadness and reprobation.

Not infrequently the excessive poorness of the wine and beer is briskly commented on, as when, for instance, Richard de Marisco, a courtier of King John, and afterwards Bishop of Durham, "taking compassion," says the chronicler, "upon the weakness of the convent's drink," gave to the Abbey of St Alban's the tithes of Englingham, in Northumberland, to help them to raise the quality of their ale. Yet for all this, the small beer of this house failed in the desired improvement, so much so that *twice* after the gift had been bestowed complaint was made that the brewing was not up to the mark, and eventually the rectory of Norton, in Hertfordshire, and two-thirds of the tithes of Hartburn, in Northumberland, were given to the monastery that no excuse could be made for the bad quality of the convent's malt liquor.

St Alban's was an abbey of the first and foremost

rank, and would therefore be, according to the Protestant historian, a great and awful example of what monasteries should *not* be in the matter of an undue participation in the good things of the world; yet it is on record that these very monks—monks of the Abbey of St Alban's, in the days of Abbot John XXI.—agreed to give up the use of wine for *fifteen years, and actually did so*, that they might be able to build their refectory and dormitory.

The various dishes were first submitted to the superior and then in order round. On the president sending any special dish to any brother, the receiver rose and bowed his thanks.

The monk drank, holding the cup in both hands, praying in silence meanwhile. The cups used were probably mazers (*murræ*), of the smaller size known as *ciphus*. The meal finished, the remaining bread was covered up to serve for supper, and knife, spoon, and salt placed in order.

The striking of a wooden tablet, or the ringing of the *squilla*, brought the meal to a close, all rising for prayer and grace, after which, signing themselves with the Cross, they left the hall.

The refectory was in the care of an officer called the REFECTIONARIUS, *refectioner*, or *refectorar*. It was his duty to see that that apartment was strewn at the proper times with mats, hay, straw or rushes. The fourteenth-century Consuetudines "In Refectorio," of St Swithin's, Winchester, charges the prior with the strewing of new rush-mats seven times in the year—three in winter and four in summer. Another monastic Consuetudinary orders him to have the refectory swept on Maundy Thursday, after Compline.

He was to see to the comely laying of the tables and

to renew the "canvas" cloths which covered them, from time to time out of the revenues apportioned to him for that purpose, as well as the napkins for the wiping of the cups of silver and wood.[1] After washing, spoons and cups were to be replaced in their "almonries" (cupboards, aumbries), and the platters returned to the attendants of the kitchener. The tables were to be wiped daily, and pots, or noggins,[2] washed (extra?) at specified feasts.

Should it happen that he combined the office of hosteler with that of refectorar, he was to introduce the invited guests to the fratry, placing their pots, according to the degree of each, at the places at which they were to dine, and ministering to them with his hood on.

In some monasteries he distributed the bread and cheese (the latter by weight) to the monks with his own hands. If the abbot dined in community, he was to place basins, water, and a towel at the lavatory before dinner and after dinner in the refectory for his use.[3]

He likewise distributed the *caritas* (charities), unless these were given by the pittancer or dispenser of allowances over commons on festivals, commemorations, anniversaries, etc.

The *caritas*, or *pittance*, that is, indulgence and extra allowance (*præbenda*) in food and drink beyond the limit of the Rule, accruing to monks through the bounty of founders and benefactors, or by gift of the dead, in connection with their commemorations, or

---

[1] At St Swithin's, Winchester, this was the chamberlain's duty.
[2] In the north of England half a pint is called a gill, and the true gill a *noggin*.
[3] The Rule of St Victor provides that the refectioner should find mats, snuffers, and cocks for the lavatory, and to clean the latter as often as was necessary.

granted on the occasion of holidays or grand functions, was dispensed in a special hall or building (erected at a later part of monastic history) called MISERICORD,[1] the eating of flesh being considered prohibited in the refectory. At Durham, the frater house was only used upon great occasions, and was called the *loft*.

By ordinance of Harold, the canons of Waltham, in the eleventh century, had pheasants every festival day from Michaelmas to Lent. By the gift of Bruce, each monk of Melrose was daily supplied with a service of boiled almonds, rice, and milk,[2] pease, or the like, beyond the ordinary quantity or quality of their every-day repast. It was called "The King's Mess."

In his charter to the Church of Lyminge, Kent, Duke Oswulf, in 798, enjoins his anniversary to be kept by the monks there, "with fastings and prayers, singing of Psalms and celebrations of Masses," with the refection of the brethren in food and drink. John Bury, in 1463, by his will left a pittance to the monks of Bury of a French loaf and a quart of wine. John Northampton, draper, left, in 1397, to each of the monks of the London Charterhouse, half a pound of ginger, and every Lent a pound of dates, a pound of figs, and a pound of raisins.[3] At *O Sapientia* (16th December), monks generally feasted on figs, raisins, cakes, and ale, and on "gaudies," or grand days, wonderful confections which the hand of the mediæval *chef* alone could produce, were set forth in the misericord by the pittancier.[4] It might have been upon such

---

[1] Applied also to the country hospital of a town or city monastery.

[2] In another house honey was given to monks in Lent to sweeten their hard pulse.

[3] Wheat and milk for "frimite" was a pittance at Barking Nunnery on St Alburg's Day.

[4] *Pitanceria*—the office of the pittancier.

an occasion in the days of King Hal that "after Evensonge" a rib of beef and a "surloin" was delivered to Master Goodnestoun "for young monks" at Christ's Church, Canterbury.[1]

In the misericord also the convalescents, after their frequent bleedings, took their extras and dispensations necessitated by their weak condition. For the use of the monks of Binham the church of Little Ryburgh paid five marks towards providing wine *in munitione* when they were bled!

As with other departments of the monastery, the food consumed in the refectory was provided from lands particularly set apart for the purpose. Manors were frequently given to abbeys for providing various things, and supplying various departments of the house. Thus the town of Sandwich was appropriated to the clothing and table of the Christ Church monks at Canterbury, being worth fifty pounds a year. The windmills of Edgefield and Wells were charged with a mark and a half to provide two cassocks and three other garments (*stragulæ*), while a further provision was made that on those days when the monks of Binham did not have gruel or cheese by custom, they were for the future to be furnished by the Church of Ryburgh. In 1198 King Richard I. gave the Old Church of St Mary, Scarborough, with the chapels, including that within the Castle, to the Abbey of Citeaux, in Burgundy, for the purpose of making three days' provision for members of the Cistercian Order attending the annual General Chapter there. Much would be received by way of rents paid by tenants of abbey lands in kind—capons, eggs, fish, fruit, etc.

---

[1] *See* a document of City of Canterbury, dated 25, Henry VIII., printed in BRENT's "Canterbury in the Olden Time."

The commons of the monks were entered in a book called "Liber Viventium"; the meat being cut into commons for each monk by an officer called *Particularius*.

That the moderate living, restricted diet, and no less the regular habits of monastic life, was conducive to longevity is amply proved by the vigorous old age so often found in members of the most severe of all orders of monastics—the Carthusian. It is on record that a deputation of twenty-seven monks of this order once visited the Pope at Avignon, the majority of whom were considerably over ninety years of age, and the youngest eighty-eight. In the English Carthusian Monastery of Witham died a certain "Brother Aynard," who had reached the remarkable age of one hundred and twenty-six years. He had spent his whole life in religion, having been received into the community when quite a child.

During dinner all the gates of the monastery were closed, and no visitor could be admitted. After dinner, in some houses, the brethren went to take their meridian sleep in the dormitory, in others to walk, talk, or read in the appointed places, or went in procession to the cemetery to pray among the graves of their departed brethren, for whom they had a continual remembrance.

The community having left the refectory, an officer called the almoner, or his servants, were to collect the fragments [1] and distribute them to the poor,[2] the widow and the orphan, the sick and infirm;[3] the poor scholars, children of the almonry, receiving their portion from the novice's table.

---

[1] Of the charity, as it was called, all monks and friars in theory lived on the alms of the faithful.

[2] WILKINS, "Concilia," vol. ii. p. 246.

[3] Anything the outside sick asked for was to be procured if possible.

"Ther was certayne poore children," says the "Durham Rites," "called the children of the almery, which was brought upp in learninge and mantayned with the almose of the house, having dyett in a lofte on the north side of the abbey gates . . . which had a long porch over the gates, . . . and at either side of the said porch there was a stair to go up to it. . . . They had their meate from the novice's table by the clerke of the convent, oute att a window where the said clerke did louke to them to see that they kept good order. And the meate and drink of the foresaid children was what the master of the novices and the monks had left and reserved, and it was carried in at a door adjoyning to the great kitchen window into a little vault at the west end of the frater house like unto a pantry, and had a window in it where one or two of the children did receive their meat and drink of the said clerke out of the covey or pantry window so called, and carried it to the almery (*aumbry* —cupboard) or loft."[1]

These doles of food and clothing to the needy was distributed in an apartment set apart for the purpose, and called the ALMONRY, or *eleemosynaria*, from the *alms* so given. Its position was invariably adjacent to a principal entrance to the monastery. At Canterbury, Durham, and other places, the choristers, or almonry children, were lodged in it.

> "The Aumanere a rod schalle have in hande,
> An office for almes, I understande ;
> Alle the broken mete he kepys in wait
> To dele to pore men at the gate."[2]

Beer was brought into the refectory to give to the poor. The allowances variated with the degree of the festival. At Glastonbury and other places, specified days were set apart for the distribution of alms—as, for instance, Wednesdays and Fridays. The daily portion of bread and beer of a deceased brother was

---

[1] Rev. J. RAINE, "Durham Rites" (1593), § 48.
[2] "Boke of Curtasye."

given to the poor for thirty days, the prayers of the receivers being asked on behalf of the dead monk.

To the maintenance of the almonry the revenues of churches and lands, in addition to the alms of the abbot, were frequently devoted, and a tenth of all the monastic proceeds were to be given in alms to the poor.

The almonry was in charge of the ALMONER, who, in addition to the distribution of alms, performed various other duties. He was to be at the expense of the processions in Lent and Rogations, finding a staff of boxwood for each monk to carry in the latter, and men to clear the way. He also provided the necessaries for the Maundy, wine for certain feasts, and especially for the clerks of St Nicholas and the Boy-Bishop; mats for various places; rushes for the dormitory; ivy leaves (at Easter) for the cloister and chapter; rods (discipline) for the chapter, chapel, and boys' school; brooms, plates, baskets, and sweepers for the refectory. He was to sweep the dormitory walls annually, and to clean it; to make out the *brevia* (or annunciation of the monks) and give them to the chantor; to send the accounts of the decease of brethren to affiliated or neighbouring houses; to have a servant on constant guard at the gates of the locutory to honourably admit visitors; and the care of the monks' garden.

In the distribution of food he was to reserve the nicest pieces left for the sick and infirm poor, and to arrange that they ate them privately, and apart from the other poor. By the "Norman Institutes" it was a part of his duty to search and find out sick, infirm, and poor persons. To aid him, he was to have the assistance of two servants who were to send out of the house all women found there before he entered to console the sick and administer to their requirements. Should the sick person be a woman, one of the servants performed this office. His alms were disposed of under the direction of the abbot or prior.

Annually, against Christmas, he provided the cloth and shoes for widows, and orphans, and others in most need, and on Maundy Thursday distributed among the monks their gift of money for the poor.

The almoner at Durham had charge of the bridges; at Lincoln he was called the hospitaller, and at St Paul's (where he was one of the minor canons) the eight singing boys were under his care. In some houses, when the business of the house required it, he could go out without asking leave for one day, but he was to return upon the same day. In the larger convents he had frequently an assistant, or assistants (*sub-almoner*).

The hospitality dispensed at a great abbey was a distinguished feature in monastic *régime*, and the cost incurred enormous. As a bounden religious duty, it was strictly enjoined and maintained, even at times when it plunged the house into debt or drove the brethren to extremely short commons.

Any *bonâ fide* traveller, whatever his position or rank, could claim food and shelter at a monastery door without any fear of refusal; bed and board being practically given free, as it was entirely left to the religious disposition of the receiver as to what "alms" he should bestow in return.

To the guest-house of a monastery, wayfaring people, clerical and lay, came in the Middle Age as nineteenth-century folk do to a large hotel. The king and his court, comprising many hundreds of persons, the bishops and the nobles with their retinues and other travelling and wandering folk, gentle and simple, would put up at a monastery for days, and in the former cases for weeks and months together.[1] It was an acknowledged custom for sovereigns to "keep Christmas," Easter, and other great feasts, at a monastery of their choice.

King Edward I., with his army, made a three months' stay at Lanercost Abbey. Peterborough Abbey spent many thousands of pounds in entertaining King Edward II. Glastonbury Abbey, on one occasion, entertained 200 knights and their retainers, and upon another, 500 travellers on horseback.

In 1378, when King Richard II. held a Parliament at Gloucester Abbey, he was entertained in the abbot's lodge, his Privy Council in the chief guest-chamber, the Common Council in the chapter house, and the Commission on the Law of Arms in the refectory. Under such an appropriation, the monks were driven from pillar to post, dining at one time in their dormitory, or sleeping apartment, at another, in their school-house, and, finally, in the orchard, as their cloister-garth was in the possession of ball-players and wrestlers who trod down the sward, and turned the whole precinct into a veritable fair.

At St Augustine's, Canterbury, in 1295, 60 knights and 4500 lesser personages, besides judges, were guests of the abbot. In 1309, £300 was spent on an installation feast, at which 6000 folk were regaled with 3000 dishes and minstrelsy.

Not only had the monasteries to provide a contingent of knights and men-at-arms for the royal service, but in times of civil war soldiers were quartered on them. Moreover, they were frequently called upon to find

---

[1] Three days was the ordinary period of entertainment.

pensions, subsidies, and gifts for the king's favourites, to endow scholars of the king's nomination, and, further, to benefice and pension them. Again, the custom of corodies was a grievous tax upon religious houses, as this method of disposal of old servants was a favourite one. Thus corodies were granted under the privy seal to yeomen, ushers of the wardrobe and chamber, clerks of the kitchen, gentlemen of the royal chapel, and royal servants in other departments.[1] Besides all this, they were the asylums or houses of noble poverty, a refuge for honourable families fallen from their high estate. The son of the Duke of Buckingham writes to King Henry VIII. that he "hath no dwelling-place meet for him to inhabit," and so was "fain to live poorly at board in an abbey this four years day, with his wife and seven children.[2]

Such lavish and indiscriminate hospitality—and no one was refused, lest perchance an angel should be passing unawares—not infrequently brought many of the houses upon the verge of bankruptcy, involving them in heavy burdens for many years very grievous to be borne, and taxing the resources of the house to the uttermost. Even great men being entertained elsewhere, would, without any qualm of conscience, send all their following of attendants to partake of the hospitality of the convent, for, in those days, the scarcity of ready money made men's wits keen in the art of getting something for nothing. What they took of the monastery, they would argue they took as a *right*. For had not all and every of these great men— and it was such as they who took the utmost advan-

---

[1] *See* GASQUET, "Henry VIII. and the English Monasteries," vol. i. pp. 28, 29.
[2] *Ibid.* vol. i. p. 34.

tage of the hospitality offered by the religious houses, and not so much the poor, every-day traveller—connections by the score who had endowed or enriched the monasteries with houses and lands, gifts, donations, and what not? Therefore, had they not a perfect right to share in the *douceurs* of their pious relations and progenitors? Some founders and donors even reserved to themselves and theirs such a right of unlimited free board and lodgment.

So great at length became these excesses and impositions, that King Edward I. forbade any such to eat or lodge in a religious house, unless formally invited by the superior, and even should he be founder, his consumption was to be moderate, the poor only to be received gratuitously.

Only those of the highest rank were actually lodged in the monastery, the guests being lodged in the GUEST-HOUSE, or hostry,[1] sometimes a part of the monastery itself, at others a separate building. In the larger monasteries it usually comprised a great hall, divided into aisles, or alleys—the guesten or guest-hall, serving as a refectory—with a number of chambers, or sleeping-rooms, or oriels, or recesses for private conversation at the sides, and extra apartments and rooms for servants. The halls of the guest-houses at Clugny and Farfa were lined with beds, those for men being arranged on one side, those for women on the other; movable tables being ranged down the centre at meal-times.[2]

At the Abbeys of St Alban's, St Edmund's at Bury, Beaulieu, and other great houses, a suite of apartments were specially set apart for the king's use. Benedictine abbots received illustrious guests at their own table in

---

[1] *Hospitium, Domus Hospitium, Hospice, Hostel.*
[2] *Vide* "Rule of St Benedict."

the refectory; those of the Cistercians dined with them in their own hostel; in the Cluniac houses the arrival of guests was unnoticed by the abbots. The larger monasteries had several houses or sets of apartments for guests, arranged for monks, for persons of gentle birth, and for poor travellers.

The guest-house appears to have had no general local position. At Westminster it was what is known as the Jerusalem chamber, and part of the abbot's lodge; at Worcester it was near the prior's house; at Furness near the gate-house; at Finchale over the gate; at Sherborne on the west side of the cloister, and so at Durham.

"There was a famouse house of hospitallitie, called the Geste Halle, within the Abbey Garth of Durham, on the weste syde, towards the water, the Terrer of the house being master thereof, as one appoynted to give intertaynment to all staits, both noble, gentle, and what degree soever that came thither as strangers, ther intertaynment not being inferior to any place in Ingland, both for the goodness of ther diett, the sweete and daintie furniture of ther lodgings, and generally all things necessarie for travcillers. This haule is a goodly brave place, much like unto the body of a church, with verey fair pillers supporting yt on ether syde, and in the mydest of the haule a most large rannge for the fyer. The chambers and lodginges belonging to yt weare swetly keept, and so richly furnyshed that they weare not unpleasant to ly in, especially one chamber called the Kyng's Chambers, deservinge that name, in that the Kyng himselfe myght verie well have lyne in yt for the princelynes thereof."[1]

In the year 1260, John (de Hertford), Abbot of St Alban's, built a noble hall for the use of the guests and strangers frequenting that abbey. It is described as having many chambers, an inner parlour having a chimney with a noble picture, an entry, and a small

---

[1] "Durham Rites." The hostry was sometimes called *palatium*—palace, cuciently meaning a place of short residence.

hall. In addition to all this luxury, this hall had a most noble entry, with a porch, and many fair bed-chambers, with their inner chambers, to receive strangers honourably. From this description we learn that this hostry was divided into two sets of apartments, one for persons of rank, the other for common travellers.

At Canterbury the guest-hall was forty feet broad and not less than one hundred and fifty feet long, and so situated that the privacy of the monks or the business of their servants should be least interfered with.

Frequently the guest-houses had chapels attached to them, where travellers returned thanks for a safe journey, and made offerings for the poor. At Finchale, Malling, and other places, it adjoined the gate-house. Peterborough preserves an example, and at Winchester is a timbered building, formerly a lesser guest house.

"Let all guests who come to the monastery," says the Rule of St Benedict, " be entertained like Christ Himself, because He will say: 'I was a stranger, and ye took Me in'[1] Let due honour be paid to all, especially to those who are of the household of the faith, and to travellers." As soon as a guest was announced, the superior or the brethren were to go to meet him "with all show of charity." After prayer together, the kiss of peace was to be offered in all humility. At the arrival or departure of all guests, " Christ—Who is received in their persons " — was to be " adored in them," by bowing the head or even prostrating on the ground. After prayer, the superior, or one appointed by him, was to sit with the guest, while the Law of God was read before him for his edification, and afterwards all kindness was to be shown him. For the sake of the guest, the superior might break his fast, except on a principal

---

[1] St Matt. xxv. 35.

fast-day. The abbot was to pour water on the hands of the guests, and both himself and the whole community wash their feet. Special care was to be taken in the reception of the poor and strangers, who were to be diligently entertained, "because in them Christ is more truly welcomed."

The kitchen for the abbot and guests was to be apart by itself, that strangers coming at unlooked-for hours might not disturb the brethren. Two capable brothers were to have charge of this kitchen for a year, with such help as they required, to avoid murmuring. Should their time not be fully occupied in this place, they were to go forth to other work.

The care of the guest-house was to be entrusted to a brother "whose soul is possessed with the fear of God."[1] He was called the HOSTILLAR, or hospitaller. He was to see that a sufficient number of beds were prepared there, and that the sheets and pillows and table-linen were kept sweet and clean. He had also annually the best of the old shoes (*Talaria— taleaparia*) for visitors that wanted slippers to wear in the morning.[2]

By the "Norman Statutes" he was to have in the hostry all things necessary for sleeping and eating, and overlook the behaviour of the servants and strange clerks dining with the abbot's consent in the refectory. No one but he was, on any account, to associate or converse with the guests, unless he was so bidden, but should he chance to meet or see them, after humbly saluting them, and asking their blessing (*petita benedictione*), he was to pass on, saying it was not lawful

---

[1] "Rule of St Benedict," chap. liii. pp. 217-21.
[2] Monasteries regularly employed and paid a shoemaker to make shoes for the poor, supplying the leather from their own tanneries.

for him to talk with a guest.[1] For the sake of sociality at request he could drink with any ordinary person without leave, but could not dine with any save by the abbot's express permission.

It would appear that his hostry duties did not exhaust his energies, for he had, moreover, the conduct of strange monks through the cloister to pray in the church; to receive parents and friends coming to see the monks;[2] to introduce seculars, or lay folk, seeking the fraternity of the house to the chapter; to take persons to the particular officer they desired to see; and to bring the novices, at their first entrance into the house, to the chapter, and instruct them in the manner of making their first petition.

In many instances the hospitality given by the monks in the hostry was supplied from lands and tithes, etc., especially given for the purpose, as, for instance, the churches of Eglingham, Hartburn, and Norton, which were granted to the monks of Tynemouth Priory "to mend their ale, and enlarge their means of hospitality."

Adjacent to the guest-house was an edifice, or a single apartment called *Pro-aula*, or GREETING-HOUSE (*Salutatorium*). It was probably a kind of general parlour for visitors, and the place where persons were first received, and must not be confounded with a very similar apartment called the LOCUTORIUM, or *spekehouse* of the monks. In this private, forensic, or outer parlour, the brethren held communication with their relatives and friends, or with persons having business with the house. In it a fugitive monk was re-invested

---

[1] "Rule of St Benedict," chap. liii. p. 221.
[2] The Feast of the Nativity of the Blessed Virgin Mary was a grand visiting day.

in his habit after his reception, and its position was invariably on the western, or south-western side of the cloister, or handy to the abbot's lodge.

### THE CALEFACTORY

There was also a very similar apartment called the CALEFACTORY, *day or common room or house*,[1] and reserved for the exclusive use of the monks. In this place they assembled for recreation and conversation (talk—*parle*—hence *Domus Conversorum*), which was prohibited in the cloister and other places. A school was sometimes held in it, processions marshalled where no galilee existed, and the banquet usual at *O Sapientia*. It would be in general use by those requiring the service of the fire, which burned every day in winter, "at snow time," for the use of the monks who were allowed no other fire [2]—"having a fyre keapt in yt all winter, for the mounckes to cum and warme them at, being allowed no fyre but that only."[3] Thus here came the precentor to dry his parchment and prepare his ink, the servants of the sacristan to fill the censers, and the acolytes for their lights. At Kirkham we learn it had a bench table, and at Thornton a series of stalls.

The calefactory frequently adjoined the refectory and the chapter house, forming a part of the substructure under the dormitory.[4] The *Domus Conversorum* of Fountains, erected towards the close of

---

[1] As at *Durham*. "Winter Hall" at *Burton*.
[2] Except the masters and house officers, who each had their own fires.—"Rites of Durham."
[3] So only one fire was allowed in the College Hall at Eton in winter, and then but seldom lighted except on feast days "in honour of God, or of His Mother, or of some other saint."
[4] It seems always to have overlooked a garth, or garden.

the twelfth century, is the largest known, being nearly 300 feet long and 44 feet wide. Above it was the dormitory, both stories communicating with the church at the northern end. At St Alban's, Durham, Westminster, etc., it was in the slype, or vaulted passage, or entry between buildings, and leading into the cloister. There is a fine example of a calefactory at Battle Abbey.

### THE CHAPTER HOUSE

The chapter house (*Domus Capitularis*) was invariably built on the east or south-east side of the cloister garth.[1] Its form was various. That built by Edward the Confessor, at Westminster, was circular, and those erected under the Norman Rule square, as Buildwas, St Mary's Abbey, York, and Wenlock. But of all plans the octagonal was the favourite,[2] although other shapes, as the polygonal, were much used, as at the Priory of Bridlington, which appears from an account taken at the suppression of that house: "It. on the est syde of the same cloister ys a very fayre chapter house, with ix fayre lights about the same, with white glass and sume imagerie, covered with lede spere facyon."

Previous to the ninth century (as at St Gall, Switzerland) an alley of the cloister had served for it, but in that and the following century a separate building was erected.

The chapter house was entered from the cloisters by a door, always within a short distance from the church.

---

[1] "Locus capitulierat claustro contiguus ad orientem."—MARTENE, "De Antiquis Monachorum Ritibus."

[2] The Cistercians subdivided their chapter houses into aisles, or alleys, by ranges of pillars.

That at Westminster is a magnificent ruin of what was once a fine piece of work.[1]

"It is a double doorway," says the late Sir Gilbert Scott, the talented architect, "the outer arch of which is of two foliated orders; one of them contains in the entwined foliage a series of figures, a 'Root of Jesse.' The tympanum is exquisitely decorated with scroll work . . . the doorway [as wide as the vaulting of the cloister] was magnificently decorated with colour and gold, traces of which are still clearly visible."

On the pedestal between the two doors stood a figure of the Blessed Virgin, with a censing angel on either side. Iconoclastic hands have shattered the beauty of the central figure, and barely left enough of the attendant angels to bear witness to their former beauty. In the central boss of the cloister above is still retained the small pulley which centuries ago kept the suspended constantly-burning lamp in position before the image.

Beneath the arch—for, as we are treating of Westminster, we may as well keep to it—the visitor passes into a vestibule—the stones of the left arcade worn away by the feet of the generations of monks walking in pairs to their weekly assemblies—and thence by a flight of steps into the chapter house, the building in which the abbot and monks met daily to consult on

---

[1] The walls of the chapter house at York bear the legend, "Ut rosa flos florum, sic est domus ista domorum."—As the rose among flowers, so this house among (chapter) houses. Over the entrance a sentence of the great founder of the Order was usually placed in some conspicuous place in every Cistercian house: "Bonum est hic esse, quia homo vivit purius, cadit rarius, surgit velocius, incedit cautius, quiescit securius, moritur felicius, purgatur citius, præmiatur copiosius;" which Wordsworth has happily translated thus (*Eccl. Sonnets*):

> Here man more purely lives, less oft doth fall,
> More promptly rises, walks with stricter heed,
> More safely rests, dies happier, is freed
> Earlier from cleansing fires, and gains withal
> A brighter crown.

the discipline of the house and the business of the convent. "It is the house of confession," says Abbot Ware in his "Custumal"; "the house of obedience, mercy and forgiveness; the house of unity, peace, and tranquillity, where the brethren make satisfaction for their faults." The name "chapter house" is derived from the reading of a chapter (*capitulum*) of the Benedictine Rule at the assembly of the monks to discuss the welfare of the house.[1]

The Westminster chapter house roof is supported by a graceful, slender central pillar of polished Purbeck marble, five-and-thirty feet high, the capital, though of marble, richly carved. Round the building, in a double row, run seats of stone under arcades, with trefoiled heads, the upper range for the professed brothers, the lower for those of lesser degree. The marble capitals are carved with foliage, the wall diapered with roses and other flowers. In the days of the monks, the walls beneath the arcades were brilliant with frescoes, some faded vestiges of which still remain in the sedilia, or eastern seats of the abbot and his chief officers, and above the seats by the left of the entrance. The subject on the eastern wall is that of the Doom, or Second Coming of Christ, Who is surrounded with cherubim and seraphim, angels and virtues, to whom He is setting forth the mysteries of redemption; those near the door representing scenes from the Apocalypse.[2]

Above, filling the intervals between the wall spaces, are set a magnificent series of windows, painted with

---

[1] LITTRÉ says, "*Capitulum*" ("little head"), "a pris le sens d'une courte leçon faite dans l'office divin; puis celui du lieu où s'assemblaient les moines et les chanoines parcequ'on y lisait des courtes leçons; et enfin celui de corps même des religieux."

[2] They are between the thirteenth and fifteenth centuries, the latter the work of a monk of the abbey, John of Northampton, in the reign of Edward IV.

the effigies of the Abbots of Westminster, and the chief events of their time; below, one of the finest encaustic tile pavements Time's destroying hand has preserved to us.

In the eyes of the monks the chapter house was no less sacred, as a building, than the church. Frequently a light burnt constantly in it, and another before the door. It may, possibly, in some instances, have contained an altar (as still at Tongres). In the centre, or some other conspicuous place, was set up a great crucifix, sometimes also a pulpit for the occasional lecture (collation), or preaching, and a large coffer called the *trunk*, at the entrance door, facing the abbot's seat, as the place for offenders.[1]

The monastic chapter was held in summer after *Prime* (6 A.M.), in winter after *Tierce* (9 A.M.). A bell rung by the prior called the community together (if they had not proceeded straight from the church to the chapter house), who proceeded in procession to the assembly. Entering the chapter house they performed the *venia*, or inclination to the cross, the abbot's seat, and to one another.

When they were all seated, a novice read out the martyrology, announced the coming festivals, and read a chapter of the Rule (*capitulum*).[2] This finished, the president says in Latin: "Let us speak, touching our Order," and they proceed to the discussion of the day's agenda, *e.g.* the nomination of celebrants and officiating priest for the ensuing week, the infliction of penance and discipline, the commemoration of benefactors, living and departed, and once a year a recital of

---

[1] Petitions were made after this fashion: "I ask and beseech God's mercy and yours for——," etc.

[2] In a visitation at Hales Abbey the monks are ordered to expound the Scriptures.

charters. At the conclusion of chapter, the "tabula" was struck to remind all present of the frailty of human life.

In the chapter house the novice was solemnly admitted to the order, the superior elected, and the great house officers confirmed. In the chapter house also the punishments due to delinquents were assigned and carried out:—for lesser offences, the ignominy of the penitent's bench (*trunculum*), standing before the chapter house door, or outside the quire;[1] for faults more grave, the sharp discipline with rod and scourge, the culprit being tied to the central pillar, or lying or sitting on the floor, and flogged before the whole assembly;[2] and for offences yet more aggravated the solitary cell, with a bread-and-water diet, relieved only by a dish of raw herbs, or the prison in the infirmary "LANTERN." At Durham, the penitential cells adjoined the chapter house,[3] and offenders were at once, on delivery of sentence, consigned to them. It appears that this prison was quite dark, and that the refectory monk was not only secluded, but chained,[4] his food being let down to him by a rope through a trap-door. That the monastic prison was by no means a pleasant abode is proved by the names by which it was known at various places—"Little Ease," "Hell" (as at Ely), etc. At Bridlington Priory Church, York, against the south wall, and near the south-west door,

---

[1] It is recorded of one so humiliated at his position that he took the stool by the leg and hurled it into the nave.

[2] The younger brethren received their due meed of chastisement not in chapter but elsewhere; at Westminster in the infirmary of St Catherine.

[3] This may have been the case at Westminster with the crypt, or underground apartments, leading from the vestibule of the chapter house.

[4] DU CANGE s. v., "Lanterna," and the Cluniac "Statutes" of PETER THE VENERABLE. It was called Isaac's Hole at Michelham Priory, Sussex.

is an iron "joug," or collar, which was used for punishment.

The stern measures taken by the men of mediæval days to repress vice and evil inclination, cause folk, in these modern and over-lenient days, to stand almost aghast. Especially is this shown in their treatment of the insane, who were really imagined to be possessed of the devil. The sad story of Alexander de Langley, at one time Prior of Wymondham, and afterwards keeper of the abbot's seal at St Alban's, is a case in point. Owing to over-study, he had the misfortune to lose his reason, and his brethren at St Alban's, being unable to endure the outbursts of his frenzy, he was publicly censured in chapter by the abbot, and flogged "to a copious effusion of blood." He was then removed to Binham Priory, where, according to the abbot's command, he was kept fettered in solitary confinement until his death, on the 26th December 1224, and was there buried in his chains.

A common way of getting rid of an obstinate or objectional brother was to send him to a distant cell belonging to the mother house, or from cell to cell— a mode of punishment thought very grievous. On the other hand, monks were sent to different cells of the house as a recreation, staying in them by turns.

In some places the Maundy, or ceremonial washing of feet on that Thursday, was performed in the chapter house, at others in the cloister (Durham), or in the presbytery (Canterbury). Here, also, was carried from the infirmary chapel the dead monk, ere he was borne out, with solemn dirge and requiem, to his last resting-place in the outer churchyard. Here, also, before interment was permitted in churches, were the abbots, laymen of rank, and principal benefactors brought for honoured burial. John of Kent, Abbot of Fountains, in 1247, was thus buried in the chapter house there, before the abbot's seat, where his grave-stone still lies in its original place.

In some convenient spot handy to the refectory door was placed a LAVATORY,[1] or washing-place—a cistern or water trough of stone, lined with lead, between the buttresses, the water being conveyed to it by means of leaden pipes. Near by was an almery, or recess for the wiping towels, shut in by a door of pierced work to admit the air. Here the monks washed and wiped their hands before entering the refectory for dinner.

"Within the cloyster garth, over against the frater house dour," says the "Rites of Durham," "was a fair laver or counditt for the monncks to wash their hands and faces at, being made in forme round, covered with lead, and all of marble saving the verie uttermost walls. Within the which walls you may walke round about the laver of marble, having many little counditts or spouts of brasse, with xxiiij cockes of brasse round about yt, having in yt vij faire wyndowes of stone-woorke, and in the top of it a fair dove-cotte, covered fynly over above with lead, the workmanship both fine and costly, as is apparent till this daie. And adjoyninge to the est syde of the counditt dour there did hing a bell[2] to geve warning, at a leaven of the clock, for the monncks to cumme, wash, and dyne, having ther closetts or almeries en either syde of the frater house dour keapt alwaies with swete and clene towels, as is aforesaid, to drie ther hands."[3]

The almeries for towels are more fully described as being "joyned in the wall, all the forepart of the almerie was carved work, for to give ayre to the towels, and there was a door in the forepart of the almerie,

---

[1] Also applied to that part of a religious house where the dead were washed immediately after their decease.
[2] The place where the bell hung can be seen at Gloucester.
[3] Remains in centre of the cloister garth.

and every mounche had a key for the said almerie, wherein did hinge clean towels for the mounches to drye their hands on when they washed and went to dinner."[1] At St Augustine's Canterbury, six towels were to be given out every Sunday morning before procession—four for the monks, one for the claustral prior, and one at the small lavatory by the church door.

Such lavatories remain in several of the old monastic cloisters, notably at Gloucester, Norwich, and Westminster, that at the former place being the largest and most ornamental in the country.[2] The *Compotus* for the Priory of Finchale has an entry under the date 1367–68 : "*Pro lotoriis factis in claustro* xxxvii$^s$." Then inventories taken in view of the suppression of the monasteries in 1539 also mention them, *e.g.* that of the treasury of Peterborough : "In the cloyster, item one conduit, or lavatory, of tynne, with divers coffers and seats there," and of Merivale, "a laver of ley mettall, and leade before the same laver."

In the Rule of St Victor it was the duty of the refectioner to find mats, snuffers, and cocks for the lavatory, and to clean it as often as necessary.

In some places, as the Chartreux, Citeaux, and Clugny, a place used for washing the dead in churches was so called.

### THE DORMITORY

The dormitory, dorter, or sleeping-place of the monks was built invariably either on the eastern (as

---

[1] Such a towel-almery, with its carved open-work door, may still be seen opposite the lavatory door in Gloucester cloisters, also at Westminster, beside the refectory door, but without its door.

[2] In the centre of the north side of the Canterbury cloister, opposite the refectory door, are two arches wider than the rest, under which runnels of water were conducted from a fountain.

at Bridlington Priory) or western (as at St Alban's and Durham) side of the cloister. Occasionally (as at Chester and Winchester) it stood at right angles to it. It always communicated direct with the church, generally by one of the transepts, a convenience of access to the minster for the night services.

At Hexham the religious descended by a noble flight of stairs; at Westminster by a bridge running accross the end of the sacristy; at Canterbury by a gallery in the west gable wall of the chapter house, over the doorway and cloister roof into an upper chapel in the north wing of the main transept; and at St Alban's by a series of wall passages along the southern wall of the east aisle of the transept and south presbytery aisle to the stairs. At Wenlock the dormitory was connected with a vaulted chamber within the church at the western end of the south aisle, and thence by means of a newell staircase, through the wall down into the church. At Fountains and Kirkstall the monks passed through the cloister.[1]

By the Rule of St Benedict[2] each monk was to sleep in a separate bed, with bedding suited to their manner of life. If it were possible, all were to sleep in one place (*in uno loco*), but should the number of brethren not allow of this, they were to repose by tens or twenties with the seniors who had charge of them, the senior or prefect being called *decanus*, or the guardian of ten. Further, the younger brethren (juniors) were not to have their beds apart by themselves, but among those of the seniors.

---

[1] The most complete specimen of an ancient monastic dormitory in existence is perhaps that of the Convent of the White Friars at Coventry, now a part of the workhouse. Cleeve and Ford Abbeys, Devonshire, afford other examples with the partitions now removed.

[2] "Rule of St Benedict," chap. xxii. pp. 119-21.

The "Decretals" of Lanfranc, Archbishop of Canterbury (eleventh century), in ordering the master of the novices so to wake the children in the morning as not to disturb the abbot,[1] shows that the superior was supposed to sleep in the common dormitory with his monks; yet the Synod of London, held in the reign of King Henry I., was obliged to order that abbots should eat and sleep in the same house with their monks, unless prevented by any necessity. That children slept in the dormitory with the religious is instanced by the nuns of Romsey and some members of religious houses in Lincolnshire taking children to sleep in their dormitories.

Anciently there were no divisions in the dormitory, the beds of the monks being exposed. The Synod of Exeter,[2] held in 1287, treats of this practice:—

"De dormitorio. *Cellas in dormitorio* esse, Benedictus papa duodecimus prohibuit; nosque hoc adjiciendum decernimus, quod ad tollatur omnis mali suspicio, lecti monachorum velaminibus, ci quæ fuerint, amotis, et perticis ita sint ordinati, ut in ipsis lectis existentes vel juxta, sine obstaculo quo cunque die noctuque continue valeaut a custodibus ordinis, et aliis transeuntibus intueri."

But in later days it became the custom to separate the bed of each sleeper from the others by means of curtains, or light erections of wood, which, eventually closed by a door, became a "cell" of wainscot, quite enclosed off from the central avenue.[3] The "Durham

---

[1] The same "Decretals" of Lanfranc order the chamberlain to change the hay in the monks' pallets once a year, and once annually to clean out the dormitory. The monastic dormitories were also usually strewn with rushes twice a year, generally on the festival days of the Nativity and Assumption of the Blessed Virgin, the walls swept yearly, and the place cleaned in some instances three days before the Feast of the Assumption of St Mary.

[2] Cap. xi. (WILKINS' "Concilia").

[3] Cells were introduced by the Carthusians, one point in whose rule was complete isolation or seclusion. The stone divisions between the cells at Durham remained till the present century.

Rites,"[1] treating of the dorter, says, that every monk had a little chamber of wainscot to himself partitioned off, and the novices likewise. The windows were towards the cloister, every chamber a window, and in every chamber a desk for their books, for reading or study at the time of the meridian or noontide repose.

The furnishing of a monk's cell was very simple—an oaken bedstead, a bed of blue saye (tester with canopy, etc.), a palliasse, bolster, rug, blankets, and coverlid of fur or sheep-skin; a round mat at the side, a bench at the foot, and a perch whereon to hang the sleeper's day clothes at the bed-head.

By the Rule of St Benedict,[2] the monks were to sleep clothed (exchanging their day for a night habit), girded with girdles or cords, but without their knives at their sides, lest they should do themselves injury in their sleep. The beds were to be frequently examined by the abbot, to see if anything might perchance be hidden away there which the occupant had not permission to have.

Entering the dormitory after Compline, each monk stood before his bed, saying privately the Compline of Our Lady. The bed was then prepared for the night, the upper garments taken off and laid aside. On getting up for midnight Matins, the *Ave Maria* was said, Christ being born at midnight. Upon the second rising for Prime, they signed their foreheads with the cross, said the *Credo* and Prime of the Little Office of Our Lady, and, having turned back their beds, went to the lavatory to wash and comb, and thence to Church for Prime.

A candle was to burn constantly throughout the

---

[1] "Rites of Durham," § 43.
[2] "Rule of St Benedict," chap. xxii. p. 119.

night in the dormitory, until the morning. In later days, this light was supplied by a standard of stone with cressets. At *Durham*, five lights were to burn from twilight to dawn. In an account of goods taken at Pipewell Abbey at the suppression of that house, in the thirtieth year of the reign of King Henry VIII., appears, entered as in the dorter, "the munkes selles and one laumpe of laten." This lamp was sometimes known as the "Vigil Lantern."

In the centre of the broad passage-way—which was covered with matting, and the remainder of the floor with hay or rushes—was generally a cross, at which any violator of the strict silence rule did the ascribed penance.[1] This strict or solemn silence commenced after the recitation of the Compline Office, and after the departure of the monks to the dormitory, all the doors of the house were rigorously locked, and all the keys handed over to the care of the responsible officer: "All the dures, both of the seller, the fratre, the dorter, and the cloisters, were locked at evin, at vi of the clocke, and the keys delivered to the sup prior untyl vii of the clocke the next morninge,"[2] who distributed them to the various officers. At the Charterhouse, the visitors of King Henry VIII. mention twenty-four keys to the cloister door in the hands of twenty-four persons; to the buttery door, twelve sundry keys in twelve men's hands.

Rigid watch was kept all night by one of the chief obedientiaries, and a responsible officer paid a visit to each monk's cell before retiring for the night. At Durham this duty was assigned to the sub-prior, whose chamber

---

[1] The "Durham Rites" expressly say "they were allowed no fyre in the dormitory."
[2] "Durham Rites," § 43.

was over the "*dorter dour,*" *i.e.* the first in the dormitory, "to the intent to heare that none should stir or go forth. And his office was to goe every nighte as a privy watch before mydnyght and after mydnyght to every mounche's chamber, and to call at his chamber dour upon him by his name, to se that none of them should be lacking or stolen furth." He had also to see that there were no disorders amongst them. In the fifteenth century complaint was made to the bishop of the diocese, of the monks of Peterborough dancing in their dormitory at night.

The WATCHERS (*excubitores*) had for their use watching chambers (*excubitoria*). In the Cathedral Church of Lincoln there is such a chamber of timber, formerly used by the searchers of the church, and under which they had, previously to watching, an allowance of bread and beer every night. In a monastic church part of the watcher's duty was to keep up the lights before the altars, awaken the monks, and ring the first peal for Matins.

The explorator's duty was to search (with a lantern, both summer and winter) and see that silence was observed in the cloister. When searching, questions were asked by signs, and replies given in the same way. The same, or a similar officer, performed a scrutiny of the quire during the night office. By the "Anglo-Saxon" and "Norman Institutes" the searcher is called *circa*, or circuitor. From his place in quire [1] he carefully watched and noted the absent and other offenders, whom he reported in chapter on the following day. Should any sleeping brother fall under his ken, he took up his dark lantern (*absconsa*) and flashed it on the sleeper's face, and if this failed to wake him he left it on the desk

---

[1] His little stone desk may still be seen near the entrance of the quire of Gloucester Cathedral.

before him, that when he awoke, he could take it up in his turn and seek out another offender.[1]

Shortly after midnight the monks were awakened by the night watcher, who went the length of the dormitory calling each monk to the Nocturns, or night services. To accomplish this he smote thrice upon each cell door with a wooden hand-mallet, exclaiming as he did so "*Benedicamus Domino,*" the newly-awakened monk replying "*Deo Gratias.*" By the time he had reached the last cell, each monk was ready at his cell door to fall into procession to the quire, headed by a novice carrying a light.

Sometimes the awakening was accomplished by the ringing of a small bell (*squilla*) hanging by a cord in the dormitory, and similar to the ones used in the infirmary and refectory.

St Benedict appointed "that monks should sleep ready clothed, that they might always be ready when the signal for rising for Matins was given, when they were to rise speedily and hasten each one to come before his brother to the work of God."

At the conclusion of Matins the monks sometimes returned again to the dormitory for a short interval, and again after dinner for repose and study. St Benedict, however, does not provide for the former, as he says "the time that remains after Matins,[2] let it be employed in study by those brethren who are somewhat behind-hand in the Psalter and lessons."[3] This was in winter-time, *i.e.* from the 1st November till Easter; but in summer, *i.e.* from Easter to the 1st November,

---

[1] The Egyptian monks had a like officer who went round the monks' cells silently and listened outside for the detection of abuses.

[2] Called *Vigiliæ*, because they were said during the night watches. *Vigiliarii*, or *Vigill-Galli*, from the wakefulness of cocks.

[3] "Rule of St Benedict," chap. viii. p. 75.

Matins having been celebrated, a short interval followed, in which the brethren went forth for the necessities of nature, and afterwards Lauds were said about the break of day.[1]

The latrines (*necessarium, gong, secretior domus*), privy, or *rere dorter* were immediately in communication with the dormitory. This apartment is always distinguishable by its position over a water-course, necessary for flushing. It was well lighted, partitioned into little openings from off a central passage, and provided with soft hay.

The officer called the CHAMBERLAIN (*Camerarius*) had the oversight of the dormitory,[2] providing from his fund clothes (both day and night), bed furniture, sheets, shirts, socks, and other necessaries. He had to see to the shaving of the monks, and had the conduct of their annual[3] bathing, prescribed by an Act of Lanfranc, "washing their bodies with warm water in the baths just before Christmas Day." For the service of the baths he was to hire a servant, and another for the bathed, who was probably the sub-chamberlain, for the monks went to the baths under his direction, and in the absence of his superior officer a use of the baths could be granted by him with the abbot's consent. He also accompanied the servant of the bathers in bringing and carrying back to the dormitory the clothes of the bathers, which were to be counted both in the bringing and the returning.

In all great monasteries the chamberlain was an

---

[1] Called *Matutini* because said in the early morning.
[2] At Abingdon his chamber was in the dormitory.
[3] At Durham three times a year. St Benedict in his Rule (chap. xxxvi. p. 159) allows the use of the baths to the sick, "but to those who are well, and especially to the young," it was to be seldom granted.

officer of some importance, frequently acting as treasurer, and general overseer of the officers of other departments. Under him were the servants of the laundry, the shoemakers, skin dressers (*peltmen*), tailors, etc. At Durham his chequer was near the abbey gates, under which was the tailors' workshop.

### THE INFIRMARY

The infirmary (*Fermory*) was not only a hospital for the sick and infirm, but an asylum for aged monks. The prison (*laterna, lying-house, helle*) of the refractory was also within it. Adjoining either it or the dormitory was a chamber set apart for the use of the bled.

Sometimes the infirmary formed part of the range of monastic buildings; at others it was a separate group of buildings ranged round a second court, or garth. It took the form of a long hall, with the beds set in the aisles. At the east end there was a chapel, and on one side a garden or court for the recreation of the sick, surrounded by little cloisters as at Canterbury, Gloucester, and Westminster. Sometimes the *Herbarium*, herbary, or herb garden was attached. It had also its special kitchen and a bathhouse. The infirmarer's house adjoined it, as still remains at Ely and Westminster. For persons not sufficiently ill to be sent to the infirmary there was the "oriel," a small room or chamber. There was one at St Alban's.

Leachcraft was a special study among monks, such as the Benedictines of St Vitalis. Ravenna, who had a *depôt* of pharmacy for all kinds of medicine, a complete surgery, anatomical subjects, and instruments for all kinds of operations. Abbots and some of the monks themselves were frequently physicians.

Flebotomy, or blood-letting (*minution*)[1] was a remedy often resorted to, necessitating a rest in the infirmary for a week or longer period. *Spiritus uberior exit per phlebotomiam* was one of its good results; another, *stomachum ventremque coercet*. It was used in lieu of physic to keep them healthy and low, thus assisting in subjugating the passions of the flesh, the coarse fare having a tendency to heat the blood.

The times of bleeding varied in the different orders. A constitution of Pope Innocent III., and another of Pope Calixtus III., obliged the monk-canons of St Peter's to draw blood six times a year *in pegno di continenza*.[2] In Premonstratensian monasteries the religious were bled six times a year; the Carthusian and canons of St Victor five times; the Cistercians and Dominicans, four times a year. The monks of Ely indulged in the luxury every six weeks, and the Augustinian canons of Barnwell (Cambridgeshire) every seven.[3]

An abbot who permitted the indulgence of bleeding, with the aftermath of a week's convalescence among the extra good things of the infirmary, or misericord, four instead of three times a year, was regarded as a great benefactor. Thus, an abbot of Peterborough was long held in grateful memory because he allowed the terms to be kept punctually. In some abbeys the bleeding operation was conducted in a chamber off the dormitory: others had a bleeding-house called FLEBOTOMARIA.

"Irksomeness of life in the cloister," "long continuance of silence," "fatigue in the quire," "extension of

---

[1] *Minutati*—those who had been bled.
[2] BARACCONI, "Rioni," p. 704.
[3] Such bleeding at fixed intervals was prevalent in the middle of the present century.

fasting," "sleeplessness and overwork," are all mentioned as causes which might compel the monks to resort to it.

Those who wished to be bled were to ask permission in chapter, and, having received a formal licence, were to attend Mass. After the Gospel they were to leave the quire, and to be bled in the fermory, where they were to remain for three days. During this period they were to be excused attendance at the daily services, except on very special occasions, and minute directions were given for their personal comfort. They were to be allowed fire and light, with suitable food—eggs and vegetables being specially mentioned—and take exercise within the precincts, and even beyond them, should leave be given.[1]

The inmates of the infirmary were to "lead a life of joy" and freedom from care, in comfort and happiness. Conversation was freely permitted, but sarcastic and abusive language was strictly forbidden, and games of dice and chess prohibited. Although women were absolutely excluded, male society, by leave of the superior, was not denied them, and the physicians might take meals with their patients.

Should it so happen that the spirit of the invalid could be cheered by the sound of music and harmony, he was to be taken into the chapel and the door shut, and some brother or other servant without the chapel was, without offence, to play sweetly upon the harp for his especial delectation. Care was to be taken, however, that the sound of melody was not to reach the infirmary hall or the cells of the brethren.

The tender care of the sick and aged especially dis-

---

[1] Observances in use at the Augustinian Priory of Saints Giles and Andrew at Barnwell, Cambridge.

tinguished the Benedictines. "Before all things," says the great founder of that order in his Rule, "and above all things, special care must be taken of the sick."[1] Nevertheless, the sick were to be careful not to "grieve the brethren who serve them by their extravagant demands."[2] Yet, should they do so, they must be patiently borne with, "because there is gotten from such a more abundant reward."[3] Therefore the abbot was to take the greatest care that they should not be neglected either by himself, the cellarer, or servers.

Moreover, he directed a cell to be set apart for the use of the sick brethren, and one who was God-fearing, diligent, and careful, appointed to serve them. As often as expedient, the use of the baths was to be allowed them, and the use of flesh meat permitted not only to the sick, but the "very weakly, with the proviso that as they got better they were to abstain from it after the accustomed manner."

In some part of the infirmary those brethren who had long left behind them the meridian of their days passed their last days in peace and quietness, untroubled by worries and fears. In the sunny infirmary garden on fine days, or the warm, comfortable parlour on cold, with a young companion to cheer and sit with them to keep all ill news from their ears, their tide of life ebbed smoothly and pleasantly away, until the day when they were carried out to join their brethren gone before, in the cemetery hard by.

The care of the infirmary, or sick-house, was entrusted to the INFIRMARIAN, or *infirmarer*. Not unusually he possessed a knowledge of medicine and surgery, as every monastic library would contain books on these subjects,

---

[1] "Rule of St Benedict," chap. xxxvi. pp. 159, 160.
[2] *Ibid.*  [3] *Ibid.*

—subjects which were the especial study of not a few of the members of the Benedictine Order, who became proficient as physicians in mediæval days.

Resident physicians were maintained at Gloucester and St Alban's, being allowed a chamber, robe, and allowance. In the museum at York is a fine specimen of a mediæval mortar, with the following inscription :—
✠ MORTARIU' SCI' JOH'IS EVANGEL' DE I'FIRMARIA' B'E MARIE EBO' — FR' WILL'S DE TOVTHORPE ME FECIT.—A.D. MCCCVIII.[1]

Should he not be trained in the art of healing himself, he was to provide the physicians and attendants both for the sick and aged, to heal and cheer them in their sickness, and their servants were to journey into the town to the apothecary when required to get the medicines. If possible, he was to have a separate kitchen and cook, so that everything for the sick might be ready in its proper season. On the other hand, if this could not be, he was to receive from the monastery kitchen daily what he wanted. He was to administer all their meals, sprinkle holy water on the beds after Compline, and before Matins to go round them with a lantern, to observe if any well enough to rise stayed in bed.[2] He himself was to lie in the infirmary, and those lying there desirous of being bled were to receive a license from him. Upon recovery, the sick person asked absolution and penance for faults and infringements of Rule while ill, went in procession to infirmary for unction, saying the Penitential Psalms.

In addition, it was the duty of the infirmarer to superintend the burials of the monks. In some places it was required that he should be in a position (the

---

[1] The *Gentleman's Magazine* for 1813 has a poor engraving of it.
[2] The infirm among the Cistercians were required to attend church.

necessary priest's orders) to receive the confession of a sick monk on an emergency. When he observed a monk at the point of death, he caused the rattle or clapper at the door of the slype to summon the community to participate in the last rites.

The Cistercians, at the approach of death, were laid in their blanket upon the ground,[1] which was strewn with ashes in the form of a cross, and covered with a mat. Having received extreme unction and the last sacrament, the brethren, by courses, watched by him,[2] and when his eyes had closed in their last sleep two of his nearest friends remained to keep vigil at his feet, the children of the almonry singing the Psalter in their stalls.

After death had taken place, the infirmarer's servants warmed the water for washing the corpse,[3] after which it was moved to the infirmary chapel, and the place where it had lain was washed and freshly strewn with straw or rushes. The care and management of the bier was in the infirmarer's hands, and after dirge and requiem, where the whole convent received it in the chapter house, the body was carried to the cemetery, to join the brethren who had gone before.

"And after there devocion," says the "Rites of Durham," "the dead corpes was caryed by the mounckes from the chapter house, through the parler (a passage, or narrow apartment, sometimes called the MORTUARY CHAMBER),[4] a place for marchaunts to utter ther waires, standing betwixt the chapter house and the church dour, and so throwghe the said parler into the sentuarie garth, where he was buryed."

---

[1] Du Cange says mats were strewn under the dead.
[2] To the dying Benedictine the Passion was read.
[3] This was done upon a stone slab "before the cross," probably in the infirmary chapel.
[4] Examples are at St Alban's, Combe, east side of cloister, and in ruins at Llanthony and Tintern.

At Durham, at the interment of a monk, his bed of blue saye was held above his grave, and became, after the ceremony, the perquisite of the barber. Monks were buried in the habit they had worn during life, without shroud or coffin. In making a vault for the burial of one Mary Stringer in the sanctuary floor of Long Crendon Church, Bucks, who died on the 7th May 1824, the remains of one of the Augustinian monks of Notley Priory—possibly of the Prior Bownde—were disturbed. The sandals were still on the feet of the skeleton, the rosary and crucifix at the side, and a plate of lead on the breast. When the body was found, it was sewn up in a hide.

One peal was rung on the bells at the completion of the interment. In some monasteries the grave was visited for thirty days; in others there was a daily procession to it, or to the cemetery itself. For the former period the dead monk's bread and beer were given to the poor, with a request for their prayers for his soul's health. In the case of an abbot or a monk of another house, and member of the chapter, the period was extended to a year.

Abbots in their last sickness caused themselves to be carried into the chapter house to absolve their monks from obedience to them, and to be absolved by them, in some such form as the following: "Wherefore I seek absolution from you, as much as appertains to you, and benediction, and I absolve you from obedience to me, and give you my benediction."

When a monk died, a bellman went round the streets, and the precentor, almoner, or other officer, whose duty it was, sent off messengers with briefs announcing the death, and giving a short account of the deceased, on the same errand to other houses, asking their prayers.

Each community visited acknowledged the receipt of the roll or brief by inscribing upon it a promise of prayer for the soul of the departed, and not infrequently adding a similar request for prayers on behalf of their own deceased brethren and benefactors.

At Westminster the abbots were buried with two candles laid crosswise upon the breast. Their burial place at this house was in the cloisters—at least, those of the early abbots, three of whose effigies—those of Vitalis (died 1085); Gervase de Blois (died 1160); and Lawrence (died 1176)—may still be delineated. In later days they found interment within the church, at Battle in the crypt, immediately before the high altar, in the chapter house or quire. Monks were generally buried in their own cemetery, sometimes in the cloisters, or cloister garth, a wooden cross inscribed with their initials being their sole memorial.[1] In the thirteenth-century cloisters of St Wandrille are many tombstones on the floor, bearing only a cross and the date.

. . . . . . . . .

St Benedict by his Rule required each monastery to be complete in itself, independent of all external aid, and supplied with workmen of every trade and industry. To this end it was the policy of the great monastic houses to multiply offices as much as possible, with the view of providing the brethren with such constant occupation and responsibility which would not only induce an interest but a zeal for the well-being of the order, and the prosperity and discipline of their own particular house.

Under the abbot would come the prior, sub-prior, and not infrequently a third, and even a fourth prior; then

---

[1] See the tombstone with incised cross and initials near the chapter house door at Gloucester.

the greater obedientiaries—cellarer, sacristan, chamberlain, almoner, hostillar, infirmarer, precentor, etc.—who have been separately dealt with in their particular department, and to each of whom separate estates were assigned, out of which they were bound to provide certain charges in their own or another department, of which they kept an account in rolls annually audited.

Under the direction of these came the officers of the subaltern class, or *quasi claustral*, being bound to put in attendance at all quire offices, but by reason of their employment permitted to quit the precincts on conventual service, *e.g.*

The TERRIER OF THE HOUSE, whose duty was to see that the guest chambers were clean and the napery used therein, to provide wine for the entertainment of strangers, provender for their horses, and all other things necessary for their comfort upon their arrival. Certain yeomen were under him to attend upon the strangers.

The SENESCHAL, an obedientiary of the abbot, often a layman of high rank, who saw to the business of the abbot with the king, paid money into the exchequer, and such-like business.

The TREASURER, or bursar, or receiver of rents. To him all other officers made their accounts. He paid the servants their wages,[1] and similar outgoings. He was sometimes called *communar*, having in charge the *commune*, or common fund of the house.

The CUSTOS OPERUM and CUSTOS FABRICÆ, the masters of the fabric and works, under whose care the constant building and repairing was carried out by

---

[1] Servants were employed in considerable number, and received as wages corn or other produce and liveries.

every generation of monks. In some houses he ranked as one of the greater obedientiaries.

The HORDARIAN, who had charge of the home or material resources of the convent; and several others—the CANCELLARIUS, REGISTRAR, AUDITOR, SECRETARY of the convent, who wrote and returned letters, etc.

To assist the SACRISTAN and PRECENTOR in their church duties were a number of minor officers, as the REVESTRAR, MASTER OF ANNIVERSARIES, LECTURER, KEEPER OF THE HIGH ALTAR, KEEPER OF RELICS, FERETRAR, or *tumbarer*—the KEEPER OF THE SHRINE,[1] OF TOMBS OF SAINTS, and OF THE LADY CHAPEL, etc., etc.

And in the domestic department, under their respective officers, the BUTLER, BAKER, and *sub-bakers*,[2] LARDENARIUS, or *keeper of the larder;* SQUELEMARII, or *keepers of baskets;* SERVANTS OF THE LAUNDRY, TAILORS, SHOEMAKERS, etc. The GRANETARIUS kept the garners, and managed the outlying farms, rendering an account weekly of the barley and malt used in the kiln.[3] The VIRGULTARIUS, or *orcharder*, had the care of the apples, which he distributed at stated times to the monks and visitors. The GARDENER and his assistants, and he who had charge of the herbary for making salves, the herbs being plucked by means of a wooden instrument. Pot herbs were not to be gathered on a Sunday. Peculiar gardens of the prior, cellarer, and infirmary are mentioned. The monks of Melrose had private gardens, as was the custom with the Carthusians. The garden had a cross in it. The best fruit trees are still found in

---

[1] He received pilgrims' offerings, etc.

[2] By the MS. constitutions of the Clugniac Order, they are directed not to sing psalms like the other monks when at work, lest any saliva should fall into the dough.

[3] At Langney, Sussex, is an ancient grange of Lewes Priory, the chapel almost entirely devoted now to farm uses. Midghall Farm, Gloucestershire, was once a grange of Stanley Abbey.

the gardens and orchards of the religious houses. Add to the porters, the keepers of courts and other places, the *Porcarius*, or keeper of pigs, the *Operarius*, who was charged wth the clearance of all filth and waste matters, and some kind of idea will be formed of the multitudinous assemblage which lived and moved within the enclosure of a great religious house.

Take as an example the servants merely at Evesham Abbey in the days of William Rufus. They numbered sixty-five (a small number compared with other houses), and were distributed as follows: Five in the church; two in the infirmary; two in the cellar; five in the kitchen; seven in the bakehouse; four brewers; four menders; two shoemakers; two in the bath; two in the orchard; three gardeners; one at the cloister gate; two at the great gate; five at the vineyard; four served the monks when they went out; four fishermen; four in the abbot's chamber; three in the hall; a servant of the parlour, and two tailors. Two servants in the vestiary, who rung bells, are also mentioned; and one for the fires, who constantly (every fifteen days) was to clean the spittings under and near the forms, and strew them. The servants of Hexham used to serve summonses, levy distress, and carry rods.[1]

The conventual chequers (the offices of the monastic officers) and workshops (*domus operaria*) were adjacent to and beyond the great cloister. They were usually undercrofts or chambers under the refectory, dormitory, and cellarer's hall. Others were utilised as chambers for storage.

The most usual arrangement was for the almoner,

---

[1] Even monks were sometimes employed in civil and external avocations, as clerks and ambassadors. A monk of Bury was a clerk of King Edward III.'s household. Henry VII. employed them as spies; others travelled as tutors and teachers of music.

chamberlain, and sacristan to live by the court gate; the cellarer by the refectory, or guest hall; the hospitaller near the hostry; the gardener near the granaries; the sub-prior near the dormitory door; the commoner near the common house; the infirmarer in the infirmary; and the under-steward next the sextry.[1] Although they dined in their offices they were bound to sleep in the common dormitory. The bursar and hostiller sometimes slept in the infirmary.

The minor offices and workships were as various as the officers and servants. Buttery, pantry, larder, fish house,[2] bake house, bulting house, mill house,[3] brew house, malt house, slaughter house, bath house,[4] barber's, or rastyr house, or shaving house, bleeding house, farmery hall, barns,[5] garners, and farm buildings.

---

[1] At Gloucester.

[2] Fish-ponds (*Vivarium*), or stews, were attached to all abbeys, the monks excelling in the culture of fish in a manner lost to us. At Stanley Abbey, Chippenham, Wilts, a chain of fish-ponds, connected at each end with the River Marden, can still be traced. At Laycock, in the same county, to the north-east of the chapter-house, lie the ponds, or stews, for fish. At Glastonbury, north of Meare, and adjoining the Brue, they covered over five hundred acres of water; at Fresco Abbey, Scilly Isles, fifty acres; whilst at Bruerne Abbey, Gloucester, they are the only remains of the monastery.

[3] Built a short distance from the monastery on the streams near to which the house was generally placed, as at St Alban's. Sometimes, in particular situations where no stream existed, a horse-mill was used in its stead, as at Bridlington. "It. On the north syde of the same Bakehouse and Brewhouse standyth a ffayre Horse Mylne newly bylded and covered w'h slatt." Waltham Abbey mills are still used to grind corn.

[4] Rather a superfluity if the Act of Archbishop Lanfranc, which prescribed *one bath* a year, just before Christmas Day, was literally carried out.

[5] Several of these fine structures remain. One built by the monks of Kingswood at Calcot is 140 feet long by 37 feet 4 inches wide. It is a fine specimen in the decorated style, with good gables, finials, and transepts in the form of low square towers, the date MCCC. being cut on a coign stone inside the south porch. At Harmondsworth is a still larger mediæval barn of probably early fourteenth-century date. Its inside length is 192 feet, its width 36 feet 9 inches, and its height 39 feet. It is divided into a dozen bays and three threshing floors. A barn of Laycock Abbey, Wilts, is of the same (fourteenth century) date, that of Glastonbury enriched with carvings of the Evangelists and other figures set upon the gables.

Forge, kiln, wax house, sextry, or chandlery, sartory for tailors, courvoiserie, or shops for shoemakers and other artificers, and stables for the convent horses and those of guests. At St Alban's these were large enough to contain nearly three hundred horses, kept in excellent condition, a lamp burning there all night.

In the stable yard, if not in the gardens, would be the dove-cote (*columbary*), no inconsiderable structure. The pigeon-house at St Pancras, Cluniac Priory, Lewes, stood upon the south-west side of the remaining ruins. It was cruciform, and "equalled in magnitude many a parish church," containing three thousand two hundred and twenty-eight pigeon-holes. It remained intact till within fifty years ago. At Boxgrove Priory, Sussex, the pigeon-house was of brick supported with buttresses; at Monks Bretton, York, it partook of the early English character, and at Bredsall was made up of four hollow, truncated, hexagonal cones, from a larger to a smaller size, placed one above another, with a little turret atop.

In the cemetery was a CHARNEL, a crypt for the reception of the contents of graves disturbed in making others. It frequently had a chapel above for Mass of Requiem. One remains at Norwich. At St Alban's, Mass was said daily in chapel for the dead.

All these buildings were arranged in no definite position with regard to the monastic structure. Thus, in the larger establishments there would be many, and in the smaller one large building (as presumably at Boxley, Kent) served for many purposes.

A word as to drains, or sewers. These were invariably good, and in sanitary arrangements the monks were far in advance of their times. The necessary office (*Necessarium*) was a comparatively large and lofty structure, with a series of seven or more wooden closets set in a row, beneath which a stream of running water drawn from an adjacent river flowed. The size and structure of these drains are still frequently associated in the minds of the ignorant with subterranean passages in communication with this or that building, or of a length absolutely unknown.[1]

Without the precincts of the monastery were grouped the "foréigns," buildings, and yards, as the Foregate of Shrewsbury and the Forbury of Reading. Here, or even within the precincts, were held the fairs, at which the monks were very fond of keeping shops.

---

[1] Reservoirs of lead and stone remain beneath the soil at Newminster Abbey.

# CONCLUSION

AS it has not been my intention to write a *history* of Monasticism, I am not called upon to deal with the dissolution of the monastic houses under "bluff King Hal," in the first half of the sixteenth century, when was brought to an abrupt close a system which had formed part of the religious life of the country for nigh upon a thousand years.

There are those who glory in the wholesale and complete destruction of the religious houses, and bless the hand that wiped them out; and there are others who as equally deplore the dastardly act, and curse the hand that accomplished it.

The dissolution of monasteries was no new thing invented by the mind of Henry VIII. He had precedent for his act in the earlier suppression of the alien priories, and the misappropriation of their revenues by his predecessors. Wolsey, too, in his own day, had suppressed several with the direct sanction of both pope and king, applying the results to the magnificent foundations he had devised.

That the monasteries had accomplished the work of their creation is asserted by some; which others as strongly deny. That they needed reform is the verdict of the best and most reliable historians; that they were abominably robbed, and their inmates barbarously treated, is a widely acknowledged fact.

For some years before their suppression the number of monks in the religious houses had been gradually diminishing. Peterborough, which had 110 monks in the thirteenth century, had only 38 at its dissolution; Winchester, founded for 60, had only 37; Canterbury, built originally for 150, had only 54: St Alban's, 40; Ely, 37; and Bath, 21, at the Suppression.

This decrease may be attributed to (1) the suspicion of what was coming; (2) the numerous advantages which the revival of English commerce was providing for the younger sons of the upper classes, who had hitherto been destined to the cloistral life; (3) that the monasteries had become sinecures for those who could pay for them, as for many years admittance to both monasteries and nunneries could only be gained by payment or influence, to the utter exclusion of the middle or lower classes, who by this time had become the backbone of the country.

Henry VIII., it must be remembered, brought forward his measures for the suppression of the religious houses on the plea of their reformation, but in reality, for their effacement and plunder.[1] Before an entirely Catholic Parliament he placed his project, and at a hint of their likely refusal, swore to have either his Bill or their heads.

It has been said Henry would have been as good as his word. Probably he would. But in that assembly there were men as determined as he; good men and true—men who feared God rather than man, though he was a king. A noble procession of these worthies—the flower

---

[1] They had been the strongest opponents to the king's divorce from Katharine of Aragon.

of the land—had gone to the block for this very cause, and there were those among them who were doomed to follow in their train.

Henry got his Bill, we are told—got it in the teeth of the almost unanimous disinclination of the House to pass it, preferring, it is added, to retain their heads to their consciences!

History records their consciences equally at fault when it came to dividing the spoil, and, moreover, when Queen Mary enticed them to return their ill-gotten gains to the coffers of the Holy Mother Church, restoring all that remained in the royal purse as an example, they obtained a dispensation from Rome to retain them.

For all this they may be readily excused, for had they not put in a claim for a share in return for their compliance, it would have been swallowed up by others less squeamish.

That robbery was the prime motive of the great reformer's move in the suppression of the monasteries is proved by the fact that the Commissioners were ready enough to allow those who would to buy back what had been taken for ready cash. In the sale of the monastic belongings nothing was lost sight of, the commonest pot or crock found on the premises being put up to auction, and its price swept into the bulk.

The monasteries suppressed, their lands were distributed among the courtiers ("cormorants," the king himself styles them, in their greediness for plunder), and the money produced by the sale of their plate and jewels squandered upon the king's favourites.

Those who held the lands were bound by the very tenure of their holdings to keep up the hospitality as of old. How they fulfilled that trust may be seen by the abundant legislation which was directed against those whom the new landlords literally drove off their holdings. This state of things continued until the reign of James I., when a complaisant parliament kindly relieved them of their obligation by striking out the objected clause, and laying the first stone of the union workhouse.

Theretofore the monasteries had been the hotels, the schools, the dispensaries, the homes of the poor and needy, a huge organisation in the hands of a single corporation, who worked it for the love of God, and without earthly fee or reward. For this purpose generation after generation of charitable people had placed in their hands huge funds, and they had not been unfaithful to the trust.

The consequence was that, when Henry VIII. robbed them of these trust funds, the country swarmed with poor and destitute persons deprived of a livelihood, and who could not be kept down although the most stringent and cruel laws were enacted against them.

Unfortunately, some tares in the course of ages had grown up with the wheat, and there were no able hands to pluck them out. Taking them as a whole, the inmates of the religious houses were everywhere better and in advance of the men of their time—pioneers in every advancement, the strong defenders of the innocent and persecuted. Even their spoilers in several instances spoke well to the king of them.

In their untiring application to work, they had very naturally drawn the monopoly of trade and commerce into their hands. In their reclamation of waste lands they had drawn people to them, and had thus created several of the largest towns. And the day only too surely came when the great question must once for all be settled, whether the monk or the secular was to be master? History has told us that the monk suffered defeat.

Some question such as this must have been the *real* point at issue, or how are we to interpret the almost unanimous complaisance with which the great majority of the people stood by and let the monasteries and nunneries be pillaged without raising a hand to help them? Were they acquiescent, or did they tremble at the frown of a despot whose equal the world has never seen?

# APPENDIX

# LIST OF RELIGIOUS ORDERS

WITH

*Name of Founder, Date of Foundation, and Colour of Habit*

———>•<———

### Monks

*Of St Anthony.*—Date, 305. Founder, St Anthony. See of Rome vacant, but St Marcellus became Pope in 308. Habit, russet and black.

*Of St Pachomius.*—Date, about 325. Founder, St Pachomius. Pope, St Sylvester. Habit, black.

*Of St Basil.*—Date, 358. Founder, St Basil. Pope, Liberius. Habit, black.

*Benedictines.*—Date, 529. Founder, St Benedict. Pope, Felix IV. Habit, black.

*Of the Order of Camaldoli.*—Date, about 1009. Founder, St Romuald. Pope, Sergius IV. Habit, white.

*Of the Order of Vallambrosa.*—Date, 1070. Founder, St John Gualbert. Pope, Alexander II. Habit, ash colour.

*Of the Order of Grandmont.* — Date, about 1076.

Founder, St Stephen of Thiers. Pope, St Gregory VII. Habit, black.

*Carthusians.*—Date, 1084. Founder, St Bruno. Pope, St Gregory VII. Habit, white.

*Cistercians.*—Date, 1098. Founder, St Robert of Molesme. Pope, Urban II. Habit, white.

*Fontevraud.*—Date, 1099. Founder, B. Robert of Arbrissel. Pope, Urban II. Habit, black.

*Celestins.*—Date, 1274. Founder, Peter Morroni, afterwards Pope Celestin V. Pope, Gregory X. Habit, white and black.

*Of Mount Olivet.*—Date, 1319. Founder, B. Bernard of Siena. Pope, John XXI. Habit, white.

*Of Monte Vergine.*—Date, 1119. Founder, St William of Vercelli. Pope, Gelasius II. Habit, white.

*Silvestrins.*—Date, 1234. Founder, B. Silvester of Osimo. Pope, Gregory IX. Habit, dark blue.

## Regular Canons

*Of St Augustine.*—Founded about 396 by St Augustine at Hippo, under Pope St Siricius. Habit, black, with narrow white sash over the shoulders, joined on the breast, and fastened on the left side.

*Of St John Lateran.*—Founded about the year 495 by Pope Gelasius at Rome. Habit, white.

*Of St Anthony.*—Founded in the year 1095 by Gasto and Girondus in the province of Vienna, under Pope Urban II. Habit, black, with the Tau cross, blue on the left breast.

*Of the Holy Sepulchre.*—Founded about the year 1110 by Godfrey of Bouillon at Jerusalem, under Pope Pascal II. Habit, black, with cloak having on the left side a red cross, with four small red crosses about it.

*Of St Victor.*—Founded in the year 1113 by Louis the Big, near Paris, under Pope Pascal II. Habit, white.

*Of the Holy Cross at Coimbra.*—Founded in the year 1131 by a secular canon of Coimbra and eleven other pious men at Coimbra, under Pope Innocent II. Habit, white, with black almuce.

*In Austria.*—Founded in the year 1140 by Leopold, Marquis of Austria, at Clooster Neuberg, near Vienna, under Pope Innocent II. Habit, white surplice, with black almuce.

*Of St Geneviève.*—Founded in the year 1147 by Pope Eugenius III. in Paris. Habit, white, with rochet, and a fur almuce over the left arm.

*Premonstratenses.*—Founded in the year 1121 by St Norbert at Premontré, under Pope Calixtus II. Habit, white, coarse black tunic, and cloak.

*Of St Gilbert.*—Founded in the year 1148 by St Gilbert at Sempringham, under Pope Eugenius III. Habit, white, black tunic, with furred cloak. Only English Order ever founded in England by an English saint.

*Of St John Baptist.*—Founded in the year 1425 (by whom unknown) at Coventry, under Pope Martin V. Habit, black, with a black cross on the scapular and mantle.

## Friars

*Carmelites.* — Date unknown, perhaps about 1100. Founder, St Albert Vercelli or unknown. Pope unknown. Habit, brown, white cloak.

*Trinitarians.*—Date, 1198. Founder, St John of Malta. Pope, Innocent III. Habit, white; cross red and blue on the breast.

*Franciscans.*—Date, 1210. Founder, St Francis of Assisi. Pope, Innocent III. Habit, brown.

*Dominicans*, or *Order of Preachers.* — Date, 1216. Founder, St Dominic. Pope, Honorius III. Habit, white and black.

*Of Our Lady of Mercy.*—Date, 1218. Founder, St Peter Nolasco. Pope, Honorius III. Habit, white; arms of Aragon on the breast.

*Servants of Mary* (*Servites*).—Date, 1233. Founders, seven citizens of Florence. Pope, Gregory IX. Habit, black.

*Alexian*, or *Cellite.*—Date, about 1300. Founder, said to be Tibias. Pope, Boniface VIII. Habit, black.

*Of St Ambrose.*—Date, uncertain. Founder, unknown. Pope (who approved them in 1376), Gregory XI. Habit, black.

*Minims.*—Date, 1435. Founder, St Francis of Paula. Pope, Eugenius IV. Habit, tawny.

*Of Charity and of St Hippolytus.*—Date, sixteenth century. Founder, Barnardin Alvarez. Pope (who first approved them), Gregory XIII. Habit, light brown.

*Of Charity.*—Date, 1653. Founder, St John of God. Pope, Paul III. Habit, dark ash colour.

*Bethlehemites.*—Date, 1653. Founder, Peter Betancur (?). Pope, Innocent X. Habit, black; Nativity painted, worn on left breast; reformed Dominicans, blazing star on breast.

*Berthold of Calabria.*—Date, 1183.

## Military Orders

*Of Knights Hospitallers, afterwards called Knights of Malta.*—Founded in the year 1104 by Raymond Dupuy at Jerusalem, under Pope Pascal II. Habit, black, with a white cross, called a Maltese cross, with eight points, on the left side.

*Of Knights Templars.*—Founded in the year 1118 by Hugo, Geoffrey, and seven others at Jerusalem, under Pope Gelasius II. Habit, black, with red cross.

*Of Knights of the Holy Sepulchre.*—Founded in the year 1120, under Pope Calixtus II. Habit, black, with red double cross.

*Of Teutonic Knights.*—Founded in the year 1190 by certain merchants of Bremen and Lubeck, under Pope Celestin III. Habit, white, with a black cross.

*Of Knights of St Hubert.*—Founded about the year 1444 by Gerard V., Duke of Cleves, under Pope Eugenius IV. Habit, black, with a gold collar with cross and image of St Hubert.

*Of Knights of St George, or of the Garter.*—Founded in the year 1330 by King Edward III. in England, under Pope John XXII. Habit, blue mantle, with collar and star, and garter round the left knee.

## Regular Clerks

*Of the Holy Ghost.*—Founded in the year 1204 by Pope Innocent III. in Saxony. Habit, black, with white double-barred cross on the left breast.

*Theatines.*—Founded in the year 1524 by St Cajetan and three others at Rome. Habit, black, like other priests.

*Of Somascha.*—Founded in the sixteenth century by St Jerome Emilian at Somascha; approved by Paul III. in 1540. Habit, black, like other priests.

*Of St Barnabas.*—Founded in the year 1533, by authority of Pope Clement VII., at Milan. Habit, black.

*Society of Jesus (Jesuits).*—Founded in the year 1534 by St Ignatius of Loyola at Paris, under Pope Paul III. Habit, black, like other priests.

*Priests of the Oratory (Oratorians).*—Founded in the year 1564 by St Philip Neri at Rome, under Pope Pius IV. Habit, black, like other priests.

*Of the Mother of God.*—Founded in the year 1574 by John Leonard at Lucca, under Pope Gregory XIII. Habit, black, like other priests.

*Priests of the Congregation for serving the Sick.*—Founded in the year 1584 by St Camillus de Lellis at Rome, under Pope Gregory XIII. Habit, black, with yellow cross on right breast.

*Priests of Christian Doctrine.*—Founded in the year 1598 by Cæsar de Bus, near Avignon, under Pope Clement VIII. Habit, black, like other priests.

*Priests of the Mission (Lazarites).*—Founded in the year 1625 by St Vincent of Paul, under Pope Urban VIII. Habit, black, like other priests.

## HERMITS

*Of St Macarius.*—Founded about 330. Founder, St Macarius, the elder of Egypt. Pope, St Sylvester. Habit, violet, with black scapular.

*Of St Augustine.*—Founded 388. Founder, St Augustine of Hippo. Pope, St Siricius. Habit, black.

*Of the Cross.*—Founded in the twelfth century. Founder, unknown. Pope, Alexander III. Habit, blue.

*Of St Paul in Hungary.*—Founded 1215. Founder, Eusebius of Strigonia. Pope, Innocent III. Habit, white; brown woollen scapular, and mantle.

*Of St Jerome.*—Founded 1366. Founder, Peter Fernandez. Pope, Urban V. Habit, white.

*Of Monte Bello.*—Founded 1380. Founder, Peter Gambacurta. Pope, Urban VI. Habit, black.

*Of Colorites.*—Founded 1552. Founder, Bernard of Rogliano. Pope, Julius III. Habit, black.

*Of St John of Penance.*— Date of Foundation and Founder uncertain. In 1572 and 1585, approved and confirmed by Pope Gregory XIII. Habit, tawny, a heavy cross of wood always hanging from the neck before them.

## LIST OF SOME MONASTIC BRASSES

1433 Cluniac Prior. *Cowfold, Sussex.*
1437 . . *St Lawrence's, Norwich.*
1438 . . *Westminster Abbey.*
1443
c1470 } Benedictines } *St Alban's Abbey, Herts.*
1531

1556 Eldest son of Hampton family as a Monk. *Minchinhampton, Glous.*

Demi-figure of a monk holding a flagellarium cowl overhead. Stourton family . . . . } *Sawtrey, All Saints, Hunts.*

1515 Austin Canon. John Stodeley of St Frideswide's, Oxford . . . . } *Overwinchendon, Bucks.*

c1460 Lectern at *Yeovil, Somerset*, has a small engraved figure of Frater Martinus Forester.

1530 Dame Elizabeth Hervey. *Elstow, Beds.* Abbess.

c1540 Dame Agnes Jordan. *Denham, Bucks.* Abbess of Syon.

1546 A Prioress (palimpsest brass). *St Stephen's, Norwich.*

1561 Margaret Dely, "a syster professed in Syon." *Isleworth, Middlesex.*

# INDEX

# INDEX.

Abbot, 119
Abbot's crooks, 147
—— dress, 147
—— —— Parliamentary, 148
—— —— Pontifical, 147
—— hall, 126
—— kitchen, 193
—— mitred, 148
—— officers, 123
—— table, 202
Abraham, Rules of, 33, 34
Admission to monasteries, 132
—— of children to monasteries, 137
Agriculturalists, monks as, 63-66, 77, et seq.
Alexandria, Macarius of, 29
Alleys, cloister, 172
—— —— (north), 175
—— —— (south), 174
—— —— (east), 174
—— —— (west), 173
Almoner, 216
Almonry, 217
Altar, keeper of high, 252
Anchorites, 41
Anglo-Saxon monasteries, 49-51
Anniversaries, master of, 252
Anthony, St, 27, 32
*Antiquarii*, 183
Apology for Monasticism, 9-17
Art skill of Celtic monks, 49
—— monastic, 61, 89, 92, 95, etc.
Arts, commerce, and trade, 89-97
Artists, monks as, 95, 110
Associated brethren, 140
*Attractius*, 204
Auditor, 252

Bacon, Friar, 108
Baker, 252
Barber, 123, 176
Barns, 254 (*note* 5)
Bartholomew de Glanville, 116
Basket-keepers, 252
Basil, Rule of St, 37
Bath, 254

Beauvais, Vincent de, 115
Bede, Venerable, 114
Benedict, St, 54
—— —— as Ruler, 55
—— —— Rule of, 58
Benedictine monks as agriculturalists, 63, 66-77, *et seq.*
—— —— civilisers, 61
—— —— creators of towns, 69
—— —— feudal lords, 73
—— —— landed proprietors, 69, 73
—— —— protectors of serfs, 74
—— —— warriors, 82
—— —— writers, 61, 100
—— Rule, 58
—— —— Cardinal Newman on the, 58
Benedictines, 64
—— in praise of, 57, 60-64
Berners, Dame Juliana, 116
Bishops *v.* monks, 87
Blood-letting, 244
Bocardo, 165
Book of Kells, 49
Books, monks' care of, 191
Brasses, list of some monastic, 272
Brethren, associated, 140
Breviaries, 146
Bridge and road-makers, monks as, 93, 94
British Monasticism, 41-51
—— nuns, 52, 53
Burial in monk's habit, 140
—— of monks, 247
Bursar, 251
Butler, 252
Buttery, 198, 201 (*note* 1)

Calefactory, 227
*Camerarius*, 242
*Cancellarius*, 252
Canonesses of the Holy Sepulchre 52
Canons, regular, list of, 266
Cardinal Newman on the Benedictine Rule, 58

275

Care of books by monks, 191
*Caritas*, 208, 213
Carrels, 188
Cellarer, 197
Cellarer's hall, 199
Cells, 237
Celtic Monasticism, 40
—— monks, art skill of, 49
—— —— Rule of, 43-47
—— —— tonsure of, 48
Cemetery, 248
Cenobites, 31
"*Cenobium*," 34
Chad and Cuthbert (Saints), Gospels of, 49
Chamberlain, 242
Chantor, 178
Chapter-house, 228
—— monks', 231
Charuel, 255
Chequers, 253
Children, admission of, to monasteries, 137
Choir duty, 151
Christian Monasticism, 9
Chronicles, 184
Cistercian monks, 65
Civilisers, monks as, 61
Claustral prior, 175
Clerks, regular, list of, 269
Cleric v. lay monks 39 (*note* [1]), 120
Cloister, 168
—— alleys, 172
—— —— (north), 175
—— —— (south), 174
—— —— (east), 174
—— —— (west), 173
—— discipline of, 149
—— garth, 171
—— spies of, 175
*Cenobium*, 34
Coining, 81
Columba, Rule of St, 48
Columbary, 255
Commerce, 89-97
Common-house, 227
"Commons," 206
Convents, double, 53
Conventual constitution, 119-256
*Conversorum, Domus*, 227
Corporal discipline, 161
Corrody, 206
Courts, monastic, 81
Creators of towns, monks as, 69
Crook, abbot's, 147
Cuthbert and Chad (Saints), Gospels of, 49
*Custos Fabricæ*, 251
*Custos Operum*, 251

DAVID (father-abbot), 32, 45, 121
Day, a monk's, 151
—— room, 227
"De Proprietatibus Rerum," 116
Death and interment of monks, 247, 250
Diet rolls, 209
Discipline, corporal, 161
—— of the Cloister, 149
Dissolution of monasteries, 257
*Domus Capitularis*, 228
*Domus Conversorum*, 227
*Domus Operaria*, 253
*Domus Secretior*, 242, 255
Donations to monasteries, 66-68
Dormitory, 235
Dorter, 235
—— Rere, 242, 255
Double convents, 53
Dovecot, 255
Drains, 255
Dress, abbot's, 147
—— —— Parliamentary, 148
—— —— Pontifical, 147
Drink, measure of, 210
Dunstan, St, 111
Duty, quire, 151


EASE, Little, 165
East (cloister) alley, 174
Eastern Monasticism, 27-38
"Egypte the fleyshe kychyn," 194
Egyptian monks, 32
—— —— habits of, 142
Eminent Monastics, 107-18
Employment of Monastics, 149, *et seq.*
Essenes, 18-21
Evesham Abbey, servants at, 253
Excommunication, 162
*Excubitores*, 240
*Excubitoria*, 240
Explorator, 160
Exterus, 176

"FABRICÆ, CUSTOS," 251
Fakirs, 10
Fasting, 33
*Feretrar*, 252
Feudal lords, monks as, 81
Fishponds, 254 (*note* [2])
Flebotomaria, 244
Flebotomy, 244
Foppery of Monastics, 143 (*note* [1])
Forbury, 256
Foregate, 256
Forensic or outdoor officers, 123
Foreigns, 256

Foundations for women, 51
Founder-monks, 66
Frater-house, 200
Friar Bacon, 108
Friars, the, 56, 57
Friars, list of orders of, 267

GARDENER, 252
Gardens, 252
Garth, Cloister, 171
Gate-house, 166
Glanville, Bartholomew de, 166
Glebe, 70
"Golden Legend," 115
Gong, 242, 255
"Gospels," 204
—— of Saints Cuthbert and Chad, 49
Gown v. Town, 84, 87
Grades of monks, 135
*Granetarius*, 252
Granges, 76
Greeting-house, 226
Guest-house, 222
"*Gyrovagi*," 31

HABIT, monastic, 141
—— —— burial in, 140
—— —— Egyptian, 142
Hall, cellarer's, 199
*Hebdomadaries*, 204, 295
"Hell," 165
Herbarium, 243
Herbary, 243
Hermits, list of orders of, 270
High altar, Keeper of, 252
Histories and Stories, 205
Holy Sepulchre, Canonesses of, 52
*Hordarian*, 199, 252
Horse-mill, 254 (*note* 3)
Hospitality, 103-7, 219
Hospitaller, 225
Hostillar, 225
Hostrey, 222
House, chapter, 228
—— common, 227
—— frater, 200
—— gate, 166
—— greeting, 226
—— guest, 222
—— lying, 165
—— pigeon, 255
—— rastyr, 176
—— shaving, 176
—— speke, 226
—— terrier of, 251
—— treasury, 180

ILLUMINATORS, 172, 182
Infirmarian, 246
Infirmarer, 246
Infirmary, 243
—— kitchen, 193
Interment of monks, 247-50
Irish Monasticism, 41, *et seq*.

JACOBUS DE VORAGINE, 115
Jewish Monasticism, 9
Juliana Berners (Dame), 116

KELLS, Book of, 49
Keeper of garners, 252
—— —— high altar, 252
—— —— relics, 252
—— —— shrine, 252
Keepers of baskets, 252
King-monks, 16 (*note* 1)
Kitchen, 192
—— abbot's, 193
—— infirmary, 193
—— servers, 195
Kitchener, 194

LAMAS, 10
Lantern, 165, 232
Larderer, 252
Latrines, 242
Laundry servants, 252
*Laura*, 34
Lavatory, 234
Lay v. cleric monks, 39 (*note* 1), 120
Lawyers, monks as, 88
*Lector mensæ*, 206
Lecturer, 252
"Legend, Golden," 115
Libraries, 117-118
—— lending, 187
*Librarii*, 183
Library, 180
Lightfoot, Peter, 111
List of military orders, 269
—— of some monastic brasses, 272
—— of orders of friars, 267
—— —— of hermits, 270
—— —— of monks, 265
—— —— of regular canons, 266
—— —— of regular clerks, 269
Little Ease, 165
Liqueurs, 80
*Locutorium*, 226
Lodge, prior's, 127
Longevity of monks, 216
Lying-house, 165

MACARIUS of Alexandria, 29
Master of anniversaries, 252
Materials, Writing, 192
Maundy, 174, 219
Measure of drink, 210
Melania, 52
*Mensæ lector*, 206
Military orders, list of, 269
Mill, horse, 254 (*note* ³)
Mills, 254 (*note* ³)
Minor officers, 252
Mints, 81
Minution, 244
Misericord, 214
Missionaries, Monks as, 97
Mitre, abbot's, 147
*Mixtum*, 172, 205
Monasteries, admission to, 132
—— admission of children to, 137
—— Anglo-Saxon, 49-51
—— donations to, 66-68
—— dissolution of, 257
—— value of, 89
Monastery of Tabennæ, 35
—— —— life in, 36
Monastic arts, commerce, and trades, 89-97
—— brasses, list of some, 272
—— chapter, 231
—— courts, 81
—— employments, 149, *et seq.*
—— foppery, 143 (*note* ¹)
—— life *temp.* St Jerome, 38
—— libraries, 117, 118
—— longevity, 216
—— officers, 251
—— prison, 165
—— recreations, 156
—— reforms, 55
—— schools, 89, 153, 173
—— travelling, 158
—— visitors, 158
Monastics, eminent, 107-18
Monasticism, apology for, 9-17
—— British, 41-51
—— Celtic, 40
—— Christian, 9
—— Eastern, 27-38
—— in praise of, 57-60
—— Irish, 41, *et seq.*
—— Jewish, 9
—— New Testament evidence of, 22, *et seq.*
—— Old Testament evidence of, 17, *et seq.*
—— Pagan, 9
—— Western, 38
Monk *v.* bishop, 87

Monks as agriculturalists, 63, 66, 77, *et seq.*
—— as artists, 95, 110
—— as bridge and road-makers, 93, 94
—— as civilisers, 61
—— as creators of towns, 69
—— as feudal lords, 81
—— as landed proprietors, 73
—— as lawyers, 88
—— as missionaries, 97
—— as physicians, 98
—— as printers, 102
—— as protectors of serfs, 74
—— as public benefactors, 58-118
—— as road and bridge-makers, 93, 94
—— as warriors, 82
—— as wine growers, 79, 118
—— as writers, 61, 90, 181
—— art skill of Celtic, 49
—— Celtic Rule of, 43-47
—— cleric *v.* lay, 39 (*note* ¹) 120
—— day, 151
—— different kinds of, 31, 32
—— Egyptian, 32
—— founder, 66
—— four kinds of, 31
—— grades of, 135
—— habit, burial in, 140
—— king, 16 (*note* ¹)
—— lay *v.* cleric, 39 (*note* ¹), 120
—— list of orders of, 265
—— longevity of, 216
Museums, 188


NAZARITES, 17
*Necessarium*, 242, 255
New Testament evidence of Monasticism, 22, *et seq.*
Newman, Cardinal, on the Benedictine Rule, 58
North (cloister) alley, 175
Novices, 130
Novitiate, 132
Nuns, 51
—— British, 52, 53
Nursery for students, 174


OBEDIENTIARIES, 123
Officers, abbot's, 123
—— minor, 252
—— monastic, 251
—— outdoor, 123
Old Testament evidence of Monasticism, 17, *et seq.*
*Operaria Domus*, 253
*Operarius*, 253

*Operum, Custos*, 251
Orcharder, 252
Orders, list of (friars), 267
—— —— (hermits), 270
—— —— (military), 269
—— —— (monks), 265
—— —— (regular canons), 266
—— —— (regular clerks), 269

PACHOMIUS, 27, 35
—— Rule of, 35
*Pactum*, 134
Pagan Monasticism, 9
Parliamentary dress of abbots, 148
Parliaments, 160, 175
*Particularius*, 216
Paul of Thebes, 27
Paula, St, 52
Penance, 161
Peter Lightfoot, 111
"Pewes," 188
Physicians, monastic, 247
Pigeon-house, 255
Pittance, 208
Pontifical dress of abbots, 147
Porcarius, 186, 229
Porter, 167
Precentor, 178
Printers, monastic, 102
Prior, 125
—— claustral, 175
Prior's lodge, 127
Prison, monastic, 165
Proctor, 126
Profession, 131
Protectors of serfs, Monks as, 74
Psalter, the, 36, 45
Pulpit, refectory, 204
*Pulsatorium*, 130

QUIRE duty, 151

RASTYR-HOUSE, 176
Reader, refectory, 204
—— weekly, 204
Recreations, monastic, 156
Refectionarius, 212
Refectioner, 212
Refectory, 200
—— abbot to dine in, 202
—— reader, 204
—— pulpit, 204
Reforms, monastic, 55
Registrar, 252
Regular canons, list of orders of, 266
—— clerks, list of orders of, 269
Relics, Keeper of, 252
*Rere Dorter*, 242, 255

*Revestrar*, 252
Road and bridge makers, Monks as, 93, 94
Rolls, diet, 209
Room, day, 227
*Rotundius*, 204
Rule of St Basil, 37
—— of St Benedict, 58
—— —— Cardinal Newman on, 58
—— of Celtic monks, 43-47
—— of Pachomius, 35
—— of St Columba, 48
Rules of Abraham, 33, 34

SACRIST, 179
Safe depositories, Monasteries as, 186
St Basil, Rule of, 37
St Benedict, 54
—— as ruler, 55
—— Rule of, 58
St Columba, Rule of, 48
St Cuthbert and Chad, Gospels of, 49
St Dunstan, 111
St Jerome, Monastic life, *temp.* 38
St Paula, 52
*Salutatorium*, 226
Sarabites, 31
Saxon (Anglo) monasteries 49-51
School, Song, 178
Schools, monastic, 89, 153, 173
Scriptoria, 188
Scriptorium, 180
Scriptures, translations of, 181
*Secretarius*, 179
Secretary, 252
*Secretior, Domus*, 242, 255
Seneschal, 180, 251
Serfs, Monks, protectors of, 74
Sepulchre (Holy), Canonesses of, 52
Servers, kitchen, 195
Servants at Evesham, 253
Shaving-house, 176
Shoemakers, 252
Shrine, Keeper of, 252
Signs used in Silence times, 160, 161
Silence, 33, 159
Silence times, signs used in, 160, 161
Song school, 178
South (cloister) alley, 174
"Speculum Majus," 115
Speke-house, 226
Spies of cloister, 175
Stables, 255
Steward, 180
Stories and Histories, 205
Students, nursery for, 174
Stylites, 29, 30
Succentor, 178

TABENNÆ, Monastery of, 35
—— life in, 36
Table, abbot's, 202
—— supply, 194
Tailors, 252
Terrier of house, 251
Thebes, Paul of, 27
Tithes, 69
Tonsure, 132, 176
—— Celtic, 48
Town v. gown, 84-87
Trade, monastic, 89-97
Travellers, 219
Travelling, monastic, 158
Treasurer, 179, 251
Treasury-house, 180

VACARIUS, 194
Value of monasteries, 89
Venerable Bede, 114

Vestiary, 146
Vincent de Beauvais, 115
Visitors, monastic, 158
*Vivarium*, 254 (*note* [2])
Voragine, Jacobus de, 115

WARRIORS, Monks as, 82
Watchers, 239, 240
Weekly reader, 204
West (cloister) alley, 173
Western Monasticism 38
Wine-growers, Monks as, 79, 118
Women, foundations for, 51
Writers, Monks as, 61, 90, 181
Writing materials, 192
Workshops, 253

CONCLUSION, 257-261

#### A Biography

By

JUSTIN McCARTHY

New and Cheaper Edition, with Portrait

*Crown 8vo.* 1s. 6d

*IMMEDIATELY*

# FRA GIROLAMO SAVONAROLA

By

The Rev. HERBERT LUCAS, S.J.

# A Benedictine Martyr in England

BEING THE

Life and Times of the Venerable Servant of God
DOM JOHN ROBERTS, O.S.B.

*By*

DOM BEDE CAMM, O.S.B., B.A., Oxon

*Priest of St Thomas's Abbey, Erdington*

---

## OPINIONS OF THE PRESS.

THE DAILY CHRONICLE (*Feb.* 14, 1898), under the heading, "A ROMANTIC MARTYR."

"Not only from the archives of the English College at Valladolid, but from many other sources—Spanish, Italian, French, Flemish, and English—Dom Bede Camm has wrought the wonderful true story of his Benedictine predecessor, Dom John Roberts; the first monk after the Reformation to risk and finally lay down his life for preaching his faith in his own country and ministering to his fellows in that faith. It is a story of pure heroism which all may admire, for unlike other Roman priests of his time, Dom Roberts was completely clear of all political intrigue or wordly treason. He is one of the men whose judicial murder has been execrated by the sober Hallam and the secular Macaulay: victims of laws concerning which Mr Beesley and Mr Lecky, no clericals in opinion, have written, the one that 'attempts to excuse such legislation as prompted by political reason, can only move the disgust of every honest-minded man;' and the other that 'many Catholics perished in England to whom it is the merest sophistry to deny the title of martyrs for their faith. . . . . .' Born in 1575, he died in 1610. He was Welsh by blood and birth, educated at Oxford, and entered as a law student at Furnival's Inn. Leaving England that same year, he conquered his religious doubts and difficulties, and was received into the Roman Church at Paris by a canon of Notre Dame. Of his life in Spain, until his departure for England, Dom Camm gives a minute and profoundly interesting account, which includes many painful incidents of dissension between Jesuits and Benedictines, impartially recorded and explained, as well as a wealth of animated detail concerning the ways and works of the English exiles, in college or cloister. Dom Roberts quitted Spain in 1602, landed in England the year following, was promptly arrested, and began the first of his six imprisonments. The story of his eight remaining years is a chronicle crowded with dramatic escapes, dangers, journeyings, of missionary labours at home and abroad, varied with intervals of the Gatehouse or Newgate. . . . . A strange life—that hunted life of proscribed priests! Now they would be ruffling it in the streets in gay disguise upon errands of charity, now saying Mass in some dark corner of a guarded house, now traversing the law of judges or the theology of bishops in open court, and at last going to their deaths with chaunts of joy. Such a life and such a death Dom Camm describes, with a strong sense of its human beauty and charm, its picturesqueness and adventurous quality, but far more with an anxious accuracy as a historian, and a reverent devotion as a martyrologist."

LITERATURE (*Feb.* 12, 1898).

"A valuable contribution to the religious history of the time. The author thus explains how he came to write the book :—

"'An Oxford convert, who had been drawn to the monastic life in a foreign country where he had gained the Faith; who had left England for a few weeks as a Protestant tourist, to return after some years a priest and a monk, would naturally feel devotion to one who had so closely preceded him on the same path.'

"Fortunately enthusiasm has not destroyed the sense of fairness to opponents or the honest presentation of facts. He does not seek to minimise the political motives of the leaders of the Jesuit propaganda, or the dissensions which raged among the Catholics themselves. . . . . His (Dom Roberts') labours were exclusively religious, and he made many converts. For six years, more or less, the Plague raged in London, and he laboured day and night in the foul and pestiferous alleys of the great city, seeking out the poor Catholics who lay in the fever dens of Westminster and Southwark, and ministering to them with entire and devoted self-forgetfulness.

"Dom Bede Camm gives a graphic account of the saintly monk's capture, trial, and condemnation, and of the manly front he opposed to his judges, and especially to the implacable Abbot, then Bishop of London and afterwards Archbishop of Canterbury. The author tells the story of the monk's sufferings in prison, and of the devotion showed him by a Spanish lady—Donna Luisa de Carvajal—with much pathos, and there is nothing in the volume to which the strongest Protestant can take objection."

### THE PALL MALL GAZETTE (*Dec.* 18, 1897).

"The pictures Father Camm gives of the Jesuit seminary at Valladolid and of the Benedictine Monastery of Santiago de Compostella are both interesting and beautiful; the account of the bitter feud between the Jesuits and the Benedictines gives us a high idea of the author's scrupulousness in matters of history . . . . The book has great historical interest. Moreover to Father Camm it was a labour of love, and is therefore written with sympathy and real feeling."

### THE TABLET (*Dec.* 25, 1897).

"This life is a welcome addition to the literature connected with our English martyrs. The author has spent considerable pains on the book, and has succeeded in adding a good deal to what we already knew from Challoner, whose account of the martyr has been hitherto almost our only source of information. The work has been a labour of love; and the task of reading it is a profitable one, not merely on account of the intrinsic value of the facts, but specially because of the spirit in which it is written. That spirit is one of peace, as indicated by the Benedictine device of 'Pax,' which is stamped upon the cover . . . . Our author gives us a short history of the Ven. Mark Barksworth, and brings up evidence to show precisely the right which he had, at the hour of his martyrdom, to call himself a professed son of St Benedict. . . . The narrative part of the present work occupies 278 pages. At the end of the book there is a series of Appendices containing some of the documents in the story. Last of all there is a good Index."

THE SCOTSMAN (*Nov.* 25, 1897).

"Roman Catholic readers who are fond of cherishing the hope that this country will go over to their communion will take a deep interest in Dom Bede Camm's biography; for that work tells us all that is known about Father John Roberts, a missionary who was sent over by the Pope to convert England at a time when attempts to convert England met with drastic treatment at the hands of the law. . . . . Little enough is known of the actual circumstances of his life; but this little has, by the careful researches and wide learning of Dom Bede Camm, been developed into a readable and instructive book . . . . Any one studying the history of the Roman Catholic disabilities or religious persecutions in England, will find it well worth reading."

THE ACADEMY (*Jan.* 15, 1898).

"Dom Camm has taken infinite pains to disinter the minutest details of his hero's biography. His book should be of service to scholars, alike for its learning and its clear expression of the Catholic view with regard to the Jacobean executions."

THE MONTH (First Notice, *Dec.* 1897).

"Father Camm's book bears marks of the most painstaking research. He seems to have consulted every possible source of information which could throw light on his subject, and in fact to have made the period with which he is concerned quite his own."

THE MONTH (Second Notice, *Jan.* 1898).

"In this interesting study, Dom Bede Camm sets before us a man of remarkable character, the fearless, active, outspoken Benedictine, John Roberts, a martyr of no ordinary kind. Until now the story of his heroic death was practically all that was known about him, but Dom Camm has ransacked Europe, one might almost say, in search of further particulars; and has succeeded so well, that we can now study in detail, not only the martyr's life and character, but his times as well. . . . . It is an illustration, too, of the thoroughness of the author's work, that he exhibits his hero to us in contact, as a missionary priest should be, with all sorts and conditions of men . . . . As a monk he embraced a life of perpetual seclusion, as a missioner he was sent on many a long and perilous journey. Then we read of escapes and banishments, of capture and recapture, of busy work in London alternately with the solitude of the monk's cell and the felon's dungeon. There is a feast in his honour in prison; there are the pleasantries of a heart at rest on the scaffold; many things, in short, stranger than those we are accustomed to find in fiction. Oftentimes there were trials from the good, sometimes the consolation of an unlooked-for conversion; always labour, occasionally success. And the end was 'a spectacle to angels and to men.' Dom Camm has given us a book which will find, we hope, many attentive readers."

### THE CHURCH TIMES (*Feb.* 11, 1898).

"It is fortunately possible to feel the utmost sympathy with Dom Roberts and to admire his devotion and courage, without assenting to his theological position. He was a man of considerable ability, piety, and courage, who devoted himself to the service of his co-religionists and kept clear of the political intrigues which afforded some excuse for the penal laws enacted against the Papal missionaries, though not for the barbarity of those laws. . . . . Fr. Camm's interesting sketch of his life and times witnesses to a considerable amount of research."

### THE USHAW MAGAZINE (*Dec.* 1897)

"Though written in a light and very interesting style, the book is the fruit of years of patient labour and research . . . . it is indeed much more than a mere memoir of the Martyr, including, as it does, the history of the revival in England of the Benedictine Order, as well as an account of the Church in England in the reigns of Elizabeth and James I. It is indeed a cheering thing to see the cause of our Martyrs, which ought to be so dear to every Catholic heart, espoused so warmly and by so talented a devotee. We trust that this work will be but the first of many of Dom Camm's upon the subject."

### THE CHURCH REVIEW (*Feb.* 17, 1898).

"The book is excellently printed, particularly the index, the names being given in thick leaded type. Dom Camm tells us that he is 'an Oxford convert,' . . . . on the whole he has not written much to give offence, and parts of his book are intensely interesting . . . . Some of our readers will be surprised to learn that under James I. the fines of recusants had risen in nine years to £371,000, which in modern figures would amount to over four million pounds . . . . The account of the last days of Dom Roberts is most interesting and very graphically told . . . . one can only wonder at his fiendish execution. Such infamous cruelty and degradation towards men or women could only damage the cause of their persecutors, not of the sufferers. What a weird picture for a great artist : Donna Luisa receiving the dismembered body of Dom Roberts late at night in her house, and depositing them on a sofa in her little oratory!"

THE CATHOLIC TIMES (*Dec.* 31, 1897).

"Dom Camm sets the career of the Benedictine martyr before us with the simplicity of language and sobriety of judgment which befit the genuine historian . . . . The biography has been written with marked ability, and with a sympathetic hand."

THE FREEMAN'S JOURNAL (*April* 1, 1898).

"The labours of Father Roberts in England, his adventurous life and hairbreadth escapes, are told in a style to which its simplicity and directness gives power ; and the closing scenes in all their sternness, lose nothing in the telling. The book has a valuable Index, and is beautifully brought out. But irrespecive of these things, the book is one to be read and 'inwardly digested' by the historical student, and will enchain the attention of the most 'general' of readers."

THE CATHOLIC NEWS (New York, *Feb.* 16, 1898).

"This is one of those fine books published by the Catholics of England whose scholarship so redounds to their credit. What a new interpretation of the English Reformation has come to us through the labours of Casquet, Morris, Pollen, Foley, and the author of this book ! . . . . That Dom Roberts was a hero of the noblest type, this book bears ample proof . . . . I know of nothing better to strengthen our faith in this new land than these books now publishing in England, reciting the sufferings of our ancestors, and of such is Dom Camm's book."
—*Walter Lecky.*

THE AVE MARIA (Notre Dame, Indiana, U.S.A., *Feb.* 19, 1898).

"Dom Camm has made a biography of Dom Roberts which scholars will read with delight. The biographer's work has been a labour of love, as one sees in every page. It is handsomely published."

THE CATHOLIC WORLD (New York, *Feb.* 1898).

"The patient and exhaustive care for historical accuracy and detail which marks every page of the work shows that Dom Camm is a worthy successor of the late Father Morris. It is delightful to see the loving pains which have been taken upon every point, the recourse which has been had, not only to books and manuscripts, but also, when these failed, to living authorities, in order that nothing may be left obscure . . . . Dom Camm, moreover, is evidently intimately acquainted with all collateral matters, and thus writes out of a full mind. He thus illuminates the surroundings, and does not, like so many writers of saints' lives, absolutely detach the subject of his work from all relation to the world in which he lived. He writes, too, as one accustomed to weigh evidence, as having the whole case before him, not as a partisan or advocate . . . . On almost every page most interesting bits of information are given . . . .

"Owing to the fact that hitherto English ecclesiastical history has been mainly written by Jesuits or secular priests, the Benedictine share of the work has been somewhat neglected; but if this most illustrious Order finds historians so fully acquainted with the facts and so well able to place them before the reader as is the author of the present work, no longer will their work remain unknown."

## APPROBATIONS

THE LORD BISHOP OF HEXHAM AND NEWCASTLE:

"Your book has perfectly delighted me; it is full of interest, and gives a knowledge of the times of the martyr that is perfectly invaluable. I will do my best to promote the sale of it."

THE ABBOT PRIMATE OF THE ORDER OF ST BENEDICT:

"It has been my ardent wish to write to you and to express the very intense pleasure your book gave me. It is really a good work; and I ask God to give you strength to continue your studies so as to be able soon to give us another volume of your series."

www.ingramcontent.com/pod-product-compliance
Lightning Source LLC
Chambersburg PA
CBHW031249250426
43672CB00029BA/1391